Psychoeducational Assessment
of Hearing-Impaired Students

Psychoeducational Assessment of Hearing-Impaired Students

INFANCY THROUGH HIGH SCHOOL

Sharon Bradley-Johnson
Larry D. Evans

pro·ed

8700 Shoal Creek Boulevard
Austin, Texas 78757

Printed in the United States of America

Library of Congress Cataloging-in-Publication Data

Bradley-Johnson, Sharon.
    Psychoeducational assessment of mainstreamed hearing-impaired
students : infancy through high school / Sharon Bradley-Johnson and
Larry D. Evans.
        p.   cm.
    Includes bibliographical references (p.   ) and indexes.
    ISBN 0–89079–455–3
    1. Hearing impaired children—Education.   2. Mainstreaming in
education—Evaluation.   3. Educational tests and measurements.
    4. Hearing impaired children—Psychological testing.   I. Evans,
Larry D.   II. Title.
HV2430.B73   1991
371.91'2—dc20   90–27491
                                    CIP

pro·ed

8700 Shoal Creek Boulevard
Austin, Texas 78757

    3   4   5   6   7   8   9   10   97

To Carl and Jason
Beth and Amy

Contents

Foreword

This small volume contains a wealth of important information regarding the psychoeducational assessment of hearing-impaired students from infancy to high-school age. The authors, Sharon Bradley-Johnson and Larry Evans, have done an excellent job of discussing the various issues and procedures related to assessment. They have also presented a comprehensive, balanced, critical review of a number of selected psychological and educational tests. There is no question that this book provides practical information for professionals who are concerned with the achievement of individuals with hearing impairments. The book will also attract the attention of researchers and theorists who are interested in developing tests and evaluating their merits. These scholars have a deep understanding of the meaning of the line on page 2: "Diagnosis is not a listing of symptoms; rather, it is a theory to explain why the symptoms exist."

In my view, Bradley-Johnson and Evans articulate two major themes that should be framed and placed on the walls of serious professionals who construct, administer, or evaluate tests. The first one seems obvious, but is sometimes forgotten: Obtaining useful assessment results on hearing-impaired students is a very complicated, time-consuming task. The second one has only recently been described in great detail: There should be an interrelationship among theory, research, instruction, curriculum, and assessment. For example, the authors state on page 2, "An assessment that does not result in improved academic performance by a student experiencing difficulty serves no useful purpose. The assessment process is a means to an end, not an end in itself." Other statements supporting this theme can be found in the chapters that review a selection of tests.

In addition to emphasizing critical general assessment issues and procedures, such as reliability, validity, selection, administration, interpretation, and the requirements of Public Law 94-142, Bradley-Johnson and Evans devote a chapter (Chapter 2) to describing the characteristics of hearing-impaired students. They realize the importance of providing complete descriptions of students, which should include degree and type of impairment, etiology, age at onset, intelligence, educational program, communication mode, and hearing status of parents and siblings. This information is necessary to understand the implications for research, instruction, and psychoeducational assessment.

The book contains three chapters that provide detailed reviews of published tests that have been (or may be) used with individuals with hearing impairments. Chapter 4 focuses on the cognitive assessment of infants and preschoolers, Chapter 5 covers assessment of school-age children and adolescents, and Chapter 6 discusses assessment of educational achievement in language, mathematics, reading, and writing. There are many types of published tests, such as standardized norm-referenced tests, criterion-referenced tests, tests that accompany academic programs, and tests that focus on classroom observations and the interactions between students and teacher. The authors' reviews of some of the more commonly used tests provide sufficient information on their relative merits for educators, psychologists, and consultants. With these reviews, Bradley-Johnson and Evans accomplish one of their major reasons for writing this book for relevant professionals: "To obtain useful assessment results, an examiner must thoroughly understand the type of information that various tests and assessment procedures can provide, as well as the limitations of the information that is obtained" (Preface, p. xi).

After reading the book, many educators, psychologists, and consultants will agree that the authors have provided "a single, comprehensive source of information regarding assessment procedures and assessment instruments for hearing-impaired students" (p. 218). It is my hope that this scholarly work will stimulate further research in this area and that "significant improvements will be made in the psychoeducational assessment of hearing-impaired students so that it will be possible to make a more helpful contribution to the education of these students" (p. 218).

Peter V. Paul
The Ohio State University

Preface

Assessment of students who are not making adequate educational progress is difficult and time-consuming. This task is even more challenging if a student has a physical handicap. Assessment results need to be educationally important, comprehensive, and obtained from tests and procedures that are reliable, valid, and appropriate for the student being tested. If these conditions are met, then the assessment results will contribute valuable information for developing programs that facilitate academic progress. If, however, assessments are not carried out well, then use of inadequate results can further hinder the progress of students. For professionals whose charge it is to conduct psychoeducational assessments, this is a tremendous responsibility.

This text is written primarily to aid psychologists, teachers, and educational consultants who are responsible for carrying out such assessments. The material is also useful to other professionals who must read assessment reports, participate in individualized educational planning meetings, and make decisions regarding educational programs for students.

To obtain useful assessment results, an examiner must thoroughly understand the type of information that various tests and assessment procedures can provide, as well as the limitations of the information that is obtained. Furthermore, with students who have a physical impairment, such as a hearing loss, one must be familiar with procedures that can circumvent a handicapping condition and understand how the handicap may affect a student's behavior. This knowledge is necessary to ensure that results accurately reflect a student's aptitude and achievement. If these procedures are not employed, the results will describe only the limiting effect of the physical impairment on performance. In other words, the examiner should use psychoeducational tests for which the student is physically able to make the responses required on the test. This is both a legal (PL 93-112) and an ethical requirement.

Thus, to provide readers with sufficient information to meet the legal requirements and ethical responsibilities involved in assessing a student with a hearing impairment, we avoided using a general survey approach to present the material in this book. Instead, material is covered in a very detailed fashion. The presentation of material, however, is practice oriented.

The book is not intended to describe procedures for assessing hearing impairments, because this is the responsibility of professionals in the medical and audiology fields. Although a number of hearing-impaired students also have other handicaps, this book does not cover assessments of students who have multiple handicaps. Because these students have many special needs, and the assessment process for them is very complex, they deserve an entire text specifically devoted to assessments that adequately address their needs. This book also does not cover vocational assessment. Assessment of interests, skills, motivation, and personality traits relevant to job training is too extensive an area to include and would require a separate text for sufficient coverage. Also, vocational assessment is relevant only for older students. The information this book does provide on assessment of aptitude and achievement, however, includes important components of any assessment of vocational potential for students.

Contained in the book are (a) material on procedures that can be used to obtain information during the process of assessment, (b) issues and background information relevant to assessment of students with hearing impairments, (c) special procedures needed to obtain information on these students, and (d) detailed reviews of published, individually administered tests.

Overview of Assessment

In selecting instruments and procedures to assess the psychoeducational needs of a student, an examiner must give considerable thought to the purposes for which the information will be used. Data from assessments can be used to make various decisions; however, different decisions require different types of information. Because of the limited time available for assessments and the need for detailed, comprehensive information, organization of the assessment process is critical. Before working with a student, an examiner must take into account the purposes of the assessment and the manner in which the assessment will proceed. This chapter addresses the various purposes of assessment and the importance of the sequence of the procedures used during the assessment process.

Purposes of Assessment

There are a number of reasons for carrying out an assessment. One reason is screening to determine which students are at risk for delays in achievement, and therefore require more individual attention. Once these students are identified, they can be referred for more in-depth assessment to determine their specific needs. Because a physical impairment is likely to interfere significantly with a student's educational progress, it is usually unnecessary to screen students with physical impairments to determine that they require special assistance.

Hammill (1987) suggested other reasons for assessment: to diagnose students' problems, to identify instructional needs, to document progress in special programs, and to provide information for research. Because these are the primary purposes for assessing hearing-impaired students, the focus of this text is on these purposes.

Diagnosis is not a listing of symptoms; rather, it is a theory to explain why the symptoms exist (Hammill, 1987). A diagnosis is usually made by a multidisciplinary team and is based on data collected from a variety of sources. A diagnosis is not helpful in directly remediating problems; however, it can be helpful in determining whether the primary cause of a student's difficulty is a physical impairment, or whether another condition (e.g., mental retardation or learning disability) is the primary cause. If mental retardation or a learning disability appears to be the primary problem, this information should be useful for determining the most appropriate placement for the student and for planning educational programs.

Making a decision regarding eligibility requires a norm-referenced interpretation of data. This type of interpretation allows comparison of a student's performance with the performance of other students of the same age or grade level. Public Law (PL) 94-142 (1975) requires norm-referenced information for determining eligibility for special education services for those who may be mentally retarded or learning disabled. Examples of norm-referenced tests include the *Wechsler Intelligence Scale for Children–Revised* (Wechsler, 1974) and the *Test of Adolescent Language–2* (Hammill, Brown, Larsen, & Wiederholt, 1987).

Identification of a student's instructional needs is an equally important purpose of assessment. An assessment that does not result in improved academic performance by a student experiencing difficulty serves no useful purpose. The assessment process is a means to an end, not an end in itself (A. Ross, 1976).

The primary goal of assessment is to plan a program that will enable a student to learn more skills. To facilitate academic progress, a student's strengths and areas of difficulty need to be determined. Both areas must be assessed in detail to identify specific skills for instruction. For example, a student's general area of difficulty may be oral expression, but the specific skills that need to be taught may be increasing vocal intensity and production of "ee," "aw," and "oi." Another example is a student whose general area of strength is addition, but the specific skill that requires instruction is double-column addition with regrouping.

Norm-referenced information can be used to identify general or broad areas of strength and difficulty. However, criterion-referenced information, curriculum-based measurement, data from systematic direct observation, and determination of problem solving strategies that the student uses also are necessary to identify specific instructional needs. Some examples of criterion-referenced tests include the *Teacher Assessment of Grammatical Structures* (Moog & Kozak, 1983) and the *Vocabulary Comprehension Scale* (Bangs, 1975). These procedures are discussed in detail in the section on The Process of Assessment.

Documenting progress in special programs and providing information for research can require any or all of the types of information previously described. For example, both norm-referenced information and curriculum-based measurement may be used to evaluate a student's progress in a reading program. If one purpose of a research project is to determine how improved academic performance affects behavior, then norm-referenced information might be used to document improvement in math and reading. Direct observation of behavior can be used to assess the frequency of certain behaviors of interest to the researchers.

The Process of Assessment

Assessment typically proceeds from the collection of general information about a student to the acquisition of data describing specific skills that have been learned, as well as the next skills that are important to teach. The process can be viewed as a funnel, because information gathering proceeds through several stages from general to specific.

Test administration is only one element of the assessment process. Additional procedures that can be employed include interviews, review of school records, use of rating scales and checklists, and direct observation. The order in which these procedures are used varies depending on the nature of a student's problem and the schedules of those involved in the assessment. The most efficient order, however, is to employ procedures that yield general information first. These procedures include interviews, rating scales and checklists, and review of school records. Based on this information, the examiner can form hypotheses about the general nature of the problems and plan which specific assessment procedures to use to test these hypotheses. The procedures that would provide more specific information are direct observation and administration of norm- and criterion-referenced tests, as well as use of curriculum-based measurement.

Interviews

The purpose of an interview is to obtain as much information as possible about a student's strengths or problem areas from the perspective of the parent(s), the teacher(s), the student, and significant others familiar with the student's performance.

An interview with parents can be helpful in terms of understanding the hearing-impaired child's level of acceptance of his or her hearing loss, as well as the parents' attitudes toward and expectations for their child. Through the interview process with the parents, examiners are usually able to determine how willing the parents are to be involved in and assist with the child's educational program.

Professionals other than the student's teacher also can provide useful information, which may differ from that given by the teacher. Other professionals, such as speech therapists or audiologists, have different perspectives because they interact with the student in settings other than the classroom and in situations with different requirements. For hearing-impaired students, it is particularly important to obtain interview information from several sources because the limitations of the hearing loss are likely to vary as a function of the requirements of different situations. Information from various sources can be useful in planning educational programs. For example, the information provided by a physical education teacher regarding a hearing-impaired child's ability to communicate with others may be quite different from the information provided by an academic classroom teacher. The physical education teacher would not be as familiar with the student and the student's communication patterns. The environment in which the physical education teacher observes the student is likely to be noisier and less structured than the regular classroom. Obtaining information on a hearing-impaired student's ability to function in this setting could be useful in planning instruction so that the student will be able to function well in a variety of settings.

Obtaining the student's opinion regarding his or her performance also can provide important information for planning programs. For example, if the student's adademic performance is poor, yet he or she does not feel that this is a serious problem, the examiner and teacher need to consider both motivational and academic issues if performance is to be improved.

When assessment involves infants or preschoolers, more information usually can be obtained from an interview conducted in the home rather than from one in a school or office setting. The home environment allows the examiner to observe the interaction of the parent(s) and child in a familiar setting.

For the school-age child with a hearing impairment, the interview with the teacher is critical, and should be conducted prior to administering tests to the student. The teacher's view of what the child's strengths and difficulties are, and what has been tried to remediate the difficulties, must be determined if intervention programs are to be effective. Furthermore, an examiner needs to determine prior to testing what special materials and procedures are used in the classroom that might be useful during testing.

It is helpful during the interview with the teacher to obtain samples of the student's work, especially for areas of difficulty. By examining these work samples, one can often determine error patterns. A remedial program can then be designed to correct such error patterns.

If rating scales or checklists are to be completed by a teacher or a parent, it is helpful to have the form filled out at the end of the interview. Thus, the examiner is present to clarify any questions that a parent or teacher might have while completing the forms. Also, the examiner will then have the information prior to directly testing or observing the student.

One such rating scale that may be of use is the *Screening Instrument for Targeting Educational Risk* (SIFTER; K. L. Anderson, 1989). SIFTER is designed for children who are identified by a hearing screening as having some degree of hearing loss or for children known to have a hearing loss. This measure addresses the areas of academics, attention, communication, class participation, and school behavior, with three items for each area. It is designed for screening purposes only, but may help to form hypotheses about areas of strength and difficulty that can be assessed further by other tests or direct observation. The measure is completed by the teacher and has been used primarily with children in grades K through 5.

Special concerns need to be addressed in an interview with the parent or teacher of a hearing-impaired student. Table 1.1, Information Organizing Checklist for Hearing-Impaired Students, is designed to help obtain and organize information regarding concerns typical of an assessment, as well as the special concerns for hearing-impaired students. Information to complete this checklist can be obtained from interviews, review of school records, or both. The following text provides the rationale for the inclusion of each item. A detailed explanation, along with a discussion of the importance of the issues included on the checklist, is presented in Chapters 2 and 3.

Importance of Information on Checklist

1. *Cause of loss.* This item alerts an examiner to the possibility of the presence of other handicaps. For example, students with inherited hearing losses tend to have more severe hearing losses, but are less likely to have additional handicaps. Prelingual losses (those occurring before the age of 2 or 3) are likely to affect negatively the acquisition of both speech and language, whereas postlingual losses are more likely to interfere with the acquisition of speech, but not necessarily language. The varying effects of both prelingual and postlingual losses depend also on the severity of the hearing impairment.

2. *Date of last audiological exam.* It is critical to keep audiological exams up-to-date. If the latest exam is not current (i.e., more than a

TABLE 1.1
Information Organizing Checklist for Hearing-Impaired Students

Student's name _____

School _____

Teacher _____

Date of assessment _____

Date of birth _____

Hearing Loss

1. Cause of hearing loss:

    Congenital _____   Acquired _____

    Cause _____

    Age at onset _____

2. Date of last audiological exam _____

    Result _____

    _____

3. Degree of loss (pure-tone average):

    for right ear _____ dB

    for left ear _____ dB

4. If hearing aids used (pure-tone average):

    Degree of aided loss for right ear _____ dB

    Degree of aided loss for left ear _____ dB

    No information available on aided loss _____

5. Type of hearing loss:

    Conductive loss _____

    Sensorineural loss _____

    Mixed loss _____

6. Loss is:

    Stable _____

    Progressive _____

TABLE 1.1 Continued

The following items in this section apply to students with hearing aids.

7. When were hearing aids first used? _____

8. Will student use aids readily?   yes _____   no _____

    If no, describe problem _____

    _____

    _____

9. Are aids used daily?   yes _____   no _____

    If no, how often _____

10. How often do batteries need to be changed? _____

    When were batteries last changed? _____

Health Issues

11. Other handicapping conditions _____

    _____

    _____

12. If student is taking medications, list _____

    _____

    _____

13. Date of most recent visual exam _____

    Result _____

14. List any allergies _____

15. Does student have colds frequently?   yes _____   no _____

Communication

In answering the following, consider various options such as signs developed by family, gestures, American Sign Language, Signing Exact English, speech reading, spoken words, total communication. (It may be necessary to clarify terms such as "total communication" to obtain an accurate understanding of the student's form of communication.)

16. What form of communication does student usually use? _____

    _____

TABLE 1.1 Continued

17. How does student receive information? _____

   _____

   _____

18. If infant or preschooler, did (does) child babble?

   yes _____   no _____

Home Situation

19. Does student have:

   parents with a hearing loss _____

   (mother _____ father _____)

   siblings with a hearing loss _____

   other relatives with a hearing loss (indicate who):

   _____

   _____

20. Family consists of:

   2 parents _____

   single parent _____

   siblings _____

   other persons _____

   _____

   _____

21. Do family members know some sign language:

	yes	no
mother	_____	_____
father	_____	_____
siblings	_____	_____
others living in home	_____	_____

22. Does student have friends in the neighborhood?

   yes _____   no _____

TABLE 1.1 Continued

23. Is home environment so noisy that it may interfere with student's hearing aid?   yes _____   no _____

    no aid used _____

24. Has family been actively involved in educational planning for the student?

    yes _____   no _____

25. Are parents involved in activities with deaf children or adults outside the home?   yes _____   no _____

26. Does home have telephone answering device, lighted doorbell, or other adaptive devices that may be of assistance to child?

    yes _____   no _____   child is infant/preschooler _____

Classroom

27. Was (Is) the student involved in either home-based or classroom preschool program?   yes _____   no _____

    Age at which student began program _____

28. Type of classroom placement:

    regular classroom _____

    special education classroom _____

        hours per day _____

29. Is a frequency modulation (FM) system used in the classroom?

    yes _____   no _____

30. Does student participate in classroom activities to about the same degree as other students?   yes _____   no _____

31. Is student teased by peers?   yes _____   no _____

32. Does student have friends in classroom?   yes _____   no _____

33. Does student interact in a positive way with peers?

    yes _____   no _____

34. Does student participate in clubs, sports?   yes _____   no _____

        If so, which _____

TABLE 1.1 Continued

35. Does student request help when needed?   yes _____   no _____

36. Does student accept help courteously?   yes _____   no _____

37. Does student display an appropriate degree of independence?

    yes _____   no _____

38. Does student require additional time to complete assignments?

    yes _____   no _____

    If yes, about how much more time is needed? _____

39. Does student seem to become more fatigued than most students?

    yes _____   no _____

40. Does teacher have concerns about student's classroom behavior?

    yes _____   no _____

    If yes, describe _____

    _____

    _____

41. Does teacher have concerns about student's academic work?

    yes _____   no _____

    If yes, describe _____

    _____

    _____

42. Prior test results:

Date	Test	Results

Permission is granted by PRO-ED, Inc., to make copies of Table 1.1.

year old), one should be obtained prior to the psychological assessment. Results of the exam may have implications for selected testing procedures.

3, 4. *Degree of unaided and aided loss.* This information suggests the type of assessment procedures that are needed. As suggested by P. V. Paul (personal communication, June 11, 1990), "many students with severe hearing impairments may need to be tested as if they were deaf, while some would not. The overwhelming majority of students with losses of 91 dB or more will require that the student be assessed as if she or he were deaf." Severe losses include those losses of 71 to 90 dB. Karchmer, Milone, and Wolk (1979) found that the majority of children with losses of 70 dB or less have intelligible speech.

5. *Type of loss.* Children with conductive losses (losses due to problems with the outer ear, middle ear, or both) *may* be able to be assessed using procedures similar to those used with hearing students, whereas children with sensorineural losses (losses due to problems with the inner ear or auditory nerve) or mixed losses (conductive and sensorineural loss) may require nonvocal instructions, cues, and signing to supplement vocal instructions. It is necessary to ensure that a student with a sensorineural or mixed loss understands test directions in order to obtain valid results.

6. *Stable or progressive loss.* This information has implications for program planning if the loss is progressive.

7. *When aids were first used.* If a child does not begin using aids quite early, it may interfere considerably with his or her learning.

8. *Aids readily used.* If a child will not wear the aids (a rather common problem), this unwillingness should be targeted for change in order to maximize the child's ability to learn.

9. *Aids used daily.* This information suggests how willing the child is to use the aids and how accustomed the student is to wearing them.

10. *Frequency of battery change for aids.* Answers to these questions are critical to ensure that the aids are operating at maximum capacity during the testing sessions.

11. *Other handicapping conditions.* If additional handicaps are present, other modifications may be necessary during testing to circumvent these problems. This information also should be considered in educational planning.

12. *Medications.* If medications are used, possible side effects should be determined so that any effect of medication on classroom performance, or performance during direct assessment, can be evaluated.

13. *Recency of visual exam.* Visual examinations need to be kept up-to-date (i.e., annual examinations are needed) because hearing-impaired students are very dependent upon vision. Visual difficulties can change rather quickly. D. D. Johnson, Caccamise, Rothblum, Hamilton, and Howard (1981) found that 30.92% of hearing-impaired persons had some type of visual pathology. Hence, if the last visual examination was not done within the year, another may be needed prior to testing.

14, 15. *Allergies and colds.* These conditions have been found to negatively affect the performance of hearing-impaired students more so than that of hearing students. Hence, if these conditions are present, testing should be delayed. This information also is useful in educational planning.

16, 17. *Form of communication used.* This information is needed to select appropriate tests and procedures, that is, to ensure that results "accurately reflect the child's aptitude or achievement level or whatever other factors the test purports to measure, rather than reflecting the child's impaired sensory, manual or speaking skills" (*Federal Register,* 1977).

18. *Did or does the child babble?* Babbling is important for the later development of speech. Hence, this knowledge may be relevant to educational planning.

19. *Family members with hearing loss.* This information may be related to the degree of acceptance of the student's handicap and suggests whether the student has been exposed to models with a hearing loss.

20. *Members of family.* This information is useful in understanding the home environment.

21. *Whether family members know sign language.* If student uses sign, this answer indicates the degree to which it is useful to the student in the home setting.

22. *Student's friends in neighborhood.* This information is relevant to the student's social development.

23. *Home environment too noisy?* If the home is noisy, this issue may need to be addressed with the parents.

24–26. *Parents' involvement in student's educational program and the Deaf community, and use of adaptive devices at home.* Parental involvement is related to the academic achievement of hearing-impaired students (Quigley & Paul, 1989). If parents have not been involved with the school and others in the Deaf community, providing further information to the parents and facilitating their involvement whenever possible may prove very helpful to them and to the student.

27. *Student's involvement in preschool program.* Earlier educational intervention is related to higher achievement for hearing-impaired students.

28. *Classroom placement.* This information is relevant to future placement decisions.

29. *Use of a frequency modulation (FM) system.* If an FM system is not used, it may be worth considering. Consultation with an audiologist is required.

30–34. *Student's participation in classroom activities and quality of interaction with peers.* These are important areas to target for instruction if problems exist. This information on social development is relevant to assessment of adaptive behavior.

35–37. *Student's ability to request assistance and degree of independence.* Students with handicapping conditions require more assistance from others. If the student has problems requesting or responding to help, this should be targeted for instruction.

38. *Additional time required to complete assignments.* This information suggests the amount of additional time that is likely to be needed in scheduling the assessment, and the information is relevant to program planning.

39. *Is student more fatigued than peers?* Because use of residual hearing is tiring, the examiner must be particularly attentive to the child's fatigue. Testing should be discontinued when fatigue is evident.

40, 41. *Teacher's concerns regarding student's classroom behavior and academic work.* These concerns need to be addressed in the assessment process and are of primary concern.

42. *Prior test results.* To assess the student's progress, a comparison of current and previous test results is needed.

Review of School Records

School records should be reviewed prior to direct observation and testing for two reasons: (a) to obtain information useful in planning how to conduct observations and testing, and (b) to avoid repeating assessment procedures that have been used recently. During this review, the examiner should take organized, comprehensive, yet concise notes so that he or she will not need to return to the files to obtain information needed for the report. The examiner should make note of the following information:

- dates and results of tests for vision, speech, and medical problems

- dates and results of prior assessments

- names and dates of schools previously attended

- relevant family information, such as the person with whom the child lives

- dates and notes regarding prior school contacts with the family

The information on the child's hearing loss is critical. Chapter 2 contains a discussion of the interpretation of an audiogram, as well as an in-depth discussion of variables that must be considered, such as age at onset and type of loss.

Observation

Systematic direct observation of a student's performance is an integral part of any educational assessment for a hearing-impaired student. Observation in the classroom environment is needed to plan a realistic educational program and is required by PL 94-142. "Classroom observation is the most neglected yet the most useful form of performance assessment that is available" (Brackett, 1981, p. 60).

Observation of a student in the home setting can be helpful, but may yield different information from that obtained in the classroom. Because the home situation is more familiar to the student, and the parents' expectations for the student may differ from those of school personnel, it is worthwhile to observe in the home environment. Comparing information from observations in both settings can help determine how the classroom environment can be changed to facilitate the student's independence.

Observation in the classroom prior to testing allows an examiner to become familiar with the student's needs, behaviors, and communication patterns. Observation is especially important for examiners who have limited experience in assessing hearing-impaired students because it will help them know what to expect during testing. This information should strengthen an examiner's confidence and help him or her to relax during testing so that more attention can be paid to the student.

Information obtained by an examiner observing in the classroom provides an additional perspective on a student's performance. Although information obtained by interviewing the teacher is obviously important, there are many reasons why the information may not be entirely accurate. For example, a teacher may describe a student's performance as better than it actually is to prevent the student's removal from the regular education classroom to a special education classroom. If a teacher is unaccustomed to working with hearing-impaired students, he or she may not understand their special needs (e.g., specialized instruction in speech and language). This lack of understanding can result in unnecessary problems and an inaccurate description of a student's abilities.

Whether data from systematic behavior observation are accurate depends on the training and experience of the examiner. The more systematic the method of data collection, the more reliable the data are apt to be. Several excellent resources describe procedures for the systematic observation of behavior (e.g., Alessi & Kaye, 1983; Gelfand & Hartman, 1984; V. Hall, 1983). A videotape that provides examiners with practice and feedback for recording accompanies the Alessi and Kaye text. These sources also contain descriptions of procedures for determining the reliability of the data, which is necessary for accurate interpretation of results.

Testing

Norm-referenced information from tests is necessary to determine eligibility for special education services for many handicapping conditions. The Ethical Principles of Psychologists (American Psychological Association, 1981) require that a test be accompanied by a manual that describes the development, rationale, reliability, and validity of the test, as well as complete information about the normative sample characteristics. In addition, PL 94-142 states that tests must be valid for their employed purpose. Thus, the use of technically adequate measures is necessary. The following criteria were used to evaluate the technical adequacy of the norm-referenced tests reviewed in the chapters that follow.

Standardization. Demographic data should be provided to demonstrate that the sample corresponds to U.S. census data in terms of sex, race, ethnicity, socioeconomic level, geographic distribution, and urban/rural residence. Approximately 100 subjects should be included at each age or grade level (Salvia & Ysseldyke, 1985). This information allows one to determine whether the normative group is an appropriate comparison group for the child to be tested.

For tests with norms for hearing-impaired students, additional demographic data are needed on the sample because this is such a heterogeneous population and many variables related to hearing loss have a considerable effect on performance. Ideally, normative samples of hearing-impaired students should be described in terms of age at onset of the loss, degree of loss, type of loss, etiology, presence of other handicaps, and type of communication used during standardization of the test.

Reliability. Internal consistency and test–retest reliability data need to be presented for each age or grade level, as collapsing data across levels may obscure low values, particularly at the extreme ages or grade levels of a test. Correlations of .85 or higher are considered adequate for eligibility decisions (Aiken, 1985; Guilford, 1978). Retest intervals should be moderate in order to minimize the effects of learning, but not so short as to be impractical. Salvia and Ysseldyke (1985) recommended a 2- to 4-week interval. Information on standard error of measurement also should be provided by age or grade level.

Validity. *Construct* validity data are required to show that the test scores conform to theory and research underlying the construct. Construct validity is particulary important for intelligence tests. *Content* validity data are necessary to demonstrate that the test items measure the area to be assessed in a comprehensive and appropriate manner. Content validity is particulary important for measures of achievement. *Criterion*-related validity data should be presented to describe the extent to which test scores are related to other acceptable measures.

Test Selection. Occasionally, an examiner may need to use tests or parts of tests that do not meet minimum criteria for technical adequacy, such as when testing hearing-impaired students who have other physical or mental handicaps that make it difficult to respond to test items. In this case, results must be interpreted with great caution, and as many test results as possible need to be obtained from a variety of sources. Another reason that data from less-than-adequate measures sometimes may be used is that the choices of tests for hearing-impaired students are fewer than for students with normal hearing. Fortunately, this situation is improving gradually as more technically adequate measures appear on the market.

Whether to use test norms for normally hearing students or hearing-impaired students is a question for which there is no simple answer. In making this decision, the examiner must consider the purpose for testing and the background of the student. If the purpose is to compare the student's current level of performance with that of normally hearing students in a regular classroom, and if the student is able to understand the instructions and make the required responses, then norms for normally hearing students might be considered. In using these norms, however, one assumes that acculturation of the student has been similar to that of normally hearing students in the norm sample, which may not be the case. For example, a student may have been overprotected because of the hearing impairment and thus have had somewhat limited experience interacting with the environment. If a student attended a residential school for hearing-impaired students, his or her educational experience differs from that of the norm group. Furthermore, if adaptations are necessary to circumvent the student's hearing impairment, the standardized administration procedures are altered and the comparison with the norms may not be appropriate. If, however, data are available on use of a test with hearing-impaired students to show that the means and standard deviations are the same as for normally hearing students, then using the hearing norms may present no problem. If the purpose is to use the information for planning an educational program, then adaptations and practice items could assist in determining strengths and difficulties.

Tests standardized on hearing-impaired students are not without problems either. Only a limited number of such tests are available, and many have problems with different aspects of technical adequacy. The requirements for responding to items, however, are more appropriate, and the normative sample may be more appropriate. The population of hearing-impaired students is very heterogeneous. Age at onset of hearing loss, degree of loss, and hearing status of parents are examples of factors that cause considerable individual variation within this population. Hence, it is important that a relatively large and representative sample of hearing-impaired students participate in the standardization of these tests to avoid bias in the norms. These issues are discussed in more detail in Chapter 3.

Because there are problems in interpreting hearing-impaired students' results on tests standardized either on hearing-impaired students or on normally hearing students, conclusions regarding educational programming and special education placement need to be based on data from other sources of information as well as on standardized tests. To determine the validity of standardized test results for a particular student, an examiner should compare the norm-referenced results with information obtained from interviews with several people who know the student well, data from review of school records, criterion-referenced tests, curriculum-based measurement, and classroom observation. Furthermore, an assessment that considers areas such as cognitive performance, academic performance, and adaptive behavior is required to draw valid conclusions about a student's abilities. Periodic reevaluation helps determine the validity of prior test results and provides data on changes in a student's performance.

If possible, the examiner should obtain data from tests standardized on both normally hearing and hearing-impaired students. These results, combined with data from other sources, provide a good information base from which to draw conclusions.

If data from norm-referenced tests, interviews, review of school records, or observation suggest that a student is having difficulty with specific academic areas, further testing with criterion-referenced tests, curriculum-based measurement, or both is likely to be needed.

Results from criterion-referenced tests are not used to compare a student's performance with the performance of others. Instead, performance is assessed in terms of whether a student is able to perform a certain task to a preset level of mastery (i.e., a student passes or fails an item depending upon whether he or she reaches a criterion). For example, a mastery level for a skill might require that three of three times a student correctly produces the "oo" and "ou" combinations. Items on criterion-referenced tests are based on a detailed task analysis of skills. These tests assess more skills than do norm-referenced tests, and each skill is usually tested three or four times. This specificity is critical for planning instructional programs.

Criterion-referenced tests have an advantage over norm-referenced tests with a hearing-impaired student because various objects and materials can be used in assessment. Adaptations can be made to determine what a child is capable of doing. Often these adaptations can be identified through classroom observation. Furthermore, because the tests are not standardized, flexible administration procedures can be used. This flexibility can help to determine the most appropriate procedures for teaching a skill to a particular student.

In curriculum-based measurement, the materials used for instruction are used in skills assessment. The primary purpose of curriculum-based measurement is to determine how well a student is progressing within a particular curriculum. This information indicates whether changes might be needed in the curriculum used, in the teaching procedures, or in both. Unfortunately, little research is available on the use of curriculum-based measurement with hearing-impaired students. Nonetheless, the procedures may be useful for assessing progress in some areas. These procedures and their technical adequacy are discussed in Chapter 6.

An examiner should also try to determine the types of strategies a student uses to solve problems (Hammill, 1987). If a teacher is aware that a student is using an incorrect strategy, then it is relatively easy to provide the student with one that works (Hammill, 1987). For many problems, more than one strategy will enable a student to arrive at a correct answer. Examples of individual-referenced interpretations follow. Both of these strategies make students' performance inefficient.

Amy uses her finger to count when completing addition problems for sums greater than 10. (Hence, Amy needs to learn these math facts.)

Jordy has difficulty comprehending what he reads if he does not sign the words as he reads. (Jordy should be encouraged to sign as he reads his assignments.)

Various procedures, including interviews, rating scales and checklists, review of school records, observation, and testing, are needed to move from general information to the specification of the exact nature of a student's academic problems. To carry out a comprehensive assessment for a hearing-impaired student, an examiner is likely to need all of these sources.

Limitations of Assessment

Educational assessment of hearing-impaired students is a time-consuming process. Despite the time requirements, interviews with teachers, parents, and students are rich sources of information, and systematic observation of a student's performance in the classroom is critical. Despite the inherent limitations in current assessment instruments, an examiner can usually obtain a considerable amount of norm-referenced information and the detailed information required for program planning. It is well worth the time required to obtain this information, which will enable professionals to make accurate decisions regarding special education placement. Detailed, comprehensive information is also necessary to plan effective educational programs that can make a difference for students.

The instruments described in the following chapters yield many benefits in the assessment of hearing-impaired students. A *major* problem in assessing hearing-impaired students, however, is that nearly all tests designed for this population fail to meet minimum standards for technical adequacy. Although many tests developed for normally hearing students are technically adequate, these tests may not be appropriate for hearing-impaired students. Authors of new tests developed for hearing-impaired students can make a major contribution to the field if the tests are well standardized and have good reliability (especially in terms of test–retest data) and validity (particulary construct validity for intelligence tests and content validity for achievement tests).

More research is necessary in the assessment of hearing-impaired students. Specifically, new tests are needed that have norms for both normally hearing and hearing-impaired students. The tests and procedures that have the greatest potential for assisting in the education of these students, however, are criterion-referenced tests and curriculum-based measurement procedures. Any progress in these areas would be important in advancing the field of education of hearing-impaired students.

2

Background and Characteristics of Hearing-Impaired Students

This chapter addresses the definition of hearing impairment according to PL 94-142 and the incidence of the impairment. Then, the various characteristics unique to hearing-impaired children are described, and the implications of the characteristics for the assessment process are discussed.

Definition of Hearing Impairment

When President Gerald Ford signed the 142nd bill of the 94th Congress on November 29, 1975, The Education of All Handicapped Children Act mandated basic levels of educational services for the 6 to 8 million handicapped children of the United States. In addition to providing public education services to handicapped children, PL 94-142 has altered and structured the way in which handicapped children are viewed. For example, definitions of *deaf* have traditionally focused on the amount or degree of hearing loss; however, from PL 94-142's educational perspective, *deaf* is defined as "a hearing impairment that is so severe that the child is impaired in processing linguistic information through hearing, with or without amplification, which adversely affects educational performance" (*Federal Register,* 1977, p. 42478). To include students whose impairment may not be as severe, *hard-of-hearing* is defined as "a hearing impairment, whether permanent or fluctuating, which adversely affects a child's educational performance but which is not included under the definition of 'deaf'" (*Federal Register,* 1977, p. 42478). Because both definitions share the words "hearing impairment," the term *hearing impaired* has become a generic term encompassing both the deaf and hard-of-hearing (Blennerhassett & Spragins, 1983; Freeman, Carbin, & Boese, 1981; Rodda & Grove, 1987; Sullivan & Vernon, 1979) and has subsequently come to incorporate the definitions of deaf and hard-of hearing in the special education laws.

Incidence

Approximately 5% of the population has hearing impairments (Vernon & Alles, 1986), which includes all hearing losses from mild to profound. Reported prevalence rates of chronic childhood hearing impairment range from about .1 to .2% (Freeman et al., 1981; Rodda & Grove, 1987; Wood, 1984), with variability reflecting primarily differences in the definitions used. Hallahan, Keller, and Ball (1986) found prevalence rates for states varied from .09 to .35% of students, with a mean of .19%. Compared with other educational handicaps, such as learning disabilities and speech impairments, the incidence of hearing impairment is low.

Characteristics

The small percentage of hearing-impaired children does not represent a homogeneous group, but rather a population that varies along several dimensions. Various authors feel that different dimensions are important to consider when working with students who have hearing losses, yet there is considerable overlap among the authors as well. Dimensions frequently noted are type of hearing loss (Blennerhassett & Spragins, 1983; Myklebust, 1964; Quigley & Kretschmer, 1982), degree of loss (Blennerhassett & Spragins, 1983; Liben, 1978; Myklebust, 1964; Quigley & Kretschmer, 1982; Zieziula, 1982), age at time of onset (Blennerhassett & Spragins, 1983; Liben, 1978; Myklebust, 1964; Quigley & Kretschmer, 1982; Zieziula, 1982), etiology (Myklebust, 1964; Quigley & Kretschmer, 1982; Zieziula, 1982), pattern of loss (Blennerhassett & Spragins, 1983; Liben, 1978), tolerance for amplification (Liben, 1978), hearing status of parents

(Quigley & Kretschmer, 1982; Zieziula, 1982), visual acuity, number of coexisting handicaps, mode of communication, speech production, and type of special education class attended (Zieziula, 1982). Knowledge of these variables can provide important information to help understand each student, provide a valid assessment, and determine appropriate placement. Although considerable overlap exists between some variables (e.g., etiology and age at onset of loss), knowledge of one variable does not always permit understanding of another variable for a particular student. As a result, examiners need to collect information regarding important variables prior to assessment from a variety of sources, including the child's audiologist, speech–language clinician, physician, teachers, and parents, as well as the child (Blennerhassett & Spragins, 1983).

To utilize the information pertaining to the hearing-impaired student's status along important variables, the examiner needs to understand each variable and its relevance to assessment. The following sections describe the variables and their relevance. It is important to remember that variables along which hearing students differ (e.g., age, race) also pertain to hearing-impaired students, and these variables should be considered when planning assessments.

Type of Hearing Loss

Description.   Types of hearing loss are classified according to the physiological site of the hearing dysfunction (see Figure 2.1). A conductive hearing loss is due to the obstruction of sound waves traveling through the outer and middle ear to the hair cells in the cochlea. Common causes of obstruction include inflammation in the middle ear (otitis media), damaged or maldeveloped tympanum or ossicles, and severe accumulation of wax. A sensorineural hearing loss is caused by a problem with the inner ear or auditory nerve (Harrison, 1985). As with conductive hearing losses, the loss may be due to disease, maldevelopment, or trauma that occurs prenatally, perinatally, or postnatally. Children with a mixed hearing loss have concurrent conductive and sensorineural hearing losses in the same ear.

A central hearing loss is due to dysfunction along the neural pathway from the auditory nerve where it enters the brainstem to the cortical areas involved in processing auditory information. This type of hearing loss may be due to acoustic tumors, brain damage associated with hemorrhage, or developmental abnormalities (Levine, 1981). Such a hearing loss is not a loss in hearing sensitivity, but a loss in the ability to interpret auditory information. A central hearing loss in itself is not generally considered to constitute a hearing impairment; however, central hearing losses and other hearing losses often occur concurrently, as many of the etiologies for hear-

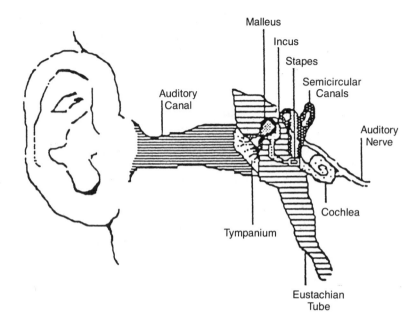

Figure 2.1.   Anatomy of the human ear.

ing loss also can affect central nervous system development (DeConde, 1984).

Relevance for Assessment.   Children with conductive hearing losses can use amplification to transmit sound to a functional cochlea. A conductive loss is limited to approximately 60 dB, the point at which bone structures can carry adequate auditory information to the cochlea. Thus, the child with a conductive loss and appropriate amplification may have a good deal of functional hearing and speech. The assessment of these children may be similar to the assessment of hearing children, although more information about the child and the hearing loss needs to be gathered before this conclusion can be drawn. Specifically, historical information is required to determine if any latency in providing amplification may have had an impact on skill development. Audiological information is needed to determine if amplification can bring hearing to a normal level. In addition, the combination of historical, audiological, and medical information may be important, as there is some indication that children with medically corrected conductive hearing losses may subsequently experience difficulty, compared with hearing children, in processing information binaurally (Hall & Derlacki, 1986).

Children with sensorineural losses are much more common to most examiners. Fewer medical interventions are available to children with this type of loss, and the mechanisms of hearing following existing interventions such as cochlear implants are not yet fully understood. Children with sensorineural losses generally utilize amplification, although some having little residual hearing may not use amplification (Karchmer & Kirwin, 1977).

Even with amplification, however, a sensorineural loss introduces distortion into audition. The distortion experienced may be similar to that heard by a hearing person trying to listen to a message from a poor public address system or from a radio that is not tuned exactly to a station. The sensorineural loss may impose intensity, frequency, and/or temporal distortion (Boothroyd, 1978), such that sounds may not be heard, may not be perceived at the correct frequency, or may not be perceived in the order of occurrence. Due to the distortion, the sensorineural hearing-impaired student may hear speech, but not understand it well. This problem is magnified by the fact that, because they have less language experience and development to understand ambiguous information using context or other cues, students with sensorineural losses are more dependent upon auditory information than are hearing students (Boothroyd, 1978).

In addition, amplifying sound involves a level of distortion that may be considerable when amplification is necessary to the degree required for most children with sensorineural losses. As a result, students with a sensorineural loss require a better signal-to-noise ratio (and less distortion in amplification) than students with conductive losses, as even small amounts of distortion can result in difficulty understanding speech (Byrne, 1986).

Even with the use of adequate amplification, the presence of distortion should be a consideration when planning assessment that includes vocal instructions. In general, students with sensorineural losses require nonvocal instructions, nonvocal cues, or signing to supplement vocal instructions, although with training a minority of students may understand speech and vocal instructions quite well without additional cues. Tests with practice and demonstration items are preferable so that the understanding of subtest requirements by a student with a sensorineural loss can be enhanced and observed. If a test does not contain such items, it may be helpful to use initial subtest items (if missed) as teaching items, to use items from skipped age levels, to compare a task to a similar task previously completed, or to have a student communicate what he or she is being asked to do. (Although repetition of instructions does not ensure understanding, inaccurate communication of requirements will reflect misunderstanding.)

Because a sensorineural hearing loss generally has more of an impact on a student's hearing than does a conductive loss, a mixed hearing loss involves the same considerations as a sensorineural hearing loss in terms of difficulty with distortion and understanding speech. The addition of a conductive loss to a sensorineural loss decreases hearing ability and increases the need for amplification (Jaffe, 1977). As a result, distortion often increases due to need for additional amplification. As with students having sensorineural losses, the examiner needs to make sure that the student understands subtest requirements before scored items are begun.

The addition of a central auditory processing problem to a hearing impairment adds to considerations when assessing hearing-impaired students. This additional problem may cause greater fatigue, distractibility, hyperactivity, frustration, speech and language delays, and difficulty following auditory information (DeConde, 1984). Central auditory processing problems are not well understood; however, it is safe to say that, by definition, students with the problem experience difficulty utilizing auditory information. As with other types of loss, the examiner will want to ensure that a student with central auditory processing problems understands subtest requirements. In addition, the examiner should be ready to adapt assessment procedures to any difficulty a student may experience due to the processing problem (e.g., a break if fatigue becomes a problem).

Degree of Hearing Loss

Description. The degree of loss experienced by a student is generally measured by an audiologist and expressed as the average number of decibels required for the student to detect a pure tone at several frequencies within the hearing range (usually 500, 1000, and 2000 Hz). The student's hearing loss is considered the average loss for the better ear and is therefore referred to as the better ear average (BEA). The BEA is obtained without the student using amplification such as hearing aids.

The dimension of degree of hearing loss is continuous; however, discrete categories are often used to describe the degree of loss and may be more accurate than a single number, given the daily fluctuations in hearing ability and the accuracy of hearing measurement. Although the category title and hearing loss range differ somewhat in the literature, losses of 0 to 25 dB are considered normal, 26 to 54 dB are mild, 55 to 69 dB are moderate, 70 to 89 dB are severe, and 90 dB or more are considered profound (Brill, MacNeil, & Newman, 1986). The term *deaf* applies to severe-to-profound or profound hearing impairments. Table 2.1 presents the prevalence of hearing impairment for each category. As noted, a positive correlation exists between prevalence and degree of hearing loss, with the highest prevalence for hearing losses in the profound range. These data were obtained from a survey of over 50 thousand hearing-impaired students in the United States. Data for preschool hearing-impaired children were reported by H. B. Craig (1983), who found 9% to have mild-to-moderate (25 to 65 dB) losses, 27% with severe (66 to 85 dB) losses, and 64% with severe-to-profound (85+ dB) losses.

TABLE 2.1

Prevalence of Hearing Impairment within Each Category of Hearing Loss

Category	Hearing loss (dB)	Prevalence (% of hearing impaired)
Normal	0–25	4.4
Mild	26–54	14.2
Moderate	55–69	13.0
Severe	70–89	24.7
Profound	90+	43.7

Note. From "Educational Significance of Hearing Loss at Three Levels of Severity" by M. A. Karchmer, M. N. Milone, and S. Wolk, 1979, *American Annals of the Deaf, 124,* p. 98. Copyright 1979 by American Annals of the Deaf. Reprinted with permission.

Relevance for Assessment. Independent of degree of hearing loss, all hearing-impaired students have some residual hearing (Quigley & Kretschmer, 1982). The residual hearing is dependent upon the number of decibels required at a given frequency (Heimgartner, 1982). Erber (1981) stated that "moderately and severely hearing impaired children hear speech, but in a somewhat distorted form. Profoundly deaf children tend to receive mainly the intensity patterns of speech and seem to respond to amplified sound through tactile perception" (p. 70). Erber further suggested that, even if profoundly hearing-impaired children can benefit only from tactile information, they can use it to supplement other receptive skills. In fact, whatever can be gained from aids can supplement other signals or can be a supplement to more primary receptive signals. Hence, whatever residual hearing a child has should be utilized during assessment and education.

Once the student's residual hearing is utilized, then some decisions can be made based on the degree of hearing loss. Vernon (1974) suggested that, for losses of 15 dB or less (unaided), a student can be given the same cognitive measures as those given to hearing students. For students with losses of 20 to 70 dB, Vernon indicated that assessment should depend on the student's amount of communication. For students with a 75 dB or greater loss, procedures for hearing-impaired students are recommended. Although these guidelines may be too general and have "grey" areas (e.g., 70 to 75 dB), some useful information can be gained from knowledge of degree of hearing loss. For example, the

> degree of hearing loss is a major consideration in determining educational placement, and it also influences such factors as the extent to which a student is judged to speak intelligibly, the particular communication methods the student is likely to use, and whether he or she will use a hearing aid. (Karchmer, Milone, & Wolk, 1979, p. 97)

As the degree of hearing loss increases, use of sign increases (Jensema & Trybus, 1978), speech intelligibility decreases, use of amplification increases (except for those with the greatest losses and least amount of residual hearing), and residential placements become more common (Jensema, Karchmer, & Trybus, 1978; Karchmer et al., 1979).

Karchmer et al. (1979) also found that speech was rated as intelligible for the majority (86%) of children with a 70 dB or less hearing loss. Just over half (55%) of those with losses of 71 to 90 dB and 23% of those with losses of 91 dB or more were rated as having intelligible speech. Jensema and Trybus (1978) found a similar pattern in that expressive language was primarily speech up to a 70 dB loss, and was primarily speech and sign for losses greater than 70 dB.

By knowing the student's degree of hearing loss, an examiner without knowledge of an individual student can make educated guesses regarding appropriate assessment procedures. For example, an examiner of a student with a 95 dB loss can hypothesize that assessment instruments with nonvocal instructions and responses are most appropriate. In most cases, however, such guessing can be avoided through direct observation and interviews with others having knowledge of the student (e.g., teacher, audiologist, speech therapist).

Knowledge of the degree of hearing loss suggests important issues that need further investigation. For a student with a 95 dB hearing loss, the examiner can focus on determining what functional receptive and expressive skills are used to supplement speech and how the student utilizes amplification. For a student with a 70 dB loss, the examiner focuses on determining whether speech or another method has been the primary form of communication and how the student utilizes amplification. For a student with a 25 dB loss, the examiner generates questions about adequacy of speech, the student's use of amplification, and the handicapping effect of the hearing impairment.

A caution regarding the interpretation of degree of hearing loss is warranted. Because categories are not used in a standard fashion, it is important to focus on the degree of hearing loss expressed in decibels rather than on the category used to describe the degree of loss (i.e., the categories normal to profound). For example, a student's degree of hearing loss that is labeled moderate may mean a loss in the 55 to 69 dB range (Brill et al., 1986), the 40 to 65 dB range (Blennerhassett & Spragins, 1983), or the 41 to 55 dB range (Rodda & Grove, 1987).

Age at Onset

Description.   The age at onset of hearing loss is relevant to both assessment and education of hearing-impaired students. A congenital hearing loss, which is present at birth, may be due to such prenatal factors as genetics, Rh incompatibility, or rubella, or may occur at birth (perinatal) due to such factors as anoxia or prematurity. Survey data reported by Rawlings and Ries (1973) indicated that approximately 78% of hearing-impaired children have congenital hearing losses.

Hearing losses that occur after birth are termed acquired (or adventitious), and may result from such factors as infections (e.g., meningitis, scarlet fever, otitis media), noise exposure, or the use of drugs that are toxic to the auditory system (e.g., streptomycin or other antibiotics). The term *acquired* can be misleading because causes of deafness can be acquired (i.e., obtained) during pregnancy (e.g., due to maternal rubella), but are considered congenital. Acquired losses comprise the remaining 22% of hearing losses (Rawlings & Ries, 1973).

Due to the impact of hearing loss upon the acquisition of language, if the age at onset occurs prior to the development of speech and language, the hearing loss is considered prelingual. For most children, this would be prior to the age of 3 years (Blennerhassett & Spragins, 1983). Spragins (1979) indicated that those "who become deaf after developing speech usually retain it, while prelingually deaf children (deaf before age three) have great difficulty acquiring speech" (p. 63).

Correspondingly, losses that occur after the child has developed speech and language are considered postlingual. Due to medical advances, the current percentage of children with postlingual losses has declined to about 5 to 10% of hearing-impaired children (Brill et al., 1986; Liben, 1978). Hearing losses due to measles, meningitis, whooping cough, pneumonia, and mumps have declined due to these advances, with a relative increase in hearing losses due to maternal rubella and heredity (Meadow, 1978).

Relevance for Assessment. Speech and language will not develop spontaneously if a child has a severe or profound loss before 12 months of age and amplification is not provided (Bernero & Bothwell, 1966; *Effect of Degree of Hearing Loss on Understanding of Language and Speech,* 1984). Because hearing losses are not usually diagnosed by 12 months of age (Freeman, Malkin, & Hastings, 1975; Shah, Chandler, & Dale, 1978), most children with congenital and early losses of 70 dB or more will experience delays in acquiring speech and language (Bernero & Bothwell, 1966). Both vocal and nonvocal measures with language requirements beyond the child's competence would be inappropriate for such children. Consultation with the child's speech–language pathologist is necessary to make such a determination.

Speech and language skills of children born with less severe losses will depend on the degree of hearing loss and the age of detection and intervention (e.g., amplification, language stimulation). Children with postlingual losses also will be variable in speech and language development as a function of degree and configuration of loss, time since hearing loss, speech and language development at the time of hearing loss, and any intervention to improve speech and language. The adequacy of verbal and language measures for those with early losses of less than 70 dB and those with postlingual losses will hinge upon the above variables. Again, consultation with the student's speech–language pathologist is important. If an examiner has any doubt that a student can provide a response for a particular measure, then that measure should not be used (except in a testing-the-limits manner), and a measure more suitable for the student's speech and language skills should be substituted.

For each individual student, examiners should determine the extent to which speech and language skills are impacted by the age of hearing loss onset. Generally, prelinguistic losses impact both speech and language skills, and postlingual losses generally result in deterioration of speech skills, but not necessarily language skills. In either case, the examiner is required to plan testing so as not to measure skills impaired as a result of the hearing loss.

Etiology

Description.   Etiology overlaps considerably with the type, degree, and age at onset of hearing loss. For example, genetic causes of hearing impairment usually result in congenital, prelingual, bilateral, sensorineural hearing losses in the severe-to-profound range. Knowledge of the type, degree, and age at onset does not completely predict etiology; in rare cases, genetic factors may produce a congenital hearing loss that is progressive (Freeman et al., 1981), allowing some degree of language acquisition.

In a survey of over 50 thousand hearing-impaired students in U.S. special education programs, Karchmer et al. (1979) obtained the percentages of the various etiologies of hearing impairment. Table 2.2 presents these findings. Of the 10 most common etiologies, 6 are generally considered congenital (maternal rubella, heredity, prematurity, pregnancy complications, trauma at birth, and Rh incompatibility). Although slightly over a quarter of the etiologies could not be determined, this may reflect either lack of genetic information that would lead to hereditary causes (Freeman et al., 1981) or inability to pinpoint the exact etiology or to make a differential diagnosis between two possible etiologies (e.g., fever or ototoxic drug treatment). In addition, 21.9% did not report an etiology. Unreported etiologies are more likely to be less detectable causes, such as heredity, or undetermined causes than such etiologies as Rh incompatibility or rubella. Freeman et al. (1981) indicated that ultimately half of the causes of hearing impairment are likely to result from heredity. Others have

TABLE 2.2
Percent of U.S. Students with Hearing Impairments Reported by Etiology

Etiology	Percent
Heredity	9.0
High fever	2.7
Infection	2.2
Maternal rubella	17.5
Measles	1.3
Meningitis	6.3
Mumps	0.4
Otitis media	1.8
Trauma after birth	0.3
Pregnancy complications	2.8
Prematurity	3.8
Rh incompatibility	2.0
Trauma at birth	2.2
Undetermined	25.8
Total	78.1*

*Cause not reported by some respondents; more than one cause reported for some students.
Note. From "Educational Significance of Hearing Loss at Three Levels of Severity" by M. A. Karchmer, M. N. Milone, and S. Wolk, 1979, *American Annals of the Deaf, 124,* p. 101. Copyright 1979 by American Annals of the Deaf. Reprinted with permission.

stated that currently the "largest diagnostic category for hearing impairment is still 'cause unknown' " (Rodda & Grove, 1987, p. 10).

Relevance for Assessment. Knowledge of the etiology of a student's hearing loss provides information about the degree of hearing loss experienced and suggests whether other handicaps may be present. Because specific data for the degree of hearing loss for a student should be available, etiological information is more relevant in terms of providing cues to potential additional handicaps. The potential for additional handicaps cues the examiner about modifications that may be needed in the assessment process. Table 2.3 presents etiologies of hearing impairment with the associated prevalence of additional handicaps in the hearing-impaired population.

Some etiologies of hearing impairment do not have published data regarding prevalence, yet these etiologies are associated with additional handicaps. For example, children whose etiology is cytomegalovirus (CMV) have a significantly greater number of behavioral problems than do non-affected children (Saigal, Lunyk, Larke, & Chernesky, 1982).

TABLE 2.3
Prevalent Handicaps for Specific Etiologies

Etiology of hearing impairment	Additional handicap	Prevalence (%)
Prematurity	Mental retardation	16.5
	Visual defect	25.0
	Emotional/behavioral	10.5
Maternal Rubella	Visual defect	33.0
	(Retinopathy)	8.2
	(Cataracts)	20–50
	(Glaucoma)	4.0
	Cardiac condition	33–76
Meningitis	Mental retardation	14.1
	Emotional/behavioral	8.0
Rh Incompatibility	Cerebral palsy	51.1
	Visual defect	25.0
	Emotional/behavioral	7.0
Heredity	Emotional/behavioral	6.2
Perinatal Trauma	Emotional/behavioral	10.7
Postnatal Trauma	Emotional/behavioral	9.4

Sources: Blennerhassett & Spragins (1983); Johnson, Caccamise, Rothblum, Hamilton, & Howard (1981); Vernon (1982); Vernon, Grieve, & Shaver (1972).

In addition to the higher prevalence of additional handicaps for various etiologies of hearing impairment, some etiologies are associated with prevalence rates for some handicaps that are less than the average for hearing-impaired persons. For example, only 5.1% of those whose hearing impairment is due to Rh factor incompatibility are mentally retarded, and only 5.7% of those whose hearing impairment is the result of meningitis have visual defects (Vernon, 1982). Similarly, behavioral problems occur half as frequently for hearing-impaired children of maternal rubella etiology than for nonrubella causes (Trybus, Karchmer, Kerstette, & Hicks, 1980).

As previously mentioned, the probable cause of undetermined impairments is likely to be hereditary (Freeman et al., 1981; Karchmer et al., 1979). Hereditary hearing impairments, although resulting in more severe hearing losses, tend to be associated with fewer additional handicaps (Conrad, 1979). Therefore, knowing that the cause of an impairment has not been determined may be useful as well.

Hence, etiological information alerts an examiner to potential additional handicaps. Examiners should make certain that hearing-impaired students with a diagnosis of prematurity, rubella, and Rh incompatibility have a complete vision examination (not simply a vision screening) prior to assessment. Emotional/behavioral assessment is indicated for all the etiologies shown in Table 2.3. Likewise, due to the high prevalence of cerebral palsy for children whose hearing impairment is due to Rh incompatibility, examiners should ascertain the degree of any motor impairment prior to testing.

Hearing Status of Parents

Description. As a group, hearing-impaired students with a hearing-impaired parent(s) have many advantages over those with hearing parents. These advantages may include earlier diagnosis, acceptance and understanding, language exposure, and visual enhancement. Schlesinger and Meadow (1972) found that interactions between deaf children and their deaf parents tended to be less stressful, more positive, more reciprocal, and more successful than interactions between deaf children and their hearing parents. Also, fewer additional handicaps tend to be associated with hearing losses that are genetic (Conrad, 1979). Yet, hearing-impaired children having a hearing-impaired parent are in the minority; about 3% of hearing-impaired children have two hearing-impaired parents, and approximately 7% have one hearing-impaired parent (Altshuler, 1974; Freeman et al., 1981; Quigley & Kretschmer, 1982).

Of children having hereditary hearing losses, 75 to 80% are caused by an autosomal recessive gene from parents who usually have no hearing loss (Freeman et al., 1981). The remaining 20% of hearing-impaired children with hereditary losses have one or both hearing-impaired parents. Because numerous genetic syndromes are known to result in hearing loss (Freeman et al., 1981; Nance, 1976), and the genetic history of a child may be difficult to trace, the incidence of hearing loss due to the genetic information of hearing parents may be higher than has been reported. If this is the case, then the percentage of hearing-impaired children with hereditary losses and hearing parents is likely to be higher than the 75 to 80% that has been reported thus far.

It would be inaccurate to conclude that all losses due to heredity are profound and of the sensorineural type. Previously, we mentioned that some hereditary losses may be progressive; however, conductive loss not due to a progressive condition and due to heredity (e.g., malformed ossicles) has been reported as well (Myklebust, 1964).

Early research showed that hearing-impaired students of hearing-impaired parents were superior to other hearing-impaired students in academic achievement, intelligence, social skills, language development, and adjustment (Meadow, 1978; Stuckless & Birch, 1966; Vernon & Koh, 1970). There is disagreement as to whether a superiority exists and what the cause of any superiority is (e.g., acceptance, auditory stimulation, and/or early language exposure). If hearing-impaired children of hearing-impaired parents show superiority in any area, it is likely to be in communication skills because, "unlike deaf children of hearing parents, many deaf children of deaf parents are experienced communicators well before preschool age. By the time the child enters school, interpersonal communication has become a way of life" (Levine, 1981, p. 63).

In addition to communication skills, emerging evidence for better performance of hearing-impaired students of hearing-impaired parents is provided from two sources. Kamphe and Turecheck (1987) reviewed the literature pertaining to reading achievement of deaf students and concluded that deaf students of hearing-impaired parents attain higher reading achievement levels than deaf students of hearing parents. Zwiebel and Mertens (1985a) compared the cognitive skills of hearing-impaired students of hearing-impaired parents with those of hearing-impaired students of hearing parents. The former were found to obtain higher scores, and their scores were comparable to the scores of hearing students.

Relevance for Assessment. For the approximately 10% of hearing-impaired students with at least one hearing-impaired parent, examiners will be likely to find that these students have a severe-to-profound loss, but established language and communication skills. For such students, the examiner must carry out the assessment in the primary mode of communication of the student, even if another examiner or an interpreter is required.

In comparison, the majority of hearing-impaired students of hearing parents are unlikely to have language and communication skills as well established as those of hearing-impaired students of hearing-impaired parents. Often, the mode of communication used in the home does not match that used in the school or with hearing-impaired peers. The examiner may have difficulty determining the student's primary mode of communication. In this case, it may be necessary to consult with communication specialists familiar with the student, or to use some other method to determine the mode of communication that is more likely to result in comprehension of test requirements and expression of responses (e.g., observation of the student, attempts to communicate with the student, presenting informal test items using various methods of communication).

Configuration/Laterality

Description. Configuration and laterality are terms that refer to the audiological profile of a student's hearing. Configuration is the pattern of hearing acuity at various frequencies tested for each ear. The human ear can hear frequencies from approximately 20 to 20,000 cycles per second (also called hertz, or Hz), but is maximally sensitive to sounds between 500 and 4000 Hz (i.e., the speech range). Harrison (1985) noted that some frequencies may be more affected than others and that loss generally is greater for high frequencies. Consonants are high frequency. "Consonants carry the information of speech; unfortunately, most deaf and hard-of-hearing have the least amount of hearing in the high frequency range" (Heimgartner, 1982, p. 13). Laterality refers to the hearing ability of each ear. A different configuration is generally obtained for each ear, although the general pattern may be similar. For example, students with sensorineural hearing losses usually have greater losses at high frequencies than at low ones (vowels are low frequency), although the exact degree may vary slightly for each ear.

Figure 2.2 provides an example of an audiological record (audiogram). The horizontal axis indicates the frequencies (in hertz) that are presented by the audiologist. As has been indicated, the better ear average is usually obtained at the frequencies of 500, 1000, and 2000 Hz, although during testing additional frequencies in the speech range generally are presented. The vertical axis indicates the degree of hearing loss (in decibels). Decibels are a measure of sound intensity, and are on a logarithmic scale, meaning that a tone of 20 dB is not twice as loud as a tone of 10 dB, but 10 times as loud (Quigley & Kretschmer, 1982). Plotted on the record are the hearing thresholds for each frequency, defined as the decibels at which a frequency is detected at least two-thirds to three-quarters of the time it is presented. Generally, frequencies are presented in 5 dB increments until the threshhold is determined.

Hearing thresholds are plotted for both air conduction and bone conduction. Air conduction refers to presentation of a tone to the auditory canal using headphones, thereby permitting the air in the auditory canal and the ossicles to transmit the sound energy to the cochlea. Bone conduction is performed by placing a vibrator against the head, usually behind the ear, which allows bone structures to transmit the sound energy to the cochlea, bypassing the outer and middle ear. Rodda and Grove (1987) pointed out that bone conduction does not completely bypass the outer and middle ear, but vibrates both the ossicles and air in the outer ear as well. Although the configuration of each student's hearing is unique, patterns do exist. Figures 2.3, 2.4, and 2.5 present audiograms indicating conductive, sensorineural, and mixed hearing losses, respectively. Audiograms are classified on the basis of average level of loss, frequency range,

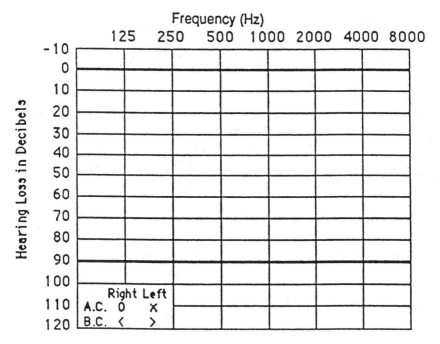

Figure 2.2. An audiogram.

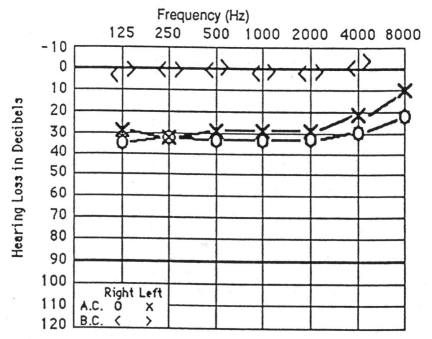

Figure 2.3. Audiogram indicating a conductive loss.

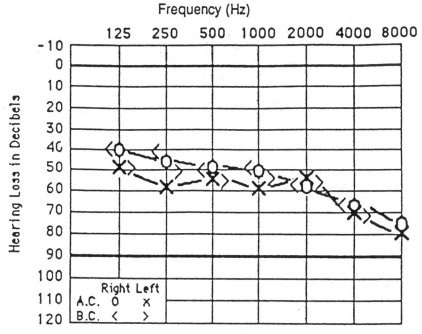

Figure 2.4. Audiogram indicating a sensorineural loss.

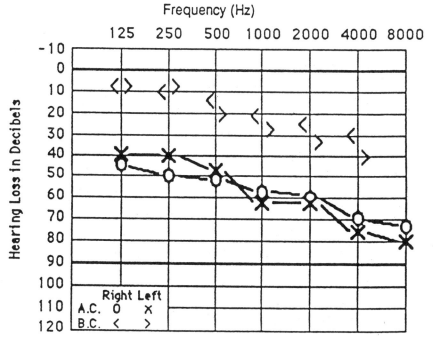

Figure 2.5. Audiogram indicating a mixed loss.

shape, and slope (Erber, 1981). These variables may provide evidence of the cause of the hearing loss and the nature of residual hearing.

Relevance for Assessment. PL 94-142 states that handicapped students are to receive support services required to assist with their special education program. For hearing-impaired students these services often include speech pathology and audiological services. Audiological services are defined as identification of hearing losses; ascertainment of the range, nature, and degree of the loss; and determination of need for, selection, fitting, and evaluation of amplification. Schools also are required to ensure that amplification systems function properly. Hence, the examiner should have access to information describing each student's hearing loss, as well as assurance that students have the necessary and proper amplification.

For the purpose of providing proper amplification, the student's *unaided* configuration and laterality are of primary importance. For the purpose of assessment, however, the student's *aided* configuration and laterality are of primary value.

Information regarding the student's aided hearing should be available to the examiner. Based on that information and knowledge of the type of hearing loss, the examiner can determine what the student is likely to experience audiologically. For example, the loudness of conversational speech is about 50 to 60 dB. With optimal amplification, a student with a profound, sensorineural hearing loss may have an aided loss of only 50 dB in the speech range (Meadow, 1978). Such a student is likely to hear speech with some degree of distortion, have trouble hearing faint or distant speech, and not detect weaker acoustic cues of speech (Boothroyd, 1987). Hence, examiners should be aware that hearing-impaired students with aided loss in the speech range of 50 dB or more have difficulty hearing and understanding speech, and the use of speech during assessment should be accompanied by the use of nonvocal cues.

A student with an unaided conductive loss of 50 dB may have an aided loss that falls in the normal range. An examiner might conclude that this student could be tested much as a hearing student. Such conclusions should be tenuous and assume that the student always had an aided loss that fell in the normal range and did not impact speech and language development. The student's speech and language skills, however, may be delayed due to lack of early amplification, and the student may have developed other methods of communication. Also, the student may be experiencing distortion that impacts speech reception. Thus, an examiner can use audiological data for aided performance to understand a student's functional hearing loss, but the information is best used in conjunction with observation and interview to determine the most valid manner of assessment.

Education

Description.   A survey of hearing-impaired students for the 1977–1978 school year (Karchmer et al., 1979) found that 35.1% of hearing-impaired students were receiving educational services in residential schools for the deaf, 16.7% received services in day schools for the deaf, 21.5% were in full-time special education classes in local public schools, and the remaining 26.6% were in local public schools integrated (mainstreamed) into regular education classes for some part of the day. The survey also found that a relationship existed between the type of program a student attended and the degree of hearing loss, with a larger percentage of students having profound and severe losses being served in special schools (residential and day) and a smaller percentage attending local public schools either in full-time or part-time special education programs.

More recent survey data regarding the educational placement of hearing-impaired students were reported by W. N. Craig and Craig (1987), who found that, at a national level, 17% were attending residential schools, with the remaining 83% attending day programs. Of those attending day programs, 20% were partially mainstreamed and 14% were totally mainstreamed. A general trend away from residential placements toward day programs was found, providing support that the gradual movement from residential schools, begun over 10 years ago, is continuing (Quigley & Kretschmer, 1982).

Relevance for Assessment.   The educational placement of a student affects the type of information required from assessment. A goal of the assessment of a hearing-impaired student in a classroom for the learning disabled, for example, would be to reevaluate the placement, which requires the selection of appropriate cognitive and achievement measures. For hearing-impaired students who are or may be appropriate for mainstreaming, a comparison of their skills with the skills of students in the integrated program may be important information to collect from assessment. This may involve the assessment of skills for which the hearing-impaired student is handicapped to some degree, yet can provide information for programming.

A survey by Rittenhouse (1987) found that the majority of regular education teachers of high-school hearing-impaired students felt prepared for mainstreaming, but did not think that adequate information was provided to develop an individualized educational program. Hence, it may be more important to provide detailed programming information for students who are eligible or currently are mainstreamed.

Language and Communication

Description.   A variety of methods are used by hearing-impaired students to receive communication. These include reading speech, sign, gesture, and/or print, and hearing (aided and unaided), either solely or in combination. In a national study of hearing-impaired students, Karchmer and Kirwin (1977) found that over 80% used some type of amplification to aid hearing. In 1976, Jordan, Gustason, and Rosen reported that 64.3% of classrooms for hearing-impaired students used total communication (combination of sign, speech reading, and hearing), 33% used an oral–aural approach (speech reading and hearing), 2.2% used the Rochester method (finger spelling, speech reading, and hearing), and .5% used cued speech (speech reading with manual cues and hearing). By 1979, these percentages had changed slightly to 64.7% using total communication, 34.6% using oral–aural, .5% using the Rochester method, and .2% using cued speech (Jordan, Gustason, & Rosen, 1979). These results indicate the continued popularity of total communication over other methods and continued prevalence of use of the major methods (total communication and oral–aural). The results also point to a distinction between total communication and other combinations of voice and hand movements, as total communication involves simultaneous expression using voice and sign, whereas cued speech, for example, uses hand movements to enhance discrimination for some words that may be difficult for speech readers to distinguish.

Hearing-impaired students may use sign, gesture, voice, or writing, solely or in combination, for expression of language. The languages used by hearing-impaired persons include English and American Sign Language (ASL). ASL is the manual system used by most deaf persons (Quigley & Paul, 1984). ASL is a distinct language, and its grammar and syntax differ from those of English (Clements & Prickett, 1986). Quigley and Kretschmer (1982) provided a breakdown of the forms of language and modes of communication used by hearing-impaired children. This information is presented in Table 2.4. Although Manual English and Oral English have the same root language, Manual English incorporates ASL in its methods of communication. For example, Signing Exact English is made up of 61% ASL signs, 18% modified ASL signs, and 21% new signs (Bornstein, 1973). Likewise, Signed English is a combination of ASL and English using English word order with ASL signs and characteristics. Hence, Oral and Manual English are separated as language systems in Table 2.4

In the 1982–1983 annual survey, Jordan and Karchmer (1986) found that two-thirds of the hearing-impaired students were reported to sign and to attend schools in which signs were used for instruction. About 35% of these students' families used sign for communication in the home setting.

TABLE 2.4
Languages and Methods of Communication Used by
Hearing-Impaired Persons

Language	Method of communication
American Sign Language	Sign
Manual English	Finger spelling
	Cued speech
	Linguistics of visual English
	Seeing Essential English
	Signing Exact English
	Signed English
	Amelish, Siglish (Pidgin)
Oral English	Aural/oral method
	Acoupedic (unisensory)
Simultaneous	Rochester method
	Total communication

Note. Adapted from *The Education of Deaf Children* (pp. 9–29) by S. P. Quigley and R. E. Kretschmer, 1982, Austin, TX: PRO-ED. Copyright 1982 by PRO-ED. Reprinted with permission.

The use of sign in this survey included any type of manual communication. The authors reported that these findings are similar to those reported over the past decade.

Relevance for Assessment. Trott (1984) stated that, "perhaps the variable that most defines the validity of the psychoeducational evaluation of an auditorily handicapped child is the mode of communication used during the evaluation and whether the child has fully understood what was expected" (p. 320). Due to the directive of PL 94-142 to provide assessment in the student's native language or other mode of communication except when not feasible, the hearing-impaired student's language skills have direct relevance to the assessment process and test selection. Ideally, a test should be administered in the student's native language using the student's receptive skills, and responses should be gathered based on the student's expressive skills. Examiners should be utilized who can effectively communicate with and understand responses of the student. Test selection is based upon standardization of these methods of communication. For example, a student whose primary method of communication is ASL would be administered tests standardized upon hearing-impaired students using ASL. Unfortunately, this often is not possible given the limited number of assessment instruments and skilled examiners.

Knowing that hearing-impaired students differ in language and expressive and receptive communication skills, examiners, with the assistance of the student's teacher and speech pathologist, must determine the student's language. The language for the majority of hearing-impaired students is either English or ASL. Next, the student's modes of reception and expression need to be identified, with primary modes targeted for use during testing. Although most classrooms use total communication (I. K. Jordan & Karchmer, 1986; I. K. Jordan et al., 1979), total communication consists of any combination of oral and manual systems, and examiner fluency with one combination does not guarantee fluency with other forms. For classrooms using total communication, however, a combination of Signed English and spoken English is most commonly used (Clements & Prickett, 1986).

Some evidence exists that hearing-impaired students often learn more than one method of communication. Eagney (1987) found that, when students were provided instruction in ASL, manually coded English, or a simplified manually coded English, no significant differences were found in comprehension. In a study of the receptive communication skills of 118 hearing-impaired children with hearing losses (unaided) greater than 60 dB, Grove and Rodda (1984) found that, although the highest comprehension was noted for reading, good comprehension was found for total communication, manual communication, and oral communication. Hence, for many hearing-impaired students, it may be possible to identify more than one method of communication that could be utilized to communicate instructions during assessment.

Oral Language and Speech Reading

Description.　As noted previously, for hearing-impaired students who use oral language, speech intelligibility appears to be related to the degree of hearing loss. Karchmer et al. (1979) noted that only 23% of hearing-impaired persons with hearing losses greater than 90 dB were found to have intelligible speech. Whether a student's speech can be understood in a particular situation is a function of several variables, which have been noted by Monsen, Moog, and Geers (1988):

> 1) the experience of the listener; 2) the context in which the sentence was spoken; 3) the visibility of the speaker; 4) the phonologic and syntactic difficulty of the material spoken; and 5) the familiarity of the speaker with the material spoken. (p. 3)

The authors suggested that the listener's experience with deaf speech is the factor that most influences the intelligibility of the speech of hearing-impaired persons.

Hearing-impaired students who attempt to obtain information via speech reading have a difficult task, especially if speech reading is used alone. One factor that makes speech reading so difficult is that 40 to 60% of the sounds of English look like other sounds or are invisible to the reader (Vernon, 1972).

Relevance for Assessment.   Knowing the degree of hearing loss for a student provides some indication as to whether the student's speech will be intelligible. Certainly, the more familiar an examiner is with a student, and with the speech of hearing-impaired persons, the easier it will be to understand a hearing-impaired student's speech. Ensuring ample time to establish rapport, especially for hearing-impaired students who use speech, is an important step in enabling an examiner to understand what the student says during testing.

It is important to recognize how difficult it is for hearing-impaired students to obtain information via speech reading. As noted by Harrison (1985), "if a child depends primarily on speechreading (lipreading) to comprehend others' speech, comprehension will be imprecise at best and fatigue will set in quickly" (p. 190). Examiners can use a number of procedures to aid speech reading during an assessment (these are discussed in Chapter 3). To assume that, because a student utilizes speech reading, he or she can understand all directions given orally would be a mistake. About half of the words in speech reading are not distinguishable by watching the mouth (Freeman et al., 1981).

Multiple Handicaps

Description.   As noted previously, the population of hearing-impaired students is heterogeneous. Many hearing-impaired students overlap with other handicapped groups, each with their own characteristics. In a survey of over 50 thousand hearing-impaired students, Karchmer et al. (1979) found mental retardation to be the most common additional handicap (7.8%), followed by visual impairment (7.4%), emotional/behavioral problems (6.7%), cerebral palsy (2.9%), brain damage (2.6%), heart disorder (2.6%), orthopedic impairment (1.9%), specific learning disability (1.6%), and epilepsy (.9%). Comparatively, the prevalence rate in school-age hearing children is about 1.9% for mental retardation, 1% for visual impairment, .15% for orthopedic impairment, and 4.5% for learning disabilities (Hallahan et al., 1986). Hence, for most handicapping conditions, hearing-impaired students show higher prevalence rates than do hearing students. According to Goldsmith and Schloss (1986), the lower prevalence of learning disabilities among hearing-impaired children may be due to diagnostic overshadowing rather than actual lower rates off occurrence. The seriousness of multiple handicaps is shown by the estimate that approximately 30% of hearing-impaired children have one or more additional handicaps (Wolff & Harkins, 1986).

There are many discrepancies in reports of the prevalence of additional handicaps. For example, Schildroth (1986) found school staff to report that less than 20% of hearing-impaired students had one or more additional handicaps, whereas Karchmer et al. (1979) found schools to report that 28% of hearing-impaired students had one or more additional handicaps. These discrepancies are likely to be a function of the definition used for "handicap" and the method used to gather data. Freeman et al. (1981) stated that the actual number of hearing-impaired students with additional handicaps is likely lower than that reported by schools in surveys. This discrepancy may be due to lack of data from mainstreamed hearing-impaired students, who may be overlooked in surveys due to less severe hearing losses and fewer additional handicaps (Karchmer et al., 1979).

Further evidence that operationalization and data collection affect the percentage of hearing-impaired students reported to have additional handicaps is provided from a number of sources. Blennerhassett and Spragins (1983) indicated that 35 to 40% of hearing-impaired students have multiple handicaps, whereas Gentile and McCarthy (1973) reported 25% to have multiple handicaps. Conrad (1979) found that attempting to use reliable definitions resulted in 11% of hearing-impaired children being identified as having multiple handicaps. In a survey of hearing-impaired students in Iowa, Shepard, Davis, Gorga, and Stelmachowicz (1981) found 13% to have additional handicaps.

The important point regarding reports of the percentage of hearing-impaired students with multiple handicaps is that these students tend to have more additional handicaps than the hearing population. Estimates of additional handicaps appear to vary from 11 to 40%, depending upon definition and data collection methods. This range (11 to 40%) is substantial. The higher incidence of additional handicaps may be directly related to the cause of the hearing loss. For example, visual deficiencies have been found in 51% of hearing-impaired children (Myklebust, 1964). Mental retardation occurs in about 15% of children with hearing impairment due to meningitis (Freeman et al., 1981). Physical disability, including cerebral palsy, occurs in 75% of children whose hearing impairment is due to Rh incompatibility (Freeman et al., 1981). Both learning disability and hearing loss are associated with prematurity. Hearing loss, cataracts and other visual impairments, and mental retardation are all associated with maternal rubella (Stein, Palmer, & Weinberg, 1982; Yarnall, 1983). Five of the major etiologies of hearing impairment (genetics, maternal rubella, meningitis, prematurity, and Rh factor incompatibility) are etiologies for a variety of cognitive, behavioral, and physical disorders (Vernon, 1982).

There may be other areas of disability not included in current esti-mates of multiple handicaps for hearing-impaired children. For example, Butterfield (1986) studied the gross motor skills of 132 deaf children 3 to 14 years of age and found that deaf children had more trouble with several skills, most noticeably those related to balance. In a study of 2- and 3-year-old hearing-impaired children, Scherer (1983) also found a higher inci-dence of motor problems in hearing-impaired children than in hearing children.

Relevance for Assessment. The presence of additional handicaps compounds assessment problems faced by examiners of hearing-impaired students. Examiners must incorporate considerations for assessing hear-ing-impaired students with those for assessing students with the addi-tional handicap. This may present various difficulties. For example, in a review of available instruments, Vernon, Bair, and Lotz (1979) found no standardized tests for deaf–blind children. In addition, information the examiner needs in order to provide valid assessment may not be available, as additional handicaps may preclude or obscure the determination of factors such as degree of hearing loss, configuration and laterality, and language and method of communication.

The lack of information regarding psychoeducational assessment of hearing-impaired students with additional handicaps highlights funda-mental guidelines for assessment. It is important for the examiner to gather as much relevant data as possible about the student prior to testing in order to determine the student's handicaps so that disabilities are not assessed. Identification of the student's method(s) of communication becomes critical to valid assessment of skills. Because appropriate standard-ized assessment instruments may not be available, observation, interviews, criterion-referenced tests, and curriculum-based measures gain impor-tance. Decisions must be based on such multiple sources of information.

Assessment of deaf–mentally retarded students requires considerable caution, given the numerous factors that contribute to the underestimate of the performance of a hearing-impaired student (e.g., failure to under-stand instructions, broken hearing aid). As Vernon and Alles (1986) noted, a low score is more likely to be inaccurate than a high one. Considerations before, during, and after testing (discussed in Chapter 3) become critical. In addition, accurate diagnosis of mental retardation in hearing-impaired students requires use of measures with norms for hearing-impaired stu-dents (e.g., *Hiskey–Nebraska Test of Learning Aptitude;* Hiskey, 1966) or measures for which hearing-impaired students have been shown to obtain the same overall mean performance (e.g., *Adaptation of the WISC-R for the Deaf;* Ray, 1979), as well as adaptive behavior information.

Assessment of students with both learning disabilities and hearing impairments also requires care. School psychologists, independent of experience, may be less likely to diagnose a learning disability for a hearing-impaired student than for a hearing student (Goldsmith & Schloss, 1986). In addition, nonverbal measures commonly used with hearing-impaired students do not correlate well with achievement (Watson, Goldar, Kroese, & Lotz, 1986), and discrepancies between nonverbal IQ and achievement may occur without indicating a learning disability.

Other Dimensions

Other potential dimensions on which hearing-impaired students vary are similar to dimensions on which hearing students vary. They include sex, race, socioeconomic status, and achievement. It is unclear, however, whether these dimensions are any more relevant to the assessment of hearing-impaired students than to that of hearing students. By a small margin, hearing impairment is more common in males than females, and the margin decreases as the degree of hearing loss becomes greater (Karchmer et al., 1979). Hearing loss appears with approximately equal frequency in children of different ethnicity (Karchmer et al., 1979; Ries, Bateman, & Schildroth, 1975). Thus, for the purpose of assessment, knowledge of a student's race generally is of equal significance for hearing-impaired and hearing students. The incidence of hearing impairment appears to be independent of social class (Rodda & Grove, 1987). A relationship does exist, however, between unclean living conditions (often associated with lowest socioeconomic levels) and conductive hearing loss.

As with hearing students, achievement scores of hearing-impaired students may assume a range of values. In contrast to hearing students, correlation of achievement scores and IQ scores of hearing-impaired students generally result in lower values, indicating that achievement provides less information (i.e., is less predictive) about the cognitive skills of hearing-impaired students. Also, data strongly suggest that achievement for hearing-impaired students tends to be less related to age (and more to other factors) than it is for hearing students (Trybus & Karchmer, 1977). Hence, a student's level of achievement may be less informative for hearing-impaired students than for hearing students.

The lower correlation found for achievement and intelligence tests for hearing-impaired than for hearing students is, however, likely to be a function of several variables. First, the correlations are usually based upon a comparison of achievement results and only the nonvocal portion of intelligence tests. Second, because of the many problems with the technical adequacy of both intelligence and achievement tests for hearing-impaired students, the low correlations may be at least partially due to the problems with the available tests for this population of students.

3

Assessment Issues
and Procedures

The first section in this chapter addresses the requirements for assessing hearing-impaired students as mandated by PL 94-142. This section is followed by a discussion of general issues that are important to consider in selecting tests and procedures so that valid results are obtained. The remainder of the chapter deals with specific issues that require consideration before, during, and after direct testing of a student; each section is followed by a detailed checklist to aid in applying the information at the appropriate time.

PL 94-142 and Requirements for Assessment

Implementation of PL 94-142 (1975) had an impact on the manner in which handicapped children are identified, as evidenced by the law's regulations pertaining to assessment. "Before any action is taken with respect to the initial placement of a handicapped child in a special education program, a full and individual evaluation of the child's educational needs must be conducted" (*Federal Register,* 1977, p. 42496). Mandated requirements for the assessment are that:

(a) Tests and other evaluative materials:
   (1) Are provided and administered in the child's native language or other mode of communication, unless it is clearly not feasible to do so:
   (2) Have been validated for the specific purpose for which they are used; and
   (3) Are administered by trained personnel in conformance with the instructions provided by their producers;

(b) Tests and other evaluation materials include those tailored to assess specific areas of educational need and not merely those which are designed to provide a single general intelligence quotient;

(c) Tests are selected and administered so as best to ensure that when a test is administered to a child with impaired sensory, manual, or speaking skills, the test results accurately reflect the child's aptitude or achievement level or whatever other factors the test purports to measure, rather than reflecting the child's impaired sensory, manual or speaking skills (except where those skills are the factors which the test purports to measure);

(d) No single procedure is used as the sole criterion for determining an appropriate educational program for a child; and

(e) The evaluation is made by a multidisciplinary team or group of persons, including at least one teacher or other specialist with knowledge in the area of suspected disability.

(f) The child is assessed in all areas related to the suspected disability, including, where appropriate, health, vision, hearing, social and emotional status, general intelligence, academic performance, communicative status, and motor abilities. (*Federal Register,* 1977, pp. 42496–42497).

These regulations signify important considerations for the assessment and subsequent planning of appropriate educational programming for hearing-impaired students. First, because hearing impairment is sometimes associated with additional handicaps, initial assessments need to include a variety of instruments and procedures to identify related handicaps, assess educational need, and plan appropriate programs. Second, valid measures for hearing-impaired students must be selected that can be administered using the student's native language or secondary method(s) of communication. Hence, in the selection of appropriate assessment measures, the language of the student must have precedence over the language of the examiner and the language used in available instruments. Examiners must be able to use the student's language and method of communication expressively and receptively. Third, selected measures must assess abilities rather than disabilities that are due to impaired hearing. Furthermore, instruments must be administered by trained examiners according to test instructions and procedures.

The result of these requirements is that examiners of hearing-impaired students often face dilemmas in providing assessments that meet legal mandates. Especially difficult is the task of identifying valid measures that can be administered using a student's communication method, a task compounded by the requirement that all areas related to the suspected disability be assessed.

PL 94-142 also has defined the procedures for providing educational services to handicapped children, most noticeably through the requirement that for each handicapped student an individual educational program (IEP) be developed. A requisite to the IEP is that handicaps, skills, and skill deficits have been identified through assessment. Given the assessment requirements of PL 94-142 as they pertain to hearing-impaired students, the dilemmas faced by examiners of hearing-impaired students can be eased through knowledge of four areas: (a) the characteristics of hearing-impaired students as described in Chapter 2; (b) the fundamental issues involved in the assessment of hearing-impaired students discussed in this chapter; (c) the available assessment instruments, their technical adequacy, and communication requirements; and (d) methods to enhance the relevance of assessment results to educational programming. These latter two areas are addressed in the chapters that follow.

General Considerations for Selecting Tests and Procedures

The following issues pertain to hearing-impaired students as a group and are less related to subgroups formed by characteristics such as type or degree of hearing loss.

Nonvocal Responses

As noted above, according to PL 94-142, assessment instruments for handicapped students must measure a student's abilities rather than disabilities related to the handicapping condition. Because loss of hearing results in delayed speech and language development for the majority of hearing-impaired students, tests of cognitive ability or achievement that require verbal skills would not be considered appropriate unless oral language was the concern.

Even before PL 94-142 was implemented, however, the literature addressed the inappropriateness of the use of verbal measures with hearing-impaired students. Vernon and Brown (1964) stated that, "to be valid as a measure of the intelligence of a deaf youngster an IQ test must be a nonverbal performance-type instrument. Verbal tests with deaf children are almost always inappropriate" (p. 415). Myklebust (1964) also stated that verbal measures are inappropriate for hearing-impaired children, particularly the prelingually deaf, and some postlingually deaf. Furth (1973) suggested that, "from what is known about the low level of language skill in deaf children, verbal tests are quite unsuitable" (p. 89).

After the advent of PL 94-142, authors continued to agree about the inappropriateness of verbal measures with hearing-impaired students. Sullivan and Vernon (1979) stated that verbal measures are inappropriate for deaf and hard-of-hearing children with even mild and moderate hearing losses. Zieziula (1982) indicated that "tests made up of verbal items are inappropriate for many hearing-impaired individuals, especially those individuals who became auditorally impaired before the normal development of language" (p. 2). Zwiebel and Mertens (1985b) noted that intelligence tests appropriate for the deaf must "avoid the heavily verbal nature of many intelligence tests" (p. 151). Similarly, Trott (1984) stated that "to report the hearing-impaired student's incorrect responses to verbal items may be again to give evidence of the child's auditory disability and its developmental impact. It does not accurately report intelligence or estimate cognitive ability" (p. 321).

Others have not been as critical of the use of verbal measures with hearing-impaired students. In a survey of examiners of hearing-impaired students in 48 states, Levine (1974) found many to use verbal items from the Wechsler scales to broaden the scope of the assessment. Earlier, Levine (1971) indicated that verbal items can be useful in making decisions regarding mainstreaming for hearing-impaired students. Sattler (1982), referring to the *Wechsler Intelligence Scale for Children–Revised* (WISC-R), stated, "a comparison of the Verbal IQ with the Performance IQ in deaf children provides an estimate of the degree to which the child has mastered verbal concepts" (p. 418). Miller (1985) reported that "it may no longer be necessary to rely solely upon nonverbal tasks to measure the intelligence of deaf individuals" (p. 134), and Boyle (1977) stated that verbal measures should be given to those with adequate verbal language skills, cautiously interpreted, and given last in the assessment to avoid undue frustration.

Due to the relationship of hearing with speech and language skills, instruments measuring speech or language skills as part of the cognitive assessment would result in an underestimate of skills for many hearing-impaired students. Given that the majority of hearing-impaired students have prelingual hearing losses and are delayed in learning either oral or sign language (Liben, 1978; Rawlings & Ries, 1973; Silverman, Lane, & Doehring, 1960), measures considered to be nonverbal in nature would be appropriate in order to measure abilities rather than disabilities related to the handicap. Ideally, such measures should have instructions and response requirements that have been standardized on hearing-impaired students, or that use a level of language attained by children and adolescents given the measure. Bragman (1982a) recommended that, in the future, test instructions be provided at two levels of language (low and high) to ensure that all hearing-impaired children understand instructions. Indeed, Ray (1979) and Ray and Ulissi (1982) provided two sets of instructions, Alternative and Supplemental, with their Adaptations of the WISC-R and WPPSI for hearing-impaired students. It may be necessary to consult with a speech–language specialist to determine if instructions for a nonverbal measure can be used with a student, or if the student's speech and language skills permit the use of verbal measures. If an examiner wishes to use verbal tests to measure a child's skills for mainstreaming or mastery of verbal skills, administration is best done by communication specialists rather than psychological examiners (Trott, 1984).

Communication of Test Instructions

PL 94-142 mandates that test instructions be provided and administered in the student's native language or other method of communication unless it is not feasible. This mandate appears to be directed more toward hearing students who speak a language other than English, than for hearing-impaired students; yet, ensuring that test requirements are understood is basic to assessment of any population. Unfortunately, the language and communication skills of hearing-impaired students are heterogeneous and the number of assessment instruments finite, creating difficulty in assessing these students.

For most instruments, instructions are frequently modified to adapt instruments for use with hearing-impaired students. In fact, Bragman (1982b) indicated that modification of the communication of test instructions is the most common method of adapting available measures for use with hearing-impaired students. Bragman further stated that the three most common modifications of communicating test instructions are the use of pantomime; demonstration; and language communication using speech, speech reading, written word, or manual communication.

Despite alteration of the method used to communicate test instructions to hearing-impaired students, the effect upon test results is often not considered, but may be a factor. Test standardization involves a standard set of materials, administration procedures, scoring procedures, and interpretation procedures (Berdine & Meyer, 1987), and departures from test standardization may have an impact on validity of results. For example, Zieziula (1982) pointed out that, "there is no doubt that standardization of instruction procedures is lacking for many tests administered to hearing-impaired people, especially for tests designed for verbal instructions. . . . Validity of results becomes a major issue when this problem arises" (p. 2). Likewise, Levine (1971) indicated that one intent of standardization is to "supply unequivocal methods of test administration and scoring so that all who take the test are given exactly the same directions and are scored according to the same criteria of performance. Deviation destroys validity" (p. 90).

A few studies have provided some information about the effect of changing the method used to communicate test instructions. Using hearing children, Graham and Shapiro (1953) found use of pantomime instructions to produce lower WISC IQs than use of verbal instructions. R. J. Anderson and Sisco (1977) found that when a variety of methods were used to communicate WISC-R Performance Scale subtest instructions to hearing-impaired children, the mean Performance IQ was significantly lower than the mean for hearing children by 4 points. Unfortunately, Anderson and Sisco did not provide the mean Performance IQ for each method of communication. In contrast, Ray (1979) utilized a standard set of instructions with hearing-impaired students and found that the mean Performance IQ did not differ significantly from the mean for hearing children.

Sullivan (1982) found that communicating subtest instructions using total communication (voice with Signed English) resulted in higher Performance IQs than use of verbal (oral) statements and gestures. In a second study, Sullivan (1982) found that use of total communication produced higher Performance IQs or subtest scores than use of visual aids or pantomime for hearing-impaired children with genetic etiologies or with multiple handicaps. In a review of studies investigating the effects of different instructions upon the performance of hearing-impaired children, Bragman (1982b) concluded that, "an analysis of the studies involving test directions for the deaf does not give a clear indication that differing directional sets can be considered equivalent or interchangeable" (p. 344).

Preliminary research with the *Kaufman Assessment Battery for Children* (K-ABC; Kaufman & Kaufman, 1983), published after Bragman's (1982b) review, indicated that use of pantomime and gestures with deaf children does not produce different scores on the Nonverbal Scale than if American Sign Language (ASL) with gestures and pantomime are used, and that use of either method of communication does not produce results different from the hearing norms (L. J. Porter & Kirby, 1986). Hence, for the K-ABC, two methods have been shown to yield results equivalent to the standardized method. Whether the methods are equivalent in other respects, however, such as standard deviation, reliability, and validity, remains to be investigated.

Because tests are to be administered in a student's native language or other method of communication, examiners may inadvertently administer a test using a nonstandardized method of communication that handicaps a hearing-impaired student's performance. Therefore, among other considerations, test selection should be based, if possible, on standardization of the test using the student's language and method of communication or on data indicating that using the student's language and method of communication is equivalent to using the standardized instructions. Hence, because the majority of tests were not standardized using nonvocal instructions and do not present data showing that other methods of communication produce equivalent results, use of these tests requires recognition that validity of tests may be compromised and that scores such as IQs may be affected by the method of communication by as much as 15 points (Sullivan, 1982).

WISC-R Instructions.   A good deal of research has been devoted to the impact of the method used to communicate WISC-R test instructions. Deaf norms provided by R. J. Anderson and Sisco (1977) were not obtained using a standard method of presenting instructions, and no evidence was provided to indicate that the method of communicating test instructions (whether by total communication, speech only, finger spelling with speech, gestures, pantomime, or another method) did not affect the Performance IQ. Ray's (1979) *Adaptation of the WISC-R for the Deaf* provides two sets of standardized instructions. With use of the instructions, Ray found that scores for children with a hearing loss did not differ from those of hearing children in the WISC-R standardization group. Unfortunately, the small number of subjects used as the basis for the *Adaptation* ($N = 127$) and the use of multiple practice items have resulted in questions about the validity of *Adaptation* scores (Evans, 1983; Phelps & Ensor, 1986). Sullivan (1982) found that the use of total communication (verbal statements and Signed English) produces higher Performance IQ scores than the use of verbal statements and gestures, and recommended using the original WISC-R norms when total communication is used. Unfortunately, while Sullivan's (1982) results imply the use of total communication over other methods, the results do not show total communication to be equivalent to the standardized instructions used with hearing children.

Language of Directions.   The purpose of test instructions is to communicate requirements without cuing the student's performance (Levine, 1971). The best method to ensure communication of requirements to a hearing-impaired student is to use the student's language and communication skills. According to federal regulation, educational agencies must ensure that tests are provided and administered in the student's native language *or* other mode of communication, unless it is not feasible. Also, tests must be given by trained examiners according to the provided test instructions (*Federal Register,* 1977). Actually, language and mode of communicating the language are separate entities, as both ASL and English can be communicated using various methods or combinations of methods. Freeman, Carbin, and Boese (1981) stated that native language implies that the student has been exposed to a language since birth, which is true for only a small percentage of hearing-impaired students. According to PL 94-142, however, "the term 'native language,' when used with reference to a person of limited English-speaking ability, means the language normally used by that person, or in the case of a child, the language normally used by the parents of the child" (*Federal Register,* 1977, p. 42479). This PL 94-142 definition of native language is taken from the Bilingual Education Act, which also includes the following directives regarding native language:

(1) In all direct contact with a child (including evaluation of the child), communication would be in the language normally used by the child and not that of the parents, if there is a difference between the two.

(2) If a person is deaf or blind, or has no written language, the mode of communication would be that normally used by the person (such as sign language, braille, or oral communication). (*Federal Register,* 1977, p. 42479)

These additions clearly indicate that a hearing-impaired student's native language is that used by the student, even if different from that of the parents. If the student does not have language skills, then the student's language is assumed to be that of the parents. The mode of communication required to provide tests to a hearing-impaired student, is that mode used by the student. Hence, the examiner's first task is to determine the student's language, then the student's method(s) of communicating the language. For students proficient in using more than one method, the examiner has some latitude in choosing a method.

If a student has no adequate communication skills, then the examiner is resigned to the use of some alternate method of communication (e.g., gestures or pantomime). Use of an alternate method is often necessary due to the delay in language development for hearing-impaired children. Levine's (1974) survey of programs for deaf students found gestures and pantomime to be commonly used during testing with children age 5 and below.

If a student has adequate communication skills, then tests should be given using those skills. If the examiner does not possess those skills, then

reasonable effort to gain skills, obtain expert help, or use a certified interpreter should be made (Braden, 1985a). If this is not feasible, then alternate methods of communication would be appropriate. Regardless of
whether the student's communication skills or an alternate method is used
during testing, tests standardized using that particular method must be
employed or tests whose results have been shown to not differ when that
method of communication is used can be administered. Otherwise, it must
be noted in the report that results may be biased due to the method used to
communicate test instructions.

Decisions Regarding Normative Data

The issue of appropriate normative data for use with hearing-impaired
students closely parallels that of the method of communicating test
instructions. Tests must be validated for the specific purpose for which
they are used (*Federal Register,* 1977). Therefore, the choice of normative
data for hearing-impaired students should result from the standardized
method of presenting instructions to such students. Deaf norms of the
Hiskey–Nebraska Test of Learning Aptitude (Hiskey, 1966) are appropriate
when the standardized (pantomime) instructions are used. WISC-R deaf
norms (R. J. Anderson & Sisco, 1977) do not have a standardized method of
presenting instructions and are less appropriate. Braden (1985a) suggested
that deaf norms for the WISC-R are not a needed alternative by showing
that hearing and deaf norms have almost identical principal factors and
psychometric characteristics. Due to criticism of sampling procedures and
the nonstandardized administration procedures, Braden argued that noth-
ing is gained (and perhaps validity is lost) by utilizing the deaf norms.

The use of norms for hearing-impaired students is not without problems. Many tests with norms for hearing-impaired students are old. Also,
comparison of a hearing-impaired student's performance with that of
other hearing-impaired students may or may not be more appropriate than
the use of hearing norms, given the heterogeneous nature of this population of students. With regard to hearing losses, M. Ross (1981) noted that
there is "such a continuum of degree and types across one or both of their
ears, that characterizing *the* average child to which other children's performance can be compared may be too great an oversimplification" (p. 7).

Because cognitive measures standardized upon hearing-impaired students are few, an alternative is to use measures in which a standard
method of presenting instructions to hearing-impaired students produces
results equivalent to those of hearing students upon which the measure
was normed. For example, the K-ABC and the *Adaptation of the WISC-R for
the Deaf* have such data. Although the method of presenting instructions
to hearing-impaired students may produce overall results that are equiv-

alent to those of the hearing for these measures, the equivalence of the standard deviation, reliability coefficients, and validity data for the hearing and hearing-impaired students must be established before scores from the measure can be considered as valid for hearing-impaired students as for hearing students.

A third choice is to use the hearing norms of measures having no data regarding equivalent results for hearing-impaired students. Obviously, this choice may render results that are not valid. As recognized by Zieziula (1982), however,

> if one were to eliminate from consideration all tests that do not have norms for hearing impaired people—or tests that do not include hearing impaired people within the general norm sample—we would in effect stop using standardized instruments to evaluate this group of people. For pragmatists, this recommendation is unrealistic. What we can do is be very cautious about results of clients who do not mirror individuals for whom the test was designed. (p. 3)

Likewise, Levine (1971) urged that common sense and caution be used to interpret results from tests standardized on hearing students. Failure to utilize hearing norms appropriately with hearing-impaired students may result in differences in scores that are significant to the child's functioning (Quigley & Kretschmer, 1982). For children with scores at the extremes of the distribution (gifted and retarded), however, the differences may be of consequence educationally (Braden, 1985a). In addition, for scales for which hearing-impaired children's distribution of scores may not be similar to that of hearing children, the use of hearing norms with deaf children would produce misleading, invalid results.

Timed Tests

There has been some concern regarding the use of tests with time limits for hearing-impaired students. For example, Sullivan and Vernon (1979) stated that tests with timed responses are less valid than tests without timed responses because hearing-impaired students respond impulsively. Likewise, Sattler (1982) stated that timed tests can be less valid with hearing-impaired students "because the added stress of time may interfere with their performance" (p. 82). Anastasi (1982) indicated that timed tests are inappropriate because "it is difficult to convey the idea of speed to young deaf children" (p. 281). Furth (1973) added that "it seems wise not to give timed tests at all, at least not to young deaf children" (p. 90), whereas Vernon and Brown (1964) wrote that young hearing-impaired children "often react to the factor of timing by working in great haste and ignoring accuracy or else disregarding the time factor completely" (p. 418). Boyle

(1977) pinpointed the creation of anxiety in hearing-impaired students as the problem with timed tasks.

The primary rationale given for the inappropriateness of timed tests is the impulsivity of hearing-impaired students. Sullivan and Vernon (1979) pointed out that "hearing-impaired children often react to being timed by trying to finish as quickly as possible even if their work is incorrect" (p. 274), and that these "impulsive response patterns" hinder the performance of hearing-impaired students.

Despite the cautions regarding impulsivity and timed tests, there seem to be contradictions to the cautions. First, popular intelligence tests used with hearing-impaired students (i.e., the WISC-R Performance Scale, and the *Hiskey–Nebraska*) have a high proportion of timed tests (e.g., all six of the WISC-R Performance Scale subtests are timed). In addition, research (e.g., Ray, 1979) has attempted to show that there is no difference between mean IQ scores of hearing-impaired students and hearing students on the Performance Scale of the WISC-R. If hearing-impaired students are penalized by timed tests, then one would expect their mean performance to be lower than that of hearing students on measures with timed tasks. Furthermore, one could hypothesize that impulsivity would be posited as an explanation of differences between mean IQs of the hearing and hearing-impaired students; however, explanations are concerned almost exclusively with method of communicating instructions.

Second, there is evidence that hearing-impaired students do not have problems with impulsivity. For example, in a study involving 192 deaf students, Schnittjer and Hirshoren (1981) had teachers complete a behavior rating scale that included a subscale measuring immature behavior, including short attention span. Findings indicated no difference between hearing-impaired and hearing students for the subscale.

Research specifically examining impulsivity of hearing-impaired students versus hearing students is not conclusive. Harris (1978) provides a review of research in this area. Although there are many anecdotal accounts of high degrees of impulsivity with hearing-impaired students, only two studies have data-based results for the critical questions of whether the distribution of impulsivity is different for hearing-impaired students than hearing students, and whether the impulsivity is of a magnitude that would affect test performance. In the first study, Altshuler, Deming, Vollenweider, Rainer, and Tendler (1976) compared the performance of hearing and hearing-impaired adolescents on a series of tasks, recording response time and errors. Overall findings were that deaf adolescents responded faster and made more errors (i.e., were impulsive). In a second study, Moores, Weiss, and Goodwin (1973; cited in Harris, 1978) found that of 70 deaf children 5 to 7 years old, 22 could be considered impulsive and 22 could be considered reflective based on scores from the *Matching Familiar Figures Test* (Kagan, 1965), a test frequently used in studies of impulsivity–reflection. The representativeness of the 70 deaf children to the deaf population is not described, so it is difficult to determine the generality of the findings. Based on the available studies, it is unclear whether hearing-impaired students are more impulsive than hearing students. Impulsivity may be related to age or simply to the nature of the measures used to assess impulsivity. In a recent study, however, O'Brien (1987) found hearing-impaired students made significantly more errors than hearing students on a measure of impulsivity, but they did not perform significantly differently on *The Porteus Maze Test* (Porteus, 1965), a measure of intelligence.

Hence, more data are needed before conclusions can be drawn regarding the use of timed tests with hearing-impaired students. For scales with norms for hearing-impaired students, or data supporting a similar distribution of scores for hearing-impaired students and the hearing, such cautions are less applicable. When norms for hearing students are used for hearing-impaired students, however, impulsivity may be a factor requiring careful observation during assessment to determine whether impulsivity may have an impact on performance.

Issues to Consider Before Assessment

In Chapter 2, a number of characteristics were identified as relevant to the assessment process. These characteristics included the type, degree, and etiology of the hearing loss, as well as the age at onset, hearing status of parents, configuration/laterality of the student's audiogram, educational factors, language and communication skills, and presence of additional handicaps. The student's location on the dimensions often has either a direct or an indirect impact on assessment procedures, requiring that this information be obtained prior to testing. Use of the checklist in Chapter 1 for organizing this information should be helpful.

A number of other issues require consideration prior to the direct testing of a hearing-impaired student. These issues are discussed below, followed by a checklist to assist in preparing for the assessment.

Nonverbal Versus Nonvocal Tasks and Responses

As early as 1964, Myklebust noted that nonverbal tests were not equally nonverbal, and that "some mental tests classified as nonverbal involve considerable ability of the type commonly referred to as verbal ability" (p. 62). This continues to be true of tests today. For example, the Picture Arrangement subtest of the WISC-R Performance Scale requires what is considered a nonverbal response, yet has a moderate loading on the Verbal

Comprehension factor of the scale (median loading of .33; Sattler, 1982). It is more accurate to indicate that the subtest requires a *nonvocal* response rather than a *nonverbal* response, as verbal skills are utilized to formulate a response. One verbal skill used to formulate a response to a nonverbal task is covert verbalization. MacMillan and Meyers (1977) stated that "research evidence indicates that nonverbal tests often require a substantial amount of covert verbalization for successful performance" (p. 50). Hence, many tests considered nonverbal may actually measure some degree of verbal ability. When the measure is given using sign language, the student's verbal skills are being used. As Freeman et al. (1981) pointed out, "languages in either modality (sign or spoken) are verbal" and "defining sign languages as non-verbal communication is not only wrong, but dangerous" (pp. 96, 97). Instead, Freeman et al. (1981) indicated that sign languages are nonoral or nonspeech forms of communication.

Hence, examiners need to recognize that a test considered to be non-verbal may assess a student's verbal ability through the test instructions, materials, or response requirements. Because language cannot be avoided when giving most tests, its role needs to be minimized by ensuring that the student's language development exceeds that required by the test. For example, a student may have begun to learn sign language at age 4 in a preschool program. At age 5 or 6, the child most likely has established language and communication skills, but not sufficiently to permit under-standing of K-ABC or WISC-R subtest instructions. Thus, the child's performance may be hindered by not understanding instructions, although the child may have the skills needed to perform the task. Avoiding this problem may require the selection of measures that supplement the language of instructions with practice items, assess primarily nonlanguage skills (as evidenced by weak loading on verbal factors or low correlations with verbal measures), and gather responses minimizing language (e.g., by pointing). When an examiner questions whether a student's current language development may be less than that required for successful test performance, the student's speech–language therapist should be consulted.

Restriction of IQ Definition

In an effort to use measures that do not assess disabilities related to a handicap, examiners of hearing-impaired students may choose to administer selected portions of an instrument (e.g., only the Performance Scale of the WISC-R). Authors of cognitive scales generally include a variety of tasks on a scale in order to assess a wide range of cognitive skills. Even use of a variety of tasks, however, may not tap a sufficiently large number of cognitive skills to provide a comprehensive sample of skills. For example, Guilford and Hoepfner (1971) indicated that the Wechsler scales tap only

11 of the 120 structure-of-the-intellect abilities, and these 11 abilities are assessed only in a superficial manner. Eliminating some portions of a scale futher restricts the range or completeness of assessed skills and subsequently reduces the number of skills represented by the overall score (e.g., the Performance IQ). Extreme caution must be used in interpreting and reporting scores such as the Performance IQ from the WISC-R as a measure of overall intelligence (Levine, 1971; Zieziula, 1982). This is not to suggest that portions of intelligence tests should not be used, but rather that test scores must be interpreted according to the skills that are measured. Because cognitive assessment of hearing-impaired students often involves giving only part of a scale, the resulting standard or scale score represents a restricted measure of the overall test score and should be interpreted accordingly. Even some measures (e.g., the *Test of Nonverbal Intelligence*) that do not generally require the elimination of any portions if given to hearing-impaired students, yet do not assess a variety of skills, should be recognized as producing an overall score based on an assessment of a limited number of cognitive skills.

Correlation of IQ and Achievement

As has been noted, minimizing the assessment of language and verbal skills by judicious test selection or eliminating portions of tests, results in a score that is not equivalent to the overall test scores for a normally hearing student in terms of the number or completeness of cognitive skills assessed. This limitation is manifested in the reduced correlation of IQ scores from what are considered nonverbal measures with measures of achievement (Boyle, 1977). As noted by Myklebust (1964), "tests requiring verbal facility correlate most closely with those abilities required for learning academic materials. Nonverbal tests are not as useful for predicting this type of learning" (p. 61). Using various achievement measures, Zimmerman and Woo-Sam (1972) found an average correlation coefficient of .33 for WISC-R Performance IQ and achievement measures, and a coefficient of .55 for the WISC-R Verbal IQ and achievement measures for hearing students. Watson, Goldar, Kroese, and Lotz (1986) found that when the Performance Scales of the WISC-R and the *Wechsler Adult Intelligence Scale* (WAIS) were correlated with achievement measures for severely and profoundly hearing-impaired students, a median correlation of only .24 was obtained. Hence, test scores from measures typically used to assess cognitive ability of hearing-impaired students often have less value in predicting overall achievement or achievement for most academic areas. By restricting the cognitive skills assessed, less relevance is found to cognitive skills required in the classroom. This does not mean that it is inappropriate to restrict assessment, but that it is necessary to recognize that doing so impacts the utility of the results for predicting achievement.

WISC-R Profile

The Performance Scale of the WISC-R continues to be one of the most popular intelligence tests used with hearing-impaired students (Trott, 1984; L. J. Porter & Kirby, 1986). Research has suggested, however, that the profile of subtest scores for a large segment of hearing-impaired students may differ significantly from that of hearing children upon whom the test was standardized.

One of the first studies providing evidence of a "deaf profile" on the WISC-R Performance Scale was conducted by R. J. Anderson and Sisco (1977). Their *Standardization of the WISC-R Performance Scale for Deaf Children* included 1,228 congenitally or prelingually hearing-impaired students with a minimum BEA of 70 dB. Results of the study indicated that subtest scaled score means for hearing-impaired students were significantly different from the WISC-R norms for all subtests except Mazes. The hearing-impaired students performed significantly higher on the Object Assembly subtest, but significantly lower on Picture Completion, Picture Arrangement, Block Design, and Coding. The mean subtest scaled score for hearing students is 10. Subtest means for hearing-impaired students were as follows: Picture Completion, 9.51; Picture Arrangement, 8.71; Block Design, 9.48; Object Assembly, 10.32; Coding, 8.03; and Mazes, 10.03.

Hirshoren, Hurley, and Kavale (1979) administered the Performance Scale to 59 prelingually hearing-impaired students. A mean IQ score of 88.07 was obtained, indicating a lower mean IQ than that for hearing students. The pattern of subtest scores, however, was similar to that reported by R. J. Anderson and Sisco (1977), although each subtest mean was lower. Highest mean subtest performance for the group was again found on Object Assembly (9.44), with lowest performance on Picture Arrangement (7.32) and Coding (7.39). Subtest means for Picture Completion (8.34) and Block Design (8.76) fell near the mean subtest performance for the group.

Ray's (1979) *Adaptation of the WISC-R for the Deaf* included 127 prelingually hearing-impaired students (BEA of 70 dB or more) given the Performance Scale with linguistically lowered and supplemental instructions. The profile of mean subtest scores closely parallels that reported by R. J. Anderson and Sisco (1977). Highest mean subtest performance was found on Object Assembly (10.71) and lowest for Picture Arrangement (9.28). Means for Picture Completion (9.90), Block Design (9.81), and Coding (9.32) complete the profile.

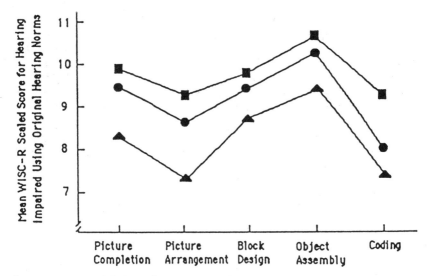

Figure 3.1.   WISC-R Performance Scale subtest score profile for hearing-impaired students.

Figure 3.1 illustrates the profiles obtained from the three studies, and provides strong evidence for a separate WISC-R profile for hearing-impaired students. The profile may be more common with students having congenital or prelingual losses of 70 dB or more, since all three studies included such students. In addition, R. J. Anderson and Sisco (1977) indicated that the profile may be more apparent with young or low scoring students. Examiners administering the WISC-R to such hearing-impaired students should consider that such a profile is commonly obtained and that, in many cases, interpretation of subtest scores may best be done in reference to the "deaf profile." Examiners reporting WISC-R subtest scores may wish to report a hearing-impaired student's pattern of scores in relation to that of the deaf profile in order to preclude or minimize questions that may arise regarding subtest scatter or variability. Also, it may be helpful to the interpretation of performance on other cognitive tasks to note that some hearing-impaired students tend to perform well on tasks similar to that of Object Assembly and have difficulty with tasks similar to Coding.

An important consideration, however, in interpreting test results is stated in the following conclusion drawn by Quigley and Paul (1984) after reviewing the literature on cognitive development of deaf children: "It is now generally accepted by researchers that any differences that do exist between deaf and hearing individuals on cognitive abilities are the result of environmental or task influences rather than being inherent in deafness" (p. 30).

Choice of WISC-R Normative Data

An issue related to that of a WISC-R profile is the choice of normative data to use when scoring the WISC-R. Original WISC-R normative data from hearing students may be used, or norms from a large group of hearing-impaired students. Use of one set of normative data over another may result in a 4- to 5-point difference in Performance IQ, and differ in interpretation of the Performance IQ due to differences in standard deviation.

Reviews of the available choices are presented in Chapter 5, including a discussion of the strengths and limitations of each choice. Examiners may give the WISC-R, adapting the verbal instructions to the hearing-impaired student, and utilize the original (hearing) norms. Another option is to utilize the norms provided by R. J. Anderson and Sisco (1977) in their *Standardization of the WISC-R Performance Scale for Deaf Children*. A third choice is to administer the WISC-R in the context of the *Adaptation of the WISC-R for the Deaf* (Ray, 1979). The Adaptation uses the original, hearing norms.

Because R. J. Anderson and Sisco (1977) found the mean Performance IQ of hearing-impaired students to be 95.7 using the hearing norms, a hearing-impaired student's Performance IQ will vary by 4 to 5 points depending upon the normative data chosen. Although 4 to 5 points may not appear large, the difference may have an impact on the number of hearing-impaired students identified as mentally retarded and gifted (Braden, 1985b).

When using the WISC-R, it is important to be aware of the consequences of the choice of normative data. It may be better to report the range into which the Performance IQ falls (i.e., Average, Borderline) rather than two Performance IQs or a single, perhaps misleading Performance IQ. When a Performance IQ falls within 4 to 5 points of the cut-off score for mental retardation or giftedness, a second IQ score will be needed to make a determination, in addition to any other necessary information (e.g., adaptive behavior scores for mental retardation).

Hearing Aids

A difficult task for many examiners is to become familiar with the student's system of amplification in order to ensure that it is functional during assessment. Systems of amplification differ in several respects. The most common system is the hearing aid, used in about 65% of classrooms (Sinclair & Freeman, 1981). Although hearing aids differ in design, function, and location worn, the basic components (microphone, amplifier, loudspeaker, power source, and gain control) are fairly standard.

Northern and Downs (1978) categorized hearing aids according to where the aid is worn. These include body aids, behind-the-ear models, eyeglass models, and all-in-the-ear aids. The most common type of hearing aid is worn behind the ear (Freeman et al., 1981; Ling, 1986).

Aids are also categorized by design. A monaural hearing aid is designed to function independently in one ear. Binaural hearing aids are two independent aids, one functioning for each ear. Matkin (1981) indicated that the number of young children wearing binaural ear-level aids is increasing. This trend is at the expense of body aids, which were more frequently used in the past. This trend is due to the decreased feedback and increased amplification of binaural ear-level aids.

Extended frequency hearing aids are designed to expand the range of frequencies that are amplified, particularly higher frequencies. Current technology is resulting in digital hearing aids (Boothroyd, 1987), bone-anchored aids (Carlsson, Hakansson, Rosenhall, & Tjellstrom 1986), and infrared aids (Leshowitz, 1982), designed to reduce distortion that accompanies amplification, improve frequency response, and reduce amplification of background noise. The development of these aids is a function of problems with current aids, even when fitted for optimal use. These problems include limited frequency amplification range, background noise, masking of weak speech sounds by stronger ones, acoustic feedback, and low signal-to-noise ratios.

An important part of each hearing aid is the earmold. Because the pinna grows in size until a child is approximately 9 years old, new earmolds are needed every 3 to 6 months prior to age 5, and approximately every year thereafter (Northern & Downs, 1978). Poorly fitting earmolds can produce feedback and irritation. Feedback is produced when amplified sound directed by the hearing aid toward the middle ear escapes through gaps between the ear and earmold, is picked up by the microphone of the hearing aid, and is reamplified. This cycle often creates a loud, high-pitched squeal. The student may turn down the gain (amplification) of the aid to reduce feedback, thereby reducing effectiveness of the aid in meeting the student's hearing needs (Matkin, 1981). The date of the most recent replacement of the student's earmold can often be obtained from the student's audiologist, teacher, or speech–language therapist.

In addition to earmolds, the student's hearing aid requires periodic checks. These checks should be performed several times a year, but it is particularly important that this check be made on the day of testing. An audiologist should perform the visual, listening, and electroacoustic checks. Sometimes a teacher, a parent, or the student performs a visual and listening check of the aid, often on a daily basis. These checks may identify broken cords and other sources of malfunction, but tend to be unreliable (Busenbark & Jenison, 1986) and do not include the electro-acoustical check necessary to determine that amplification is meeting the student's needs. If the audiologist cannot check the aid on the day of testing, then the aid should be checked as close to the evaluation date(s) as possible, and the trained teacher, parent, or examiner can perform a check on the day of testing. The fact that a check was performed and the date of the check should be recorded in the psychoeducational report.

The importance of checking the condition of hearing aids was shown in a survey by Worthington, Stelmachowicz, and Larson (1986). They found that 40% of students' hearing aids were nonfunctional, and that the majority of aids were nonfunctional for children under 7½ years old. A listening check was not sufficient to locate these problems. These results are consistent with findings of Musket (1981), who found that up to 50% of students' hearing aids were malfunctioning.

Weak batteries are often the source of malfunctioning aids and may result in loss of amplification, restriction of frequency response, and distortion. Old batteries may appear to hold an adequate charge when tested in the morning due to having been recharged or not used for several hours; however, they may not maintain proper voltage during the school day (Diefendorf & Arthur, 1987). A student's hearing aid batteries should be checked after the aid has been used for several hours on the day before or of testing. It may be a good rule to use fresh batteries before testing begins, as some hearing aids (e.g., high gain hearing aids) more frequently require fresh batteries to maintain adequate power levels.

Other problems that can occur include wax blocking the tubes, cracks in plastic tubing for earmolds, loose screws, dirt, and movement of cords for body aids.

Frequency Modulation Systems

Another system of amplification that may or may not include aids is a frequency modulation (FM) system. Using an FM system, the teacher has a microphone and students ordinarily wear headphones. The teacher's voice is amplified and broadcast to the students' headphones using radio waves. The headphones may be set to provide amplification as a hearing aid, or as a complement to the students' hearing aids. A major advantage of the system is the reduction of background and extraneous sources of noise (Boothroyd, 1987). Examiners assessing students using an FM system should become familiar with the system's operation before the assessment. Like hearing aid batteries, batteries for the FM receiver require voltage checks before use, as the batteries may weaken during the day and adversely affect amplification.

In a survey of 1,871 classrooms, Sinclair and Freeman (1981) found that FM systems are used in approximately 57% of classrooms, with FM systems combined with personal hearing aids in 54% of these classrooms and FM systems alone in the remaining 46%. Hearing aids alone are reportedly used in 34% of classrooms. Less than 10% of classrooms use methods other than hearing aids and/or FM systems. These include personal-loop (6%), desk-mounted (2%), and room-loop (1%) types of amplification systems. Examiners planning assessment of students using these types of systems need to determine whether and how the system can be adapted for individual use. Also, because loop-type systems involve the use of hearing aids, use of these systems requires the considerations described above for hearing aids.

Vibrotactile Devices

Vibrotactile devices are used mainly to supplement speech reading. Vibrators that receive speech sensations are placed on the body, such as on the back of the hand or on the wrist. M. Ross (1986) noted that those who benefit most from these devices are those who cannot benefit from hearing aids.

Willingness to Use Aids

Some children for whom amplification is prescribed may refuse to use the system. This problem needs to be dealt with prior to testing. Often a correctable reason for the refusal can be found (e.g., irritation, squeal, amplification too high, weak batteries) and the situation remedied. Once correctable factors are addressed, the examiner can deal with factors such as aesthetics and acceptance with a short-term goal of using the amplification during testing, and a long-range goal of increasing use of amplification.

Testing Room

An important consideration is the room chosen for testing. Not only does the room need to be relatively free of background noise and reverberation, but the room also should have ample diffuse lighting that minimizes glare.

Because any noise can interfere with the use of residual hearing, it is important to minimize extraneous noise. The following factors should be taken into consideration:

- If possible, select a room with carpeting, acoustical tiles, and draperies (M. Ross, 1978).

- Keep doors and windows closed (M. Ross, 1978).

- Avoid use of rooms with noisy air conditioners and heating ducts. Also, fluorescent lights that hum or buzz are potential distractions.

- Place a sign on the door, such as "Quiet please. Testing in progress."

Because hearing-impaired students rely heavily on visual input, it is important to maximize their use of vision. Consideration of the following issues should help:

- Select a room without patterned wallpaper and without numerous items on the wall, such as mirrors and pictures.

- Lighting should be from above or located in front of the examiner.

- Avoid testing materials that are plastic coated as the plastic may cause glare.

- Seat the student so that he or she is not facing a window.

- Arrange the room so that testing materials are placed conveniently for the examiner but so that only materials currently in use are visually available to the student.

Use of Interpreters

Conveying test instructions through an interpreter, especially one who is familiar and experienced in communicating with the student to be tested, may appear to overcome communication differences between the examiner and student. Levine's (1974) survey of psychologists at schools for the deaf found that interpreters were used in 4% of assessments. Trott's (1984) review of 74 evaluations of hearing-impaired students in a northeastern state found that parents or teachers were used as interpreters in over 33% of evaluations.

Freeman et al. (1981) noted that there are four different types of interpreters for hearing-impaired students: oral interpreters mouth words so that the words can be speech read more easily, simultaneous interpreters mouth and sign information to the student, manual interpreters sign what is said, and voice interpreters say what the hearing-impaired student signed. Furthermore, Freeman et al. stated that in some cases two interpreters may be needed during assessment, one to convey instructions and a second to translate a student's responses. Two interpreters may be necessary when a student is not proficient at his or her method of communication or uses many nonstandard signs, and a person highly skilled in the student's method, such as the student's classroom interpreter (for some mainstreamed students), native deaf person, teacher, or parent is required to interpret responses.

It has been suggested that use of interpreters results in loss of rapport between the examiner and the student, and in loss of validity for the results obtained (Sullivan & Vernon, 1979; Vernon & Brown, 1964). Other potential problems with interpreters include their unfamiliarity with standardized test procedures, alterations of test instructions that affect test validity if direct translation is not possible, and confusion when the student must simultaneously attend to both the examiner and the interpreter (e.g., on demonstration items).

Despite potential problems with the use of interpreters, they may be necessary in some circumstances (Sattler, 1982). For such cases, an interpreter certified in psychological assessment is highly recommended in order to deal with the serious challenges to validity when noncertified interpreters are used. Trott (1984) deemed the practice of using parents or teachers as interpreters as "unacceptable" and recommended use of a certified interpreter when an interpreter is required. A list of certified interpreters for a region can be obtained from state or local agencies that use interpreters (e.g., the Rehabilitation Service Commission or Community Centers for the Deaf) or from the Registry of Interpreters for the Deaf (814 Thayer Avenue, Silver Springs, MD 20910).

In many cases, it may be more practical and efficient to have a student assessed at a state or regional agency that routinely provides assessment and related services to hearing-impaired students. This practice may offer other advantages over an interpreter because of the examiner's familiarity with test selection, administration, and interpretation, and it may avoid the challenges to validity that exist with the use of certified interpreters. Brill, MacNeil, and Newman (1986) stated that use of an interpreter during assessment is neither satisfactory nor valid; instead, they indicated that

> it is recognized that a complete assessment may have to be carried on in a different locale from where the educational services may ultimately be provided, as every program serving educational needs may not have the facilities and personnel to conduct a complete assessment. (p. 71)

Ideally, when an examiner is unable to communicate with a hearing-impaired student, the examiner should have the student assessed by an examiner who can. When this is not feasible, then certified interpreters can be used, recognizing that introducing a third party may influence results. In the only published study comparing skilled examiners and interpreters, Watson, Sullivan, Teare, and Thompson (1984) tested 154 hearing-impaired students and found higher WISC-R subtest scores and Performance IQs when examiners used total communication to administer the scale than when interpreters used total communication. Examiners using interpreters should ensure before testing that the right type of interpreter(s) has been selected, and that the interpreter can communicate with the student, given the variability that exists in the language and communication skills of hearing-impaired students. If an examiner chooses to use another examiner or an interpreter to obtain a more valid assessment, the examiner should strive to retain the right to provide input into the selection of measures, assessment procedures, and interpretation of results.

Of course, an examiner may choose to select tests that do not require communication with the student (e.g., *Arthur Adaptation of the Leiter International Performance Scale;* Arthur, 1950) to circumvent the need for an interpreter or another examiner. This approach is not likely to be wise and may create problems, including difficulties in establishing rapport, disciplining the student, and praising effort. Imagine the dilemma faced by an examiner unable to communicate with a student when the student continues to attempt to solve an item and a reasonable amount of time has elapsed. The examiner can neither allow the student to continue indefinitely and become frustrated, nor simply gather up the task items.

Students have a legal right to be tested in one of their methods of communication (preferably their most fluent method), unless it is not feasible. Taking the student to an examiner who can communicate with the student, obtaining an interpreter, or learning the student's communication method are feasible alternatives.

Checklist for Considerations Prior to Assessment

Table 3.1 is a checklist of issues that should be addressed prior to testing a student. Addressing these issues should increase the likelihood of obtaining valid results, assist in making the assessment process proceed smoothly, and enhance the educational usefulness of the results. If, at the scheduled time, preparations for assessment are not complete or the student may not be able to perform well, testing should be postponed (Boyle, 1977; Levine, 1971).

TABLE 3.1

Checklist of Considerations Prior to Assessment

_____ Complete the Information Organizing Checklist for Hearing-Impaired Students (Table 1.1), using information from review of school records and from interviews.

_____ Carry out systematic classroom observation.

_____ Select appropriate assessment instruments, considering the test selection issues presented in this chapter and the reviews presented in the following chapters.

_____ Discuss the appropriateness of the selected assessment instruments and procedures with the student's teacher, if there are any concerns.

_____ If the student wears glasses, be sure he or she will bring them on the day of testing.

_____ Become familiar with the student's amplification equipment.

_____ Check with the teacher, speech pathologist, or audiologist regarding proper volume and tone settings for the student's aid.

_____ On the day of testing, ensure that the amplification system is operating properly. An audiologist should perform the visual, listening, and electro-acoustic check. The date of the check should be included in the psycho-educational report.

_____ Select a room for testing that will maximize the student's use of vision and residual hearing.

_____ On the day of testing, check with the student's teacher and parents to determine that the student does not have a problem with a cold, allergies, or other factors that might interfere with the use of residual hearing.

_____ If the student uses manual communication, wear plain clothing on the day of testing to maximize contrast of your clothing with your use of manual communication.

_____ If necessary, make arrangements for an interpreter, keeping in mind the limitations of this approach.

Permission is granted by PRO-ED, Inc. to make copies of Table 3.1.

Issues to Consider During Assessment

The direct assessment of a hearing-impaired student is complex and time consuming if the assessment is to be comprehensive and the results are to be valid. Examiners can employ a number of procedures during test administration to enhance the validity and aid in obtaining comprehensive information for eligibility and program planning. A detailed discussion of several considerations that merit elaboration follows.

Rapport

Hearing-impaired students are likely to require more time to establish rapport than hearing students. Furth (1973) indicated that it takes both time and ingenuity to establish rapport with a hearing-impaired student, and recommended allowing the student to play or otherwise become comfortable in the testing environment. Allowing the student to explore the room before being directed to a chair may be helpful. Although some degree of rapport may have been established before testing, it is important to use ample time to ensure that the student understands why testing is being carried out and what will happen during testing. For some students, the entire initial session may be required to establish adequate rapport. When establishing rapport, it is important to be certain that the student is comfortable physically and with their amplification.

Ensuring Proper Amplification

The examiner must make sure that the amplification setting is appropriate. If squealing occurs, the examiner should consult the teacher, speech pathologist, or audiologist. The volume (gain) should not be turned down below the proper setting. Also, the examiner should ask the student about background noise and echoes.

Praise for Effort

The examiner should encourage the student's effort by using the student's method of communication, rather than by facial expressions. Furth (1973) warned that, if expressions are used, "the child will then naturally look for continued approval and will pay more attention to the face of the examiner than to the task" (p. 90).

Communicating Directions

Additional examples or practice items are often necessary to help a hearing-impaired student understand the requirements of a task. Many subtests have sample items. If it is apparent that a student does not understand the task after communication of directions and sample items, additional practice items may be necessary. It is critical, however, not to provide too many items and contribute to a practice effect. As mentioned previously, to aid the student's understanding of task requirements, the examiner may wish to compare a new task with a previously completed task, ask the student to indicate what he or she is being requested to do, or use failed initial items or items skipped at an earlier age level as teaching items.

Hearing-impaired students may sometimes act as if they understand task requirements when they do not (Vernon & Brown, 1964). Thus, it is important to encourage a hearing-impaired student to ask questions during testing whenever the student feels uncertain.

Problems understanding directions may cause hearing-impaired students to demonstrate what Vernon and Alles (1986) referred to as a neutral response that can be misleading to examiners. To cope with difficulty, the student may smile, say "yes," and nod that he or she understands, when the student does not understand. Vernon and Alles suggested that the student may appear to be withdrawn and nonresponsive, and to have flat affect. Hence, conclusions regarding the student's emotional status and understanding of directions, must be made only after a considerable amount of evidence is obtained that the student in fact understood the directions (e.g., use of practice items, similar performance on several measures).

J. W. Birch (1975) and Gildston (1973) both noted that if hearing-impaired students who speech read request to have directions repeated, it helps for the examiner to repeat directions using phrases rather than single words because single words are more difficult than phrases to speech read.

Fatigue

Trying to understand instructions requires extra effort for many hearing-impaired students, and signs of fatigue should result in breaks or discontinuation of testing when appropriate. Use of speech reading or residual hearing can be very tiring (Gildston, 1973). It is important that the examiner be sensitive to changes in background noise or other factors that may change during the course of testing.

Behavior of Students

Examiners may have different expectations for a handicapped student's behavior during testing than for that of a nonhandicapped student, and may be less willing to discipline a handicapped student. Regardless of the presence of a handicap, a student's inappropriate behavior may hinder test performance (Bradley-Johnson, 1986), and examiners should strive to maintain discipline throughout the testing of a hearing-impaired student. It will not be to the student's benefit to do otherwise.

Visual Cues

The examiner needs to be aware of visual information that is provided to the student. Hearing-impaired students are more attentive to facial expressions, hand movements, gestures, and extraneous body movements than are hearing students. Not only might these movements be distracting, but they might cue a student to select a particular response. On multiple-choice tests, examiners must be careful not to cue a student by visually fixating too long on an alternative or by placing a finger on or near an alternative when turning pages in a flip book.

Checklist of Considerations During Assessment

In addition to the issues addressed above, several other considerations need to be made during assessment, including methods to maximize speech reading and manual communication. All of the issues that are useful to consider during the direct testing of a hearing-impaired student are noted in Table 3.2.

Issues to Consider After Assessment

Issues after assessment also can enhance validity and the usefulness of the information obtained. These issues are addressed below, followed by a checklist to aid in applying the information.

Notes on the Session

Because there are many special considerations when assessing hearing-impaired students, the examiner should document difficulties encountered during testing, as well as any other factors that may qualify the student's

TABLE 3.2
Checklist of Considerations During Assessment

___ Allow ample time to establish rapport.

___ Ensure proper amplification settings for aids.

___ If needed, be sure the student is wearing glasses.

___ Encourage the student's efforts using the student's form of communication.

___ Ensure the student's understanding of directions by using a moderate number of practice items, comparing with prior tasks, or asking the student to explain the directions.

___ Encourage the student to ask questions when uncertain.

___ Keep materials not in use out of sight.

___ Use transitions between tests (e.g., explain how the next test is the same or different, indicate why the next test will be used).

___ Keep a pad of paper and a pencil at hand. The student may use these materials if he or she becomes confused.

Be sensitive to fatigue by:

    ___ scheduling frequent breaks, if needed.

    ___ allowing ample time and several sessions for testing.

___ Use behavior management procedures to maintain appropriate behavior and optimize test performance.

___ Avoid giving unintended visual cues.

To optimize speech reading:

    ___ Avoid exaggerating mouth movements because exaggeration may make speech reading more difficult.

    ___ Avoid chewing gum or cough drops, and avoid putting other objects, such as pencils, near or in your mouth.

    ___ Consider that mustaches or beards may interfere with speech reading.

    ___ Face the student directly, and be sure the student is looking at you when you speak.

    ___ Sit about 2 to 3 feet from the student. This is the optimal distance between an examiner and a speech reader (Sullivan & Vernon, 1979).

    ___ Avoid looking down when speaking.

TABLE 3.2 Continued

To optimize use of residual hearing:

_____ Speak in a normal tone of voice. When speech is raised more than moderately, intelligibility decreases (Byrne, 1986).

_____ Sit close to the student or close to the microphone of the acoustic system used (M. Ross, 1981).

_____ Avoid making unnecessary noise in handling materials.

To optimize use of manual communication:

_____ The student should be seated no more than 60 degrees to the side of the examiner's dominant hand for signing (Cacamise, Meath-Lang, & Johnson, 1981).

_____ Avoid extraneous hand movements or other motions that may interfere with communication.

Permission is granted by PRO-ED, Inc., to make copies of Table 3.2.

performance. It is especially important to note any communication difficulties and problems with impulsive behavior. Problems with amplification and the date the student's system was evaluated for proper functioning are worth noting. These notes should be made immediately after testing, or as soon thereafter as possible, when recall of the sessions is best.

Summarizing Procedures

Just as a hearing-impaired student may not have an initial understanding of testing and may benefit from an explanation and overview, it is important to promote understanding by informing the student that assessment is completed or when it will resume. In either instance, the examiner can reduce anxiety by thanking the student for participating and by providing information as to what will happen next.

Following the model of J. Porter and Holzberg (1979), the teacher should be consulted at the end of the testing sessions to discuss the general findings, and to plan any additional testing. The model is intended to increase the relevance of test results to the student's educational program.

Many caregivers tend to be overprotective of their hearing-impaired child (Baum, 1981) and may be anxious about the child's performance. The anxiety oftens concerns fears that the child's communication skills may have impaired performance and that results will not accurately represent the child's abilities. It may be helpful to communicate with the caregivers to indicate when assessment is underway or completed, and to provide some positive comments about the student's efforts. This contact also would provide caregivers an opportunity to ask any questions they may have.

Reporting Results

It is more accurate to report test results using the standard error of measurement and to give results in terms of a range of performance, than to report a single score from a test. This is particularly important when handicapped students are assessed, because many of the tests used lack sufficient technical adequacy and because many other factors may affect test performance. Allen, White, and Karchmer (1983) noted that, when student progress is slow, the use of the standard error of measurement is particularly important. As discussed in detail in Chapter 6, growth in academic performance is delayed for hearing-impaired students. Hence, use of the standard error of measurement is strongly recommended in reporting results of norm-referenced tests for these students.

When scores of questionable validity are obtained, some examiners report the scores with a qualification as to why the score is questionable. Simply reporting a quantified test score implies accuracy and authority (Levine, 1971), and the quantification is prone to greater attention than the qualification, too often resulting in misinterpretation. If scores of questionable validity are reported, it is recommended that performance ranges (e.g., Below Average Range) be substituted for the scores along with appropriate qualification.

An additional consideration for reporting test scores has to do with the age of the test used. Because it is sometimes necessary to administer out-of-date tests (i.e., older than 15 years) to hearing-impaired students, inflated test scores may be obtained. Flynn (1984) found that, on the average, intelligence test scores tend to increase .3 of a point per year. Hence, a test that is 20 years old may yield a score that is inflated by as much as 6 points.

Although test results may be inflated due to the age of a test, Vernon and Alles (1986) noted that, for hearing-impaired students, low scores are more likely to be in error than high scores because of the number of factors that may hinder performance (e.g., understanding of directions, expressing responses, timed items, and fatigue).

If discrepancies are found between tests given to a student, these differences must be resolved to make appropriate decisions regarding the student's needs. Usually, resolution can be accomplished by using the standard error of measurement, considering the age of the tests used, noting that low scores are more likely to be in error for hearing-impaired students, and considering other test characteristics. One characteristic of tests that might account for differences in results is differences in technical adequacy, with the more technically adequate test being more likely to be accurate. Other test characteristics include differences between skills tested, differences in the way in which instructions are presented, and differences in the type of responses required. Item-by-item comparisons also may help resolve differences.

Follow-Up

It is important to provide follow-up for the recommendations resulting from the asessment and to decide when the next assessment should be scheduled (Levine, 1971). Hearing-impaired students may require more frequent assessments to determine suitability for increased mainstreaming or other programs.

Checklist for Consideration After Assessment

Table 3.3 provides an overview of issues to consider once direct testing is completed. Use of the checklist should aid in applying the information addressed above.

TABLE 3.3
Checklist of Considerations After Assessment

_____ Record any difficulties that occurred during testing.

_____ Communicate the status of the assessment to the student and his or her caretakers.

_____ Consult with the student's teacher regarding assessment results, interpretations, and need for additional testing.

_____ Use assessment information to make recommendations for program planning, placement, teaching procedures, and behavior management strategies.

_____ Use the standard error of measurement to report norm-referenced test results.

_____ It test scores must be qualified, use ranges of performance rather than scores.

_____ Resolve differences in results from different tests, considering age of tests, remembering that low scores are more likely to be in error for hearing-impaired students, and considering differences in technical adequacy, test construction, and task requirements.

_____ Follow up on recommendations to evaluate their effectiveness.

Permission is granted by PRO-ED, Inc., to make copies of Table 3.3.

4

Cognitive Assessment of Hearing-Impaired Infants and Preschoolers

This chapter first addresses the legal mandates for assessment of infants and preschool children with a hearing loss. Then detailed reviews of available instruments are presented. The first section of each review includes information regarding administration of the test, method of presenting instructions, type of response required, and a general description regarding the type of child for whom the test is appropriate. Next, a description of the subtests or items is presented to explain the range of skills tested. This is followed by a detailed evaluation of the test's technical adequacy, including standardization, reliability, and validity information. Information regarding use of the test with hearing-impaired children is included, when this information was available in the literature. In the final section of each review, the strengths and limitations of the test for use with hearing-impaired children are discussed.

Legal Issues and Availability of Services

Although PL 94-142 is directed toward providing free appropriate public education to handicapped children from age 3 to age 18, it is concerned primarily with children from 6 to 17 years of age. Services for children from 3 to 5 are not mandated unless a state or public agency in the state meets certain conditions. Also, PL 94-142 defines handicaps according to their impact on a child's educational performance. Because most infants and preschoolers do not receive formal educational services, it is not known at that young age whether a child with a hearing loss has impaired educational performance due to the loss and can, therefore, be labeled handicapped. However, infants and preschoolers with hearing losses, especially severe and profound losses, are at risk for being labeled hearing impaired when they reach school age.[1] For these hearing-impaired infants and preschoolers, assessment and intervention services may be a crucial factor in the development of speech, language, and other preacademic skills. Unfortunately, there are two reasons why such services may not be received.

First, hearing losses are usually not identified until a child is between the ages of 1 and 2 years (Harris, 1978). Although parents often suspect their child has a hearing problem before the age of 1, actual diagnosis may not occur until some time later. In a study of Canadian families with hearing-impaired children, Freeman, Malkin, and Hastings (1975) found that deafness was suspected before 10 months of age for infants with profound losses, and by 16 months for infants with severe losses. In a similar study, Shah, Chandler, and Dale (1978) found that 76.5% of hearing losses were first suspected by parents, and 13% first suspected by physicians. The mean age of suspicion was 16 months (median age of 13 months), but actual diagnosis of the hearing loss by a hearing specialist was delayed for an average of 11.5 months (median delay of 8 months). Delays may be attributed to several factors, including hesitation in seeking a physician once a loss is suspected, initial physician misdiagnosis and reluctance to refer to a hearing specialist, and difficulty obtaining an immediate appointment with a hearing specialist. These delays were found to be greater for children with less severe hearing losses and for multihandicapped children (Shah et al., 1978). By the time a child is suspected of having a hearing loss and is then diagnosed, the child is usually into the second year of life, having missed opportunities for amplification, speech, language, and other intervention services.

---

[1] For the purpose of this text, the term *hearing impaired* is used for infants and preschoolers with a hearing loss. This is not meant as a departure from, or disagreement with, the technical definitions of deaf and hard-of-hearing provided by PL 94-142. It is merely a recognition that education begins before a child enters school and that a hearing loss can adversely affect early learning opportunities.

The exception to this pattern is the high-risk infant who is diagnosed early and provided with assessment and intervention services. A number of methods are used to diagnose hearing losses in a child's initial weeks of life; however, at present, these methods are practical for use only with newborns and infants identified as high risk because of prenatal factors (e.g., maternal rubella) or hereditary factors (e.g., family history of hearing loss). Methods used to diagnose hearing losses in infants are not completely accurate, but are most accurate for children between 5 and 12 months of age and with severe and profound losses (Kraus, Ozdamar, Stein, & Reed, 1984; Riko, Hyde, & Alberti, 1985; Shah et al., 1978). Presently, however, 92 to 95% of infants are not screened, including some high-risk infants (Marlowe, 1987).

The second reason why early assessment and intervention services may not be received is that only limited services are available for hearing-impaired infants and preschoolers who are less than 6 years old. Given that 90 to 95% of all hearing-impaired children and adolescents have prelingual hearing losses (Liben, 1978; Rawlings & Ries, 1973), there is a considerable need for early services. However, less than 10 percent of 3- to 5-year-old children with hearing losses are currently being served through the approximately 250 parent–infant home programs and 550 preschool programs for hearing-impaired children in the United States (American Speech–Language–Hearing Association, 1987; W. N. Craig & Craig, 1987). The lack of early services often means that children who are diagnosed as having a hearing loss at an early age may not receive an assessment and appropriate level of intervention.

Although hearing-impaired infants and preschoolers currently appear to have two strikes against them, PL 99-457, an amendment to PL 94-142 that was passed by Congress in 1986, was designed to provide funds for states to identify and serve developmentally delayed and at-risk children between the ages of birth and 5 years. The law requires the development of an individualized family service plan (IFSP) that must contain a number of components, among them a statement of the child's present level of cognitive development, specification of early intervention services required, and the manner in which those services will be delivered.

Hence, large-scale improvements in the identification and service of developmentally delayed infants and preschoolers including those with hearing impairments are under way as states develop plans and apply for funds. These improvements will highlight the need for psychoeducational assessment of infants and preschoolers. For hearing-impaired infants and preschoolers, there will be a need to identify assessment instruments that can be employed and to determine their appropriateness and technical adequacy for use with this population.

Cognitive Measures

A number of measures of cognitive ability used with hearing-impaired infants and preschoolers have been identified from published reviews (Boyle, 1977; Sullivan & Vernon, 1979; Trott, 1984; Vernon & Brown, 1964; Zieziula, 1982), surveys (Levine, 1974; McQuaid & Alovisetti, 1981), test manuals, and published reports. These tests are listed in Table 4.1, along with the ages for which each test was developed. Measures of vocabulary and language (e.g., *Peabody Picture Vocabulary Test–Revised, Quick Test*) that were erroneously given as cognitive measures (Trott, 1984) are not included in Table 4.1. Measures included in Table 4.1 are divided into norm-referenced tests, as well as criterion-referenced tests and informal measures. The primary purpose of norm-referenced tests is to compare a child's performance with that of other children on the same measure, whereas the purpose of criterion-referenced and informal measures is to indicate skills the child has mastered or the degree of mastery (Sattler, 1982).

Review Criteria

Although Table 4.1 lists a number of measures that may be used with hearing-impaired children, not all the tests have been selected for review because of several factors. First, screening measures do not meet the legal requirements for identifying handicapped students, and these measures (e.g., *Developmental Activities Screening Inventory–II, Slosson Intelligence Test*) have been excluded from review. Second, tests published over 15 years ago have been excluded to ensure that normative data are not out-of-date. Exceptions to this are those measures that continue to be used often with hearing-impaired children despite the age of the norms (e.g., *Hiskey–Nebraska, Arthur Adaptation of the Leiter,* WPPSI) (McQuaid & Alovisetti, 1981; Trott, 1984) or tests that cover ages for which there are few alternative measures (e.g., *Bayley Scales of Infant Development, Smith–Johnson Nonverbal Performance Scale*). Third, for measures that have been revised (e.g., *Stanford–Binet Form L-M*), only the more recent versions were reviewed. The *Wechsler Preschool and Primary Scale of Intelligence* (Wechsler, 1967) was revised in 1989; however, because a considerable amount of research has been carried out on the use of the 1967 version with hearing-impaired children, and no research is available at this time on the more recent version for hearing-impaired children, the older version was reviewed.

Reviewed measures are presented in Table 4.2 according to one of four categories: measures with norms for hearing-impaired children; measures with hearing norms, nonvocal instructions, and nonvocal responses; measures with hearing norms, verbal instructions, and nonvocal responses; and criterion-referenced and informal measures. Criteria used to review the tests were presented in Chapter 1 under Direct Testing.

TABLE 4.1
Cognitive Ability Measures for Hearing-Impaired
Infants and Preschoolers

Norm-Referenced Tests	
Adaptation of the WPPSI for the Deaf (Ray & Ulissi, 1982)	4-0 to 6-6 years
Arthur Adaptation of the Leiter International Performance Scale (Arthur, 1950)	3-0 to 7-11 years
Battelle Developmental Inventory (Newborg, Stock, Wnek, Guidubaldi, & Svinicki, 1984)	Birth to 8 years
Bayley Scales of Infant Development (Bayley, 1969)	2 to 30 months
Cattell Infant Intelligence Scale (Cattell, 1960)	2 to 36 months
CID Preschool Performance Scale (Geers & Lane, 1984)	2-0 to 5-5 years
Cognitive Abilities Scale (Bradley-Johnson, 1987)	2-0 to 4-0 years
Columbia Mental Maturity Scale (Burgemeister, Blum, & Lorge, 1972)	3-6 to 9-6 years
Denver Developmental Screening Test (Frankenburg, Dodds, Fandal, Kazuk, & Cohrs, 1975)	2 weeks to 6 years
Developmental Activities Screening Inventory–II (Fewell & Langley, 1984)	6 months to 5 years
Hiskey–Nebraska Test of Learning Aptitude (Hiskey, 1966)	3-0 to 16-0 years
Kaufman Assessment Battery for Children (Kaufman & Kaufman, 1983)	2-6 to 12-6 years
Leiter International Performance Scale (Leiter, 1969)	3-0 to 16-11 years
Merrill–Palmer Preschool Performance Test (Stutsman, 1931)	19 months to 4-0 years
Ontario School Ability Examination (Amoss, 1936)	4 to 10 years
Pictorial Test of Intelligence (French, 1964)	2-6 to 8-6 years
Randall's Island Performance Tests (Poull, Bristol, King, & Peatman, 1931)	2 to 5 years
Slosson Intelligence Test (Armstrong & Jensen, 1981)	2 weeks to adult
Smith–Johnson Nonverbal Performance Scale (Smith & Johnson, 1977)	2-0 to 4-0 years
Stanford–Binet Intelligence Scale Form L-M (Terman & Merrill, 1973)	2 years to adult
Stanford–Binet Intelligence Scale (4th ed.) (Thorndike, Hagen, & Sattler, 1986)	2 years to adult
Wechsler Preschool and Primary Scale of Intelligence (Wechsler, 1967)	4-0 to 6-6 years
Criterion-Referenced Tests and Informal Measures	
Ordinal Scales of Psychological Development (Uzgiris & Hunt, 1989)	Birth to 2 years

TABLE 4.2
Reviewed Tests of Cognitive Ability for Hearing-Impaired
Infants and Preschoolers

Norm-Referenced Tests with Hearing-Impaired Norms

Hiskey–Nebraska Test of Learning Aptitude (Hiskey, 1966)	3-0 to 16-0 years
Smith–Johnson Nonverbal Performance Scale (Smith & Johnson, 1977)	2-0 to 4-0 years

Norm-Referenced Tests with Hearing Norms, Nonvocal Instructions, and Nonvocal Responses

Adaptation of the WPPSI for the Deaf (Ray & Ulissi, 1982)	4-0 to 6-6 years
CID Preschool Performance Scale (Geers & Lane, 1984)	2-0 to 5-5 years

Norm-Referenced Tests with Hearing Norms, Verbal Instructions, and Nonvocal Responses

Battelle Developmental Inventory (Newborg, Stock, Wnek, Guidubaldi, & Svinicki, 1984)	Birth to 8 years
Bayley Scales of Infant Development (Bayley, 1969)	2 to 30 months
Cognitive Abilities Scale (Bradley-Johnson, 1987)	2-0 to 4-0 years
Kaufman Assessment Battery for Children (Kaufman & Kaufman, 1983)	2-6 to 12-6 years
Stanford–Binet Intelligence Scale (4th ed.) (Thorndike, Hagen, & Sattler, 1986)	2 years to adult
Wechsler Preschool and Primary Scale of Intelligence (Wechsler, 1967)	4-0 to 6-6 years

Criterion-Referenced Tests and Informal Measures

Arthur Adaptation of the Leiter International Performance Scale (Arthur, 1950)	3-0 to 7-11 years
Ordinal Scales of Psychological Development (Uzgiris & Hunt, 1989)	Birth to 2 years

Norm-Referenced Tests with Hearing-Impaired Norms

Hiskey–Nebraska Test of Learning Aptitude

Author: M. S. Hiskey
Publisher: Marshall S. Hiskey
             5640 Baldwin Ave.
             Lincoln, NE 68507
Copyright: 1966

General Description.   The *Hiskey–Nebraska Test of Learning Aptitude* is a general intelligence test with separate norms for hearing and hearing-impaired children age 3-0 to 16-0 years. Instructions for hearing-impaired children are pantomimed, and all subtests require nonvocal responses (i.e., pointing to pictures or manipulating objects). Three subtests have time limits. Approximately 45 to 50 minutes are required to administer the test. There is one form of the test, and there are practice items. Scores for hearing-impaired children include age rating for each subtest and an overall learning age based on the median subtest age rating, or a learning quotient. Materials consist of the examiner's manual, a record book, and a case of numerous materials, including pictures and items such as beads and blocks.

Description of Subtests

The *Hiskey–Nebraska* is composed of the 12 subtests listed below. The first 5 are for ages 3 to 10, the next 3 are for all ages, and the final 4 are for ages 11 to 16. Many of the subtests require visual memory skills.

Bead Patterns.   This subtest consists of three parts: the number of beads strung in 1 minute, copying and comparing a sequence of beads from the examiner's pattern for three different patterns, and copying a sequence of beads from memory for four patterns.

Memory for Color.   This subtest involves short-term memory for up to six different colors presented visually. There are eight trials for remembering one color, four trials for two colors, two trials for three colors, two trials for four colors, two trials for five colors, and two trials for six colors.

Picture Identification.   Seven items require matching a picture with one of five similar pictures.

Picture Association. This subtest, which has 14 items, involves the selection of a third picture that corresponds to a relationship expressed by two stimulus cards. For example, the child is shown two pictures of objects that fly and is asked to choose a third related picture from several alternatives.

Paper Folding. The child is asked to reproduce a series of paper folds (up to nine folds) from memory.

Visual Attention Span. The nine subtest items involve reproducing a sequence of pictures (from one to seven pictures) from memory.

Block Patterns. This 14-item subtest requires the child to build a block structure to match a pattern.

Completion of Drawings. The 28 subtest items require drawing the missing part on a picture.

Memory for Digits. The subtest involves visual memory for reproducing a series of numbers. The child reproduces the sequence using a set of plastic numerals. Series vary from two to nine digits, with three opportunities given for each sequence.

Puzzle Blocks. This seven-item subtest requires the child to construct a cube from a varying number of pieces.

Picture Analogies. The 12 subtest items involve the selection of a picture to complete a relationship modeled by two stimulus pictures. For example, two pictures illustrate a transportation vehicle and its mode of locomotion (i.e., air, water, road, rail). The child is shown a picture of another type of vehicle and asked to select the picture of the appropriate mode of locomotion for the vehicle.

Spacial Reasoning. The 10 items of this subtest require the child to select an unassembled figure to match a completed design.

Technical Adequacy

Standardization. Normative data for both normally hearing and hearing-impaired children are available. Normative data for hearing-impaired children are based on 1,079 hearing-impaired children from 2-6 to 17-5 years of age. The basis of subject selection was primarily attendance in a state school for the deaf. Information regarding degree and type of hearing loss, onset of loss, or method of communication is not indicated. The number of subjects at each age level ranges from 25 to 106, with over 100 subjects only at age levels 6, 7, and 15. Data are not reported according to sex, race, socioeconomic status, ethnicity, or urban/rural residence. Of the 10 states from which subjects were obtained, 5 are Western states.

Reliability. Internal consistency coefficients are provided for two age groups of hearing-impaired children: ages 3 to 10 ($r = .95$) and ages 11 to 17 ($r = .92$). No test–retest data or information on standard error of measurement are presented.

Validity. Evidence of the *Hiskey–Nebraska*'s construct validity with hearing-impaired children is provided through correlation of subtest and total scores (above .5 for each subtest) for the standardization group. Evidence of criterion-related validity is presented through correlation coefficients between the *Hiskey–Nebraska* and the *Stanford Achievement Test*, the *Metropolitan Achievement Test*, the *Gates Reading Test*, and the *Teacher Rating Scale* in a study of 225 hearing-impaired children in grades 2 through 12 (Giangreco, 1966). Coefficients with achievement tests by grade level ranged from –.09 to .72. Coefficients with teacher ratings of achievement ranged from .06 to .64.

Use of the Test with Hearing-Impaired Children. The *Hiskey–Nebraska* is standardized on hearing-impaired children and has been used with the population since its publication. Levine's (1974) survey found the *Hiskey–Nebraska* to be the sixth most popular assessment instrument with hearing-impaired children. Additional surveys, reviews, and reports have indicated use of the *Hiskey–Nebraska* with hearing-impaired students (e.g., Bragman, 1982b; McQuaid & Alovisetti, 1981; Smith & Johnson, 1977; Trott, 1984).

Test–retest stability data for the *Hiskey–Nebraska* have been reported by Watson (1983) for three groups of hearing-impaired students. The first group ($n = 13$) was retested within 24 months (mean = 9 months), and yielded a coefficient of .79. A second group ($n = 14$) was retested between 25 and 48 months (mean = 34 months), resulting in a coefficient of .85. A final group ($n = 16$) was retested 49 or more months later (mean = 62 months), providing a coefficient of .62. Although two of these stability coefficients are at or near .85, it is difficult to determine from these data whether the test has adequate test–retest reliability for eligibility decisions due to the small number of subjects and lengthy retest intervals.

Concurrent validity data for the *Hiskey–Nebraska* have been reported in two studies with the WISC-R Performance Scale. Using hearing-impaired norms for the WISC-R, Phelps and Ensor (1986) obtained a coefficient of .91 for 49 students. Using hearing norms, Hirshoren, Hurley, and Kavale (1979) found a correlation of .89. Concurrent validity with achievement measures was reported by Watson, Sullivan, Moeller, and Jensen (1982). Coefficients of the *Hiskey–Nebraska* and *Test of Language Development* ($r = .57$), *Reynell Expressive Scale* ($r = .40$), and *Reynell Recep-*

tive Scale ($r = .30$) were obtained from a group of 25 hearing-impaired children.

Watson, Goldar, Kroese, and Lotz (1986) found results for the *Hiskey–Nebraska* to correlate at .42 with various measures of achievement for hearing-impaired students. This correlation was higher than the correlation of .24 found with the WISC-R and WAIS and measures of achievement with these students.

Although the *Hiskey–Nebraska* may be useful with students who are functioning in the broad average range of intelligence, Watson, Goldar, and Kroese (1983) found an unusually high number of hearing-impaired students with extreme performances. Because of this, these authors caution that the *Hiskey–Nebraska* may be problematic when used to identify mentally impaired or gifted hearing-impaired students.

Conclusions. The *Hiskey–Nebraska* is one of the few cognitive assessment instruments standardized on hearing-impaired children. Other strengths of the test include its applicability to a wide range of hearing-impaired children due to the use of pantomime instructions, limited use of time limits, and provision of a learning quotient rather than an IQ (Zieziula, 1982). Also, the use of a median age rating helps compensate for subtests for which the hearing-impaired child may not fully understand directions.

Limitations of the test include the age of the norms. Given that Flynn (1984) found that intelligence test performance increased about .3 of a point per year, it would not be surprising to find scores on the *Hiskey–Nebraska* inflated by about 7 points. Zieziula (1982) reported that scores from the *Hiskey–Nebraska* appear to be too high.

Lack of representativeness of the norms in terms of sex, race, ethnicity, residence, and geographic distribution is another problem. Furthermore, data are lacking on the description of the children's hearing losses. All children were from residential schools, and today most hearing-impaired children are not attending residential schools. The emphasis on assessment of visual memory skills for several subtests, and dated materials (e.g., pictures) also are problematic. An additional limitation that has been reported is the lengthy administration times with some students (Zieziula, 1982).

Based on these limitations, primarily the age of the norms, it is recommended that test scores be considered as supplemental to scores from other measures; *Hiskey–Nebraska* scores should not be used as the sole basis for eligibility decisions. Also, the test can be of value as an informal measure of skills, including matching (e.g., Bead Patterns), memory (e.g., Memory for Color, Paper Folding), sequencing (e.g., Memory for Digits), and synthesis (e.g., Puzzle Blocks, Spacial Reasoning).

Smith–Johnson Nonverbal Performance Scale

Authors: A. J. Smith and R. E. Johnson
Publisher: Western Psychological Services
               12031 Wilshire Blvd.
               Los Angeles, CA 90025
Copyright: 1977

General Description. The *Smith–Johnson Performance Scale* is intended for hearing and hearing-impaired preschool children from 2-0 to 4-0 years of age. The purpose of the scale is to permit interpretation of tasks already established as measures of cognitive ability with language- and/or hearing-impaired children. Items on the *Smith–Johnson* were adapted from *Hiskey–Nebraska, Ontario School Ability Examination, Merrill–Palmer, Stanford–Binet,* and other scales. The test requires about 30 to 45 minutes to administer. There is one version of the test.

A total of 14 tasks (65 items) are included in the *Smith–Johnson*. Items are scored pass/fail, refused, or omitted. Separate norms are provided for hearing and hearing-impaired children. Scores for the scale are reported in terms of percentages of children at a given age who passed each item. The performance on each task can be summarized as average, below average, or above average based on the most difficult item passed within a task. An overall score, however, cannot be obtained.

No vocal instructions are given for any item. Instructions are given primarily through pantomime. Only three items have time limits. Materials included in the scale are the examiner's manual, a record form, and a number of testing materials, such as blocks, scissors, beads, and form-boards.

Description of Tasks

Formboard. The three formboard items require the child to place the inserts in the three-hole formboard when the position of the formboard is unrotated, rotated, or inverted.

Block Building. Of the six items, three require the child to build an object following the examiner's demonstration, one requires building while viewing the examiner's model, and two require building from memory after exposure to the model for 10 seconds.

Pencil Drawing. The child draws designs with a pencil following the examiner's demonstration(s). The eight items range from a vertical line to a pentagon.

Bead Stringing. The five items involve the number of beads the child strings in 2 minutes, and copying a bead pattern from a model or from memory.

Knot Tying. This task requires tying a single knot and a double bow knot following demonstration (two items).

Color Items. Using Kohs blocks, the child is required to match the color pattern of the examiner's blocks (three items) or the pattern on a printed card (one item).

Scissors. The single item requires the child to make a ½-inch or larger cut in paper following demonstration.

Paper Folding. Following examiner demonstration, the child makes a rectangle with a single paper fold, a square using a double fold, then a triangle using a double fold (four items).

Cube Tapping. The child imitates the examiner's tapping of one block on top of other blocks. The number of blocks tapped varies from two to four, and the sequence of taps also varies. There are nine items.

Form Discrimination. The child matches designs on form cards to identical designs on a large template card (four items).

Completion Items. Each of the two items contain two puzzles the child solves by joining two pieces. Demonstration is provided for the first puzzle, and a model is shown for the third and fourth.

Manikin. The child uses six plywood puzzle pieces to form a manikin. No demonstration is given. The task contains six items, based on the possible responses in forming the manikin.

Block Patterns. The four items require building a block structure from a printed pattern. Demonstration is provided only for the first item.

Sorting. The child is required to sort black and white buttons by color; pennies, nickels, and quarters by denomination; and buttons and money by type (button or coin). There are four items.

Technical Adequacy

Standardization. Normative data for normally hearing children were obtained in 1960. A total of 602 children were included, with 44 to 95 children at each 3-month interval from 24 to 48 months. Males comprised 55% of the sample. Children were from the West coast, had higher socioeconomic status and parent education levels than the U.S. population according to 1958 U.S. census data, were Caucasian, and did not have a language or hearing impairment. No information is given regarding urban/rural residence.

Normative data for hearing- and/or language-impaired children were obtained between 1960 and 1970. A total of 632 children were tested, with 32 to 115 children per 3-month interval. Equal numbers of males and females were included. Although all children were tested at the same clinic, the geographic regions from which children came are not specified. No data are provided pertaining to socioeconomic status, residence, race, or ethnicity. Thus, it is not possible to determine whether a representative national sample was obtained. Profoundly deaf children comprised 36% of the sample, with the remaining 64% being hard-of-hearing.

Reliability.   Test–retest reliability data are presented for a subset of hearing children from the 1960 standardization sample (135 males, 94 females). The retest interval was approximately 1 week. Coefficients are presented by item for both males and females. Values range from .27 to .83 for males and from .06 to .83 for females across the items. Values are not presented for items that were passed by most children age 2-0 or failed by most children age 4-0 due to the pass/fail scoring and assumptions of the reliability coefficient statistical procedure. No reliability data for hearing-impaired children are presented.

Validity.   Evidence of the scale's content validity is based on the selection of items from published measures of intelligence. Of the 65 items, only 6 were original items. The remaining items were adapted primarily from *Hiskey–Nebraska, Ontario School Ability Examination, Merrill–Palmer, Stanford–Binet,* and *Pintner–Paterson Performance Tests.* The manual reports one study that provides criterion-related validity data. The preliminary form of the *Smith–Johnson* and the *Leiter* were given to 27 children 3 to 6 years of age, resulting in an overall correlation coefficient of .73 between the scales. It is not specified whether the children had normal or impaired hearing.

Use of the Test with Hearing-Impaired Children.   The *Smith–Johnson* is designed to be used with hearing-impaired children and includes normative data from a hearing-impaired standardization sample. Additional published reports of use of the scale with hearing-impaired children were not found; however, Sullivan and Vernon (1979) reported the scale to be useful with hearing-impaired children, particularly those with mild to moderate losses.

Conclusions.   The *Smith–Johnson* has the potential to be helpful for evaluating the cognitive skills of hearing-impaired preschool children. The majority of items have been selected from established scales, and some items adapted from verbal scales. Items are grouped into tasks, combining items requiring similar skills. Rather than provide an overall score, the scale can be interpreted according to tasks or items. Also, the scale permits comparison between the skills of hearing and hearing-impaired children.

Nevertheless, the *Smith–Johnson* has not fulfilled its potential. Data to support the hearing-impaired standardization sample as representative of the nation's population are not provided in terms of geographic distribution, socioeconomic level, race, ethnicity, and residence. Furthermore, lack of description of the children's hearing losses is a problem. Reliability data for hearing-impaired children are not given (and correlations are less than .85 for hearing children), only limited validity data are presented, and normative data are out-of-date and may yield inflated results. Given these limitations, the *Smith–Johnson's* best use may be as a criterion-referenced measure to support findings from other scales. Examiners may wish to present selected tasks and observe performance as items become more difficult, thereby gaining information regarding emerging skills and skills requiring remediation.

Norm-Referenced Tests with Hearing Norms, Nonvocal Instructions, and Nonvocal Responses

An Adaptation of the Wechsler Preschool and Primary Scale of Intelligence for Deaf Children

Authors: S. Ray and M. Ulissi
Publisher: Steven Ray
              P.O. Box 5003
              Northwestern State University
              Natchitoches, LA 71457
Copyright: 1982

General Description.   The *Adaptation of the Wechsler Preschool and Primary Scale of Intelligence for Deaf Children* is designed as a standardization of the WPPSI Performance Scale with hearing-impaired children. The *Adaptation* uses the same Performance Scale items and materials as the WPPSI, but modifies WPPSI instructions to better convey subtest instructions to hearing-impaired children. The *Adaptation* contains two sets of modified instructions. The Alternative Instructions are WPPSI instructions with less complex syntax and vocabulary. These linguistically lowered instructions are signed or spoken. The Supplemental Instructions provide additional demonstration and practice items to four of the five Performance subtests to ensure comprehension of task requirements. The Supplemental Instructions are spoken or signed and are intended for hearing-impaired children with limited communication skills. The instructions have been standardized on a sample of hearing-impaired children, and data are presented to indicate that scores from the sample are not significantly different from those of hearing children included in the standardization of the WPPSI. As a result, norm tables from the WPPSI are used to obtain subtest scores and the Performance IQ.

The *Adaptation* is designed for the same ages as the WPPSI, 4 to 6½ years, and produces the same scores. The only additions are that the *Adaptation* includes a manual and materials for the extra examples (crayons, sample sheets, pointer, sample cards, and red-and-white two-dimensional patterns) for the Supplemental Instructions. If the Supplemental Instructions are used, the *Adaptation* may take longer to give than the 25 to 40 minutes of the WPPSI Performance Scale. Once subtest items are given, however, the same time limits as those of the WPPSI subtests are used.

Description of Subtests.   The review of the WPPSI Performance Scale later in this chapter describes individual subtests. *Adaptation* Supplemental Instructions add two sample items to the Animal House subtest, five sample items to the Picture Completion subtest, three sample items to the Mazes subtest, and three sample items to the Block Design subtest.

Technical Adequacy

Standardization.   Subjects included 120 prelingually hearing-impaired children with a minimum loss of 70 dB in the better ear. Further basis for subject selection is not provided. The number of subjects per half-year age level ranged from 16 to 30.

Comparison of sample characteristics to the 1960 U.S. census data, upon which the WPPSI was based, indicates several discrepancies. Discrepancies are due primarily to the small number of subjects, which allows a few subjects to greatly influence percentages. Compared with the census data, approximately equal numbers of males (46.7% of sample) and females (53.3%) were included. White subjects, however, were underrepresented in the sample (68.3% of sample vs. 85.8% of population), and nonwhites were somewhat overrepresented (20% vs. 14.2%). Subjects of urban residence were somewhat overrepresented (76.7% vs. 68.0%); consequently, those of rural residence were underrepresented (23.3% vs. 32.0%). Subjects from Southern and Western geographic regions were overrepresented (43.0% vs. 31.9% and 25.1% vs. 16.0%, respectively), and those from Northeastern and North Central regions were underrepresented (10.9% vs. 22.7% and 21.0% vs. 29.4%). Parents of moderate socioeconomic status, as defined by occupation, were underrepresented (28.3% vs. 43.7%).

Reliability.   No reliability data for scores obtained using either set of *Adaptation* instructions are included in the *Adaptation* manual.

Validity. No validity data from use of the *Adaptation* are reported in the *Adaptation* manual.

Use of the Test with Hearing-Impaired Children. The *Adaptation* was designed to be used with hearing-impaired children and was standardized on hearing-impaired children. Additional use of the test with hearing-impaired children was not found in a review of the literature.

Conclusions. Standardization of established measures of cognitive ability, such as the WPPSI, on hearing-impaired children offers many advantages. Among these advantages are the comparisons between hearing and hearing-impaired children for overall performance, factor structures, validity, and reliability. In addition, such standardization permits a degree of overlap in use of common materials, administration procedures, and scoring.

Given the many advantages, the *Adaptation* has the potential to be a valuable tool for evaluating the cognitive skills of hearing-impaired children. However, the *Adaptation*'s standardization sample is too limited in number and demographic characteristics to represent adequately a national population. According to Sullivan (1985), attempts to equate the sample with the WPPSI sample lack necessary power and use inappropriate analyses. Furthermore, the *Adaptation* contains two sets of instructions, and the effect of each set on performance has yet to be examined. Questions remain regarding a practice effect due to the extra sample items contained on the Supplemental Instructions. Presently, these shortcomings and lack of reliability and validity data seriously hinder the value of the *Adaptation* in providing a valid measure of cognitive ability. Use of the *Adaptation* as a supplement to other measures providing an overall score is recommended, however, due to the small number of available alternative measures.

Central Institute for the Deaf Preschool Performance Scale

Authors: A. E. Geers and H. S. Lane
Publisher: Stoelting Company
               620 Wheat Ln.
               Wood Dale, IL 60191
Copyright: 1984

General Description. The *CID Preschool Performance Scale*, based on a revision of *Randall's Island Performance Series* (Poull, Bristol, King, & Peatman, 1931), is a measure of intelligence for children from 2-0 to 5-5 years of age. Both the test instructions and the child's responses are nonvocal. Administration requires 30 to 60 minutes. Although items are timed, it is suggested in the manual that the limits are "generous" (p. 3). The test consists of six subtests. Standard scores are provided for subtests, and a Deviation Quotient is used to describe overall performance on the test. There is one form of the *Preschool Performance Scale.* Instructions are conveyed by gesture and modeling. Prompts and practice may be employed to ensure understanding of the tasks. Optional verbal directions can be used, but only to supplement nonvocal directions. Materials consist of the examiner's manual, a record book, and a set of toys, including puzzles, blocks, cards, color chips, and pegboards.

Description of Subtests

Manual Planning.   This subtest consists of four items requiring building with blocks, one item requiring placing graduated (Montessori) cylinders into corresponding holes in a casing, and one item using the Pintner Two Figure Board.

Manual Dexterity.   This subtest consists of three items requiring a child to button buttons (one-button piece, two-button piece, and four-button piece), and two items utilizing both the round and square Wallin Peg Boards.

Form Perception.   This subtest consists of matching pictures using the Decroly Picture cards and completion of the 10-piece Sequin Formboard.

Perceptual–Motor Skills.   This subtest involves imitating sequences of tapping blocks, copying figures (circle, square, triangle, inverted triangle, and diamond), and folding paper (one, two, and three folds).

Preschool Skills.   This subtest involves sorting colors and matching different quantities of sticks (one to nine).

Part/Whole Relations.   This subtest consists of completion of a manikin and two-, three-, and four-piece puzzles. The manikin and puzzles are those from the *Merrill–Palmer Scale.* Pictures for the puzzles are dated.

Technical Adequacy

Standardization.   The standardization consisted of children evaluated at the Central Institute for Deaf's clinics. Of the 978 children, 521 had hearing losses greater than 30 dB, 294 had normal hearing, and 163 children had no recorded audiologic information, but they had passed a hearing screening. No additional information is provided on the children's hearing losses. Boys made up 53% of the sample. No information is provided on the geographic distribution, race, ethnicity, socioeconomic level, or urban/rural residence. Data were collected from 1965 to 1980.

Reliability. Test–retest reliability was examined with 92 children retested from 4 months to 3 years, 5 months after the initial test. A correlation of .71 was obtained for the overall IQ. No information is given for other types of reliability.

Validity. Scores generally were shown to increase with age. Scores were shown to correlate with the WISC-R at .485 for 112 children. Because the interval between administration of the tests ranged from 1 year, 5 months to 10 years, 8 months, this seems to reflect predictive validity. No additional information on validity is provided.

Use of the Test with Hearing-Impaired Children. The *Preschool Performance Scale* was designed and standardized on both hearing-impaired and normally hearing children. No additional reports of use of the test with hearing-impaired children were available.

Conclusions. Based on tasks involved in the *Preschool Performance Scale,* the test appears to have included some items useful in the assessment of intelligence for preschool children. The use of the measure since 1932 also lends support to the use of the test. Because each subtest has only a few items, interpretation of performance on subtests is highly questionable, although the overall score could provide some useful information if interpreted cautiously. A considerable amount of work remains to be done before the measure would meet the criteria for technical adequacy. For standardization, a sample that is representative in terms of geographic distribution, socioeconomic status, race, ethnicity, and urban/rural residence is needed. Furthermore, background information on hearing loss of the children in the sample, and their method of communication, is needed. Data on internal consistency, short-term test–retest reliability, and standard error of measurement are needed for reliability. Also needed is support for the construct validity of the test and the criterion-related validity. The *Preschool Performance Scale* seems to have potential as a measure of intelligence for hearing-impaired children, but until the important aspects of technical adequacy are addressed, it cannot be recommended except as a measure to provide supportive data to other more technically adequate measures.

Norm-Referenced Tests with Hearing Norms, Verbal Instructions, and Nonvocal Responses

Battelle Developmental Inventory

Authors:	J. Newborg, J. R. Stock, L. Wnek, J. Guidubaldi, & J. Svinicki
Publisher:	DLM Teaching Resources One DLM Park Allen, TX 75002
Copyright:	1984

General Description. The *Battelle Developmental Inventory* (BDI) is a measure of developmental skills for children from birth to 8 years of age. The purpose of the BDI is to identify handicapped children, strengths and weaknesses of nonhandicapped children, and appropriate instructional plans for individual children, as well as to monitor student progress. The BDI contains five domains, Personal–Social, Adaptive, Motor, Communication, and Cognitive. A screening test containing 28% of the test items is also provided.

Administration time is approximately 1 to 2 hours for the entire BDI and 10 to 30 minutes for the screening test. There is one form of the test. Approximately 30 minutes are required to give the Cognitive Domain. Items are scored based on an interview of caregivers or teachers, observation, and/or task performance. Items are scored 2, 1, or 0 according to whether the child meets, attempts, or does not attempt (or poorly approximates) criterion performance. Hence, emerging skills can be identified. Test scores include percentile ranks for the overall test, domains, and subdomains; and age equivalents for the overall test, domains, and some subdomains. Standard scores and normal curve equivalents can be obtained from conversion of percentile scores.

Test materials include six manuals (an examiner's manual and one manual for each domain), test books, scoring booklets, and an envelope of visual stimuli. Additional materials must be provided by the examiner and are listed in an appendix. Five Cognitive Domain items require supplemental materials when the BDI is given to a hearing-impaired child.

General information for testing hearing-impaired children is provided in the manual. The information includes considerations during assessment, as well as cautions when employing an interpreter.

Description of the Cognitive Domain.   The Cognitive Domain contains 56 items. The majority of items (52 of 56) are completed through structured administration of the inventory; the remaining items are completed through interview and observation. Because children are not given each age level of the inventory, not all 56 items are scored. Three to 12 items are included at each age level. The items of the Cognitive Domain "measure those skills and abilities that are conceptual in nature" (p. 6). Four subdomains comprise the Cognitive Domain.

Perceptual Discrimination.   This domain (10 items) measures exploration of the environment, ability to match objects, and ability to visually discriminate between similar objects. Six items have verbal instructions; however, instructions for hearing-impaired children using gestures are provided for 5 of these items. The majority of subdomain items (8 of 10) are for children 4 years or younger.

Memory.   This domain (10 items) requires tracking an auditory stimulus, tracking a visual stimulus, locating a hidden object, repeating digits, and recalling information. Nine items require the use of hearing or language (e.g., tracking auditory stimuli and repeating digits), yet additional instructions for hearing-impaired children are not included for these items. Again, the majority of items (7 of 10) are for children 4 years or younger.

Reasoning and Academic Skills.   This domain (16 items) includes items such as reaching around a barrier to get a toy, answering logic questions, identifying missing parts of objects, and demonstrating addition and subtraction skills. Fifteen items require language skills (e.g., answering logic questions). Eight of these items have additional instructions for hearing-impaired children. Only 3 items of the subdomain are for children younger than 4 years of age.

Conceptual Development.   This domain (20 items) requires the child to identify objects, shapes, colors, and sides; demonstrate understanding of various concepts; tell time; sequence; join; categorize; group; assemble; and conserve. Although most items do not require a verbal response, language skills are needed to communicate response requirements (e.g., identifying the middle object). As with other tests assessing knowledge of concepts, use of sign language may cue the hearing-impaired child to the correct response (e.g., asking the child to identify the longer of the two sticks). Three subdomain items are for children younger than 4 years.

Technical Adequacy

Standardization.   Subjects were selected through "stratified quota sampling" along the variables of geographic region, sex, race, and urban/rural residence according to 1981 U.S. census statistics. A total of 800 children were selected, with 49 to 108 at each 6-month age level. The percentage of children selected corresponds to the statistical data for the variables of geographic region, sex, and race (white/minority); however, no data are presented for socioeconomic level, ethnicity, or residence.

Reliability. Internal consistency reliability data are not presented because it was deemed that such data would not be appropriate for an inventory that measures several skills.

Test–retest reliability coefficients are presented for 183 children. Time between testings was 4 weeks or less. Coefficients, presented at 6-month age intervals, range from .84 to .98 for the Cognitive Domain. Coefficients for Cognitive subdomains across age intervals range from .72 to .97. An overall coefficient of .99 is reported for the Cognitive Domain.

Interrater reliability data for 148 children are also presented by 6-month age levels. Coefficients for the Cognitive Domain across age intervals range from .86 to 1.00. Coefficients for subdomains across intervals range from .70 to 1.00. An overall Cognitive Domain coefficient of .99 is reported.

Standard errors of measurement are presented by 6-month age intervals for subdomains, domains, and the total test. Values are not based upon internal consistency reliability, but were obtained by dividing the standard deviation by the square root of the sample size. It appears that such a quotient is directly related to sample size (i.e., sample size is controlled in the numerator, but not in the denominator) and that values may vary with sample size.

Validity. Evidence of content validity for the BDI is provided through item selection from published and unpublished tests, item review by professionals, pilot testings and revisions, and item analysis. Data supporting construct validity are presented, indicating that BDI scores correlate moderately to highly with each other. Factor analysis of scores provides general support for the five domains, although the number of factors varies with age. Additional data support hypotheses that BDI scores increase with age, distinguish between groups expected to differ in development, and do not distinguish on the basis of sex or race.

Criterion-related validity data are presented through correlational data for the BDI and the *Vineland Social Maturity Scale* (Doll, 1965), *Developmental Activities Screening Inventory* (DASI; Dubose & Langley, 1977), *Stanford–Binet Intelligence Scale* (Terman & Merrill, 1960), WISC-R (Wechsler, 1974), and PPVT-R (Dunn & Dunn, 1981) for a clinical sample of handicapped children. Correlation of the Cognitive Domain with the various scales produced coefficients of .79 with the *Vineland,* .78 with the DASI, .50 with the *Stanford–Binet,* .43 with the WISC-R Verbal IQ, .02 with the WISC-R Performance IQ, .44 with the WISC-R Full Scale IQ, and .63 with the PPVT-R. Hence, the Cognitive Domain does not correlate as highly with other cognitive measures as it does with noncognitive measures. This may be a function of both the developmentally delayed sample and the lack of a consistent cognitive factor across ages (e.g., Cognitive Domain items tend to measure primarily communication skills at ages 2 through 5, but additional skills for older children).

Use of the Test with Hearing-Impaired Children. Although the inventory is designed for children with various handicaps, including hearing impairment, use of the test with hearing-impaired children is not reported in the manual. Of the five case studies presented in the manual, none included a hearing-impaired child. A research review did not identify a study reporting use of the inventory with hearing-impaired children.

Conclusions. Because the BDI is a relatively new test, additional information regarding its use with hearing-impaired children is needed before its utility as a cognitive measure with this population can be assessed. Although the test has fair technical adequacy, the Cognitive Domain has too few items to yield what can be considered an overall IQ score. Additionally, data are necessary to show that scores for hearing-impaired children do not differ significantly from those of the standardization sample, and that adequate reliability and validity can be demonstrated with hearing-impaired children. Additional information for assessing hearing-impaired children with limited language and communication skills is needed before the test can be used adequately with younger hearing-impaired children.

In its present form, the Cognitive Domain may be of value with hearing-impaired children with good language skills to identify strengths and difficulties, and to plan programs. The limited number of items, however, restricts the utility of the information, necessitating further testing. Use of the overall Cognitive Domain score is recommended only as a supplement to another cognitive measure, due to the limited number of items and questions pertaining to criterion-related validity and the area that the Cognitive Domain is assessing.

Bayley Scales of Infant Development

Author: N. Bayley
Publisher: The Psychological Corporation
              555 Academic Court
              San Antonio, TX 78204
Copyright: 1969

General Description. The *Bayley Scales of Infant Development* (BSID) is designed for children from 2 to 30 months of age. BSID consists of three parts: the Mental Scale (163 items), the Motor Scale (81 items), and the Infant Behavior Record. Stated purposes of the BSID are to assess current developmental skills and provide limited prediction of later skills, identify areas for intervention and formulate hypotheses for developmental delays, identify retardation, assess a broad set of behavioral variables, and provide a suitable measure for research with infants.

Approximately 20 to 40 minutes are required to administer the Mental Scale. There is one form of the test. Scores for the Mental Scale include a standard score and an age equivalent. Items are scored Pass, Fail, or Other (Omitted, Refused, or Reported by Mother). Materials consist of the examiner's manual, a record book for each scale, and numerous testing materials, including blocks, puzzles, and dolls. Materials not included in the kit should be readily available to most examiners (table, paper, facial tissue, stopwatch, stairs), with the possible exceptions of a crib and a walking board. Concern has been raised about the safety of some items included in the kit for use with young children, and close supervision is recommended with the materials, particularly those that could be swallowed (Bradley-Johnson, 1986).

Description of the Mental Scale. The 163 items of the Mental Scale tap a variety of skills, including "shape discrimination, sustained attention, purposeful manipulations of objects, imitation and comprehension, vocalization, memory, problem solving, and naming objects" (Sattler, 1982, p. 253). The majority (152) of the Mental Scale items are grouped according to "situations." Items comprising one of the 35 situations involve the same materials and/or other stimuli (e.g., voice). Within a situation, items are sequenced according to the age that the item is passed by most (50%) children. Thus, grouping items according to situations adds continuity to testing, and enhances interpretation.

The 11 items that are not included in a situation either do not share materials with other items or involve behaviors topographically different from items using the same stimuli. For example, items requiring the naming of one, then two, then three objects form a situation, whereas finding two objects is not included in a situation.

Eight of the 35 situations contain items that involve an auditory stimulus other than a verbal instruction (e.g., bell, rattle, whistle doll). Other situations contain instructions that can be presented orally and/or manually; however, the use of sign language may cue certain responses (i.e., "Show me the dolly's hair"). Furthermore, several items require a vocal response (e.g., jabbers expressively, says two words).

Technical Adequacy

Standardization. Subjects were selected using a stratified sample design according to the variables of sex, race, residence, and parent education in accordance with 1960 U.S. census data percentages. A total of 1,262 children were included in the standardization sample, with 83 to 95 (mean = 90) children at each of the 14 age levels (2, 3, 4, 5, 6, 8, 10, 12, 15, 18, 21, 24, 27, and 30 months). Only nonhandicapped children were selected.

The sample closely approximates census data percentages for the variables of sex, race (white/nonwhite), and parent education. Further socioeconomic status information is provided by data indicating that the percentage of heads of households in each of the eight census occupational categories conforms to census data percentages.

Rural children, however, are underrepresented in the sample, particularly rural white children (11.1% of sample vs. 26.7% in the population). Children from the South are also underrepresented (17.0% vs. 31.6%). Correspondingly, children from the West are overrepresented (37.3% vs. 15.9%).

Reliability. Internal consistency reliability data are presented by split-half correlation coefficients and are based on the standardization sample. Values for the Mental Scale range from .81 to .93 across the 14 age levels, with a median value of .88. Coefficients are at or above .85 at the ages of 3 to 6 months and 15 to 30 months.

Test–retest reliability data are provided for an earlier version of the BSID given to 28 8-month-old infants. Only a 1-week retest interval was used. A percentage of agreement of 76.4 is presented for the Mental Scale. This value likely underrepresents a correlation coefficient, as a percentage of agreement is based upon item-by-item scoring.

Interrater reliability also is presented for an earlier version of the BSID with 90 8-month-old infants. A percentage of agreement for items of 89.4 is reported.

Standard errors of measurement are presented by age level for each scale and are based on internal consistency reliability values.

Validity. Evidence of criterion-related validity is presented by data indicating that scores from the Mental and Motor Scales correlate to a moderate degree (values from .24 to .78 based on raw scores). Further criterion-related data are provided in a study of 120 children at three age levels given the BSID Mental Scale and the *Stanford–Binet.* An overall correlation coefficient of .57 was obtained.

Use of the Mental Scale with Hearing-Impaired Children. The BSID manual does not indicate use of the Mental Scale with hearing-impaired children. Hearing-impaired children were not included in the standardization, and a literature review did not reveal studies employing the scale with these children. Boyle (1977) stated that the test may be used with hearing-impaired children, and is more appropriate for children functioning in the average range, but may be used with retarded children.

Sullivan and Vernon (1979) also reported that the test can be used with hearing-impaired children, but cautioned that the results indicate current performance and are not useful in prediction of later ability.

Conclusions.   Although the BSID Mental Scale may be the best available cognitive test for infants, its use with hearing-impaired infants is restricted, as a large number of items require hearing, or speech and language skills. Examiners may choose to omit these inappropriate items and score as neither pass nor fail, but as "other." Doing so will produce a score; however, only items passed contribute to the score, and according to the test manual, "omitted items tend to invalidate test scores" (p. 31).

Use of the BSID with hearing-impaired children, however, may be valuable in three instances. First, compared with items for older children, items for children 2 to 6 months of age rarely require hearing or speech and language skills. For example, approximately 65 of the first 78 items do not require hearing, speech, or language skills, and it may be possible to obtain a valid score for 2- to 6-month-olds. Second, as with the BDI, the entire Scale may be appropriate with children using amplification and having speech and language skills. Third, for hearing-impaired children older than 6 months and without adequate hearing or speech and language skills, some information may be gained from individual items and from situations that do not rely on hearing, language, or speech. By using selected situations and interpreting according to item age level, the examiner may obtain a range of age levels for items passed that can describe cognitive development.

Use of scores from the BSID should be used only to supplement results of other tests, due to the age of the normative data; lack of representativeness of the sample in terms of geographic distribution, ethnicity, and urban/rural residence; lack of demonstrated validity; lack of reliability for the current version of the test; and lack of information on the performance of hearing-impaired children on the test.

Cognitive Abilities Scale

Author: S. Bradley-Johnson
Publisher: PRO-ED
               8700 Shoal Creek Blvd.
               Austin, TX 78758-6897
Copyright: 1987

General Description.   The *Cognitive Abilities Scale* (CAS) is a measure of cognitive ability for 2- and 3-year-olds. The scale has been designed to produce both norm-referenced assessment data and specific information for planning educational programs. The CAS comprises five subtests: Language, Reading, Mathematics, Handwriting, and Enabling Behaviors. Scores include a standard score and percentile for each subtest, plus an overall scale score, either the Cognitive Quotient or a Nonvocal Cognitive Quotient (from items requiring a nonvocal response). Administration time is about 30 to 45 minutes. Materials include the manual, record book, child's book, picture cards, and toys. Toys required for administering the scale are included with the scale and have been selected to be safe for 2- and 3-year-olds.

Description of Subtests

Language. The 30 items of this subtest assess the child's knowledge of concepts, expressive and receptive vocabulary, expressive and receptive knowledge of pronouns, and expressive and receptive knowledge of syntax. Except for concepts, the format of this subtest allows the child to respond initially orally. If the child refuses to speak, has unintelligible speech, or misses items, these items may be readministered by requiring a nonvocal response from the child. Unfortunately, the use of sign, gesture, or pantomime may cue the correct response for many items that can be responded to nonvocally.

Reading. This 16-item subtest assesses prereading skills (e.g., turning book pages), listening comprehension, and knowledge of letter names and sounds. Only the initial 3 items of this subtest require nonvocal responses. Thus, the subtest is of extremely limited use with hearing-impaired children.

Mathematics. The 22 items of this subtest assess math concepts, counting, sequencing, matching equal quantities, number identification, and matching numbers with quantities. As with the Language subtest, the use of sign, gesture, or pantomime may cue the correct response for many items on the Mathematics subtest that have nonvocal responses (e.g., "Show me the little cup").

Handwriting. The six items of the Handwriting subtest measure the child's writing posture and pencil grip, and ability to copy designs necessary for letter formation (e.g., circle, vertical line). The entire Handwriting subtest could be used with hearing-impaired children.

Enabling Behaviors. This 14-item subtest assesses the child's willingness to imitate speech, ability to imitate physical movements, memory for sentences, and memory for words. The author indicates that these skills are assessed due to their importance for efficient learning. Only the imitation of physical movement requires nonvocal responses; however, no subtest score can be assigned if only the physical imitation items are given.

Technical Adequacy

Standardization. Over 100 children were included in the standardization sample at each age level (203 2-year-olds, and 333 3-year-olds). The sample closely approximates 1980 U.S. census data on the variables of sex, residence, socioeconomic status, ethnicity, and race. The sample underrepresents the West geographic region (13% of sample vs. 20% of U.S. population) and the Northeast region (15% vs. 21%). Correspondingly, the North Central and South regions are overrepresented (33% vs. 25%, and 39% vs. 34%, respectively). The inclusion of handicapped children in the sample, other than the 3% who were mentally retarded, is not stated.

Reliability. Internal consistency reliability data are presented for each subtest at each age level. Coefficients are above .80 except for the Handwriting subtest at the 3-year age level ($r = .75$). Coefficients for the Cognitive Quotient and Nonvocal Cognitive Quotient are above .90 at both age levels.

Test–retest reliability data are presented by age level from two studies. For both studies, a 2-week interval was used between testing. The first study involved children from a single state. Coefficients are above .80 for each subtest except the Reading subtest at the 2-year level, and the Mathematics and Handwriting subtests at the 3-year level. Cognitive Quotient and Nonvocal Cognitive Quotient coefficients are above .90 except the Nonvocal Cognitive Quotient at the 3-year level ($r = .88$). The second study involved 30 children randomly selected from the standardization sample. Coefficients range from .69 to .98 for subtests and .90 or higher for the Cognitive Quotient and Nonvocal Cognitive Quotient at both age levels.

Standard errors of measurement using internal consistency reliabilities are reported in the manual.

Validity. Evidence for the scale's content validity is provided from selection of test items from review of published tests and literature, and from field testings with subsequent item analyses. Additional evidence is shown by the manner in which test items directly assess a skill. For example, children are required to demonstrate knowledge of concepts using toys, to draw symbols, and to use a book. Guessing is minimized, as the child directly demonstrates skills rather than pointing to an answer or giving only a verbal response. Also, due to the restricted age range of the scale, a large number of items (there are 88 total test items) are given to each child, compared with the number given to children with a test designed for a larger age range.

Evidence of concurrent validity is provided from correlational data from the CAS and the *Stanford–Binet*. A coefficient of .79 was found for 2-year-olds, and .74 for 3-year-olds. A coefficient of .69 was found between the *Kaufman Assessment Battery for Children* (K-ABC) Mental Processing Composite and the CAS. A higher coefficient was found between the K-ABC Achievement Score and the CAS ($r = .84$), whereas a lower value was found between the K-ABC and the CAS Nonvocal Cognitive Quotient ($r = .59$). Also, a coefficient of .70 was found between the *Test of Early Reading Ability* and the CAS Reading subtest. A coefficient of .67 was found between the *Test of Early Language Development* and the CAS Language subtest.

Additional data are presented for predictive validity. A correlation coefficient of .66 was found between CAS scores for children tested at age 2 and retested at age 3. A coefficient of .59 was found for children given the CAS at age 2 and the *Stanford–Binet* at age 3.

Evidence of construct validity is provided by data indicating that CAS scores correlate with age as hypothesized and that subtests correlate moderately with each other (coefficients range from .38 to .75), and from a study in which CAS scores discriminated a group of retarded children from a group of nonretarded children.

Use of the Test with Hearing-Impaired Children.   No studies using the CAS with hearing-impaired children are reported in the manual or the literature. Use of this new test with hearing-impaired children has not been explored yet.

Conclusions.   Although a nonvocal score can be obtained from the CAS, the score was intended not for hearing-impaired children, but for those who can comprehend the vocal instructions yet who "will not talk or whose speech is unintelligible" (p. 48). One subtest, however, the Handwriting subtest, can be given to hearing-impaired children, and a standard score and percentile can be obtained. Although the subtest is similar to the Draw-A-Design subtest of the *McCarthy Scales*, it samples a wider range of prehandwriting skills. Thus, the Handwriting subtest may have some utility as a criterion-referenced measure with hearing-impaired children, recognizing that, without data to validate its use with hearing-impaired children, scores must be interpreted cautiously.

Kaufman Assessment Battery for Children

Authors: A. S. Kaufman and N. L. Kaufman
Publisher: American Guidance Service
                    Circle Pines, MN 55014
Copyright: 1983

General Description. The *Kaufman Assessment Battery for Children* (K-ABC) comprises both cognitive ability and achievement scales. The cognitive ability scale is divided into the Sequential Processing Scale and the Simultaneous Processing Scale. Together, the Sequential and Simultaneous Processing Scales provide a measure of general intelligence based on neuropsychology and cognitive psychology theory. Furthermore, the two Mental Processing Scales are designed to measure distinct types of fluid, noncrystallized cognitive ability. The K-ABC is intended for ages 2½ to 12½ years. Ten subtests, three for the Sequential Processing Scale and seven for the Simultaneous Processing Scale, make up the Mental Processing Scales; however, the number of scales a child receives varies with age and ranges from five (ages 2½ and 3) to eight (ages 6 to 12½). Correspondingly, Mental Processing Scale administration time varies with age, ranging from about 25 to 60 minutes. There is one form of the test. Practice items are included for each subtest. Results from the Sequential and Simultaneous Scales are combined to form an overall index, the Mental Processing Composite. In addition, the Nonverbal Scale comprises three to five subtests from the Sequential and Simultaneous Scales. Standard scores are provided for each of the four scales (Mental Processing Composite, Simultaneous Processing Scale, Sequential Processing Scale, and Nonverbal Scale) and for subtests. Percentile ranks and age equivalents are provided also for subtests. Percentiles, sociocultural percentiles (for black and white), and stanines are provided for scales. Materials for K-ABC include the manuals, test records, administration easels, and subtest materials (moveable cardboard wheel within a slotted jacket, rubber triangles, photographs, plastic squares).

The Nonverbal Scale is designed for children who are hearing impaired, speech and language impaired, and non-English speaking. It is for ages 4 to 12½. Instructions are provided in "any reasonable verbal or nonverbal technique" (p. 35), and responses are nonvocal. Some sections are timed. As Nonverbal Scale subtests represent a subset of the 10 Mental Processing subtests, test authors indicate that the Nonverbal Scale may be thought of as a short form of the Mental Processing Composite, useful with children having communication problems. Administration time is less than the Mental Processing Scales and requires the same materials, except the cardboard wheel.

Description of Subtests. Six subtests comprise the Nonverbal Scale; however, depending on age, only three to five subtests are given to a child. Unlike the Mental Processing Scale, subtests are not divided or interpreted according to simultaneous or sequential processing. Instead, it is stated that Nonverbal Scale subtests integrate both types of processing.

Four-year-olds receive three subtests—Face Recognition, Hand Movements, and Triangles—when given the Nonverbal Scale.

Face Recognition. This subtest exposes a photograph of a face for 5 seconds. The child then chooses the same face in a different pose from a photograph including several faces (15 items).

Hand Movements. The 21 items of this subtest require the child to reproduce a sequence of hand movements performed by the examiner.

Triangles. This subtest is similar to the WISC-R Block Design subtest. Children arrange rubber triangles that are blue on one side and yellow on the other to match a pictured design (18 items).

At age 5, the child is given four subtests. The first two subtests are Hand Movements and Triangles. The next two subtests are Matrix Analogies and Spatial Memory.

Matrix Analogies. The 20 items of this subtest are similar to those of the *Raven Progressive Matrices* and the *Test of Nonverbal Intelligence.* Unlike those scales, however, the child indicates a response by placing a plastic chip with the picture or design that completes the matrix directly on the matrix.

Spatial Memory. Twenty-one items require the child to look at a page divided into quadrants with randomly placed pictures appearing in a subset of quadrants. At the end of 5 seconds, the child is shown the same page without pictures and is asked to indicate the quadrants that contained pictures.

Ages 6 to 12½ are administered five subtests. The first four are Hand Movements, Triangles, Matrix Analogies, and Spacial Memory. The fifth subtest is Photo Series.

Photo Series. This 17-item subtest is similar to the Picture Arrangement subtest of the WISC-R, but color photographs are used instead of printed pictures. The child is asked to arrange pictures into a logical temporal sequence.

Technical Adequacy

Standardization. Because the subtests of the Nonverbal Scale represent a subset of the scales of the K-ABC, the standardization sample for the Nonverbal Scale is identical to that of the K-ABC.

Subjects were included in the standardization based on a sample stratified on the variables of age, sex, geographic region, socioeconomic status, race, community size, and educational placement. Two hundred children were included at each age level and 100 at the half-year levels from 2½ to 3 years and 12 to 12½ years. Equal numbers of males and females were included at each age level. The standardization approximates 1980 U.S.

census data on the variables of geographic region, socioeconomic status, race, community size, and educational placement.

The sample included 108 educationally handicapped children. The number of children with hearing impairments is not specified; however, the number was less than 15.

Reliability. Internal consistency (split-half) and test–retest reliability coefficients are presented for each subtest of the Nonverbal Scale and for the Nonverbal Scale itself. Internal consistency coefficients were obtained from the standardization sample and are given for each age level, ranging from .70 to .92 for subtests and from .87 to .92 for the Nonverbal Scale. Across the ages, the mean internal consistency coefficient for the Nonverbal Scale is .87 for preschool children and .93 for school-age children.

Test–retest reliability coefficients are reported for the Nonverbal Scale at three age groupings, 2½ to 5 ($r = .81$), 5 to 9 ($r = .82$), and 9 to 12½ ($r = .87$). Subtest coefficients across the groups range from .59 to .83. Test–retest reliability coefficients are based on a total of 246 subjects with a 2- to 4-week retest interval. Because test–retest coefficients are reported by age groupings, it is difficult to determine if the scale has adequate reliability for eligibility decisions involving a given age. Coefficients may be above .85 for some ages between 2½ to 9 years, and below .85 for some ages between 9 and 12½ years. Hence, more data are needed before the scale can be considered to have adequate reliability for use in making eligibility decisions.

A third type of reliability, alternate-levels reliability, also is provided to demonstrate that test scores remain stable despite changes in subtest name and number at different age levels. For example, at ages 4 and 5, 7 of the 10 Mental Processing subtests are given, but of those 7, 5 subtests are common to both ages, and each age receives 2 subtests the other does not. Alternate-levels reliability data are presented from a study of 41 4- and 5-year-olds tested twice. Correlation coefficients of .92 (Mental Processing Composite) and .83 (Nonverbal Scale) were obtained.

Standard errors of measurement are presented by age level for subtests and scales and based upon internal consistency reliability coefficients.

Validity. Evidence of content validity is provided from field testing and subsequent item analysis, internal consistency, item bias, and factor analyses, and through a review of items by independent reviewers and examiners.

Concurrent validity data are presented from a large number of studies. Sixteen studies compare WISC-R and K-ABC scores using nonhandicapped, handicapped, and Native American populations. Collapsing the 16 studies into 9 groups based on population resulted in correlation coefficients for the K-ABC Nonverbal Scale and the WISC-R Full Scale ranging from .36 to .74 (mean = .60). Correlation of the Nonverbal Scale and the *Stanford–Binet* (1973) for eight studies (collapsed into 6 groups) found correlations ranging from .31 to .51.

Correlation of the Nonverbal Scale with other measures of cognitive ability include coefficients of .33, .53, and .70 for three studies involving the total score of the *McCarthy Scales of Children's Abilities,* a coefficient of .36 with the total score of the *Woodcock–Johnson Psychoeducational Battery* (Volume 1), .40 and .68 with the Nonverbal Scale of the *Cognitive Abilities Test,* and .50 and .51 with the *Luria–Nebraska* Intelligence variable.

Additional studies investigated the correlation of the Nonverbal Scale with the *Columbia Mental Maturity Scale* (r = .36), the *Slosson Intelligence Test* (r = .61), the *Bender–Gestalt* (r = .30 & .42), and the *Developmental Test of Visual–Motor Integration* (r = .54). Nine studies provide correlational data for the Nonverbal Scale and the *Peabody Picture Vocabulary Test–Revised.* Coefficients range from .24 to .71 (mean = .48).

Additional concurrent validity data are provided from correlational data from achievement tests. Standardization of the Passage Comprehension subtest of the *Woodcock Reading Mastery Test* and the Written Computation subtest of the *Keymath Diagnostic Arithmetic Test* produced coefficients of .58 and .46, respectively, with the Nonverbal Scale.

Studies investigating predictive validity report correlational data for K-ABC with the following four achievement measures: *Peabody Individual Achievement Test, Woodcock–Johnson Psychoeducational Battery, Iowa Test of Basic Skills,* and *California Achievement Test.* Coefficients for the Nonverbal Scale and the total achievement score range from .18 to .63 (mean = .44) across the tests. A 6-month to 1-year interval elapsed between administration of the predictor (K-ABC) and the criterion achievement measures.

Evidence of construct validity is given through data showing that subtest scores increase as hypothesized with age, significant correlation coefficients exist between subtest scores and age, and coefficients between subtest scores and sex or race are not significant. Subtest scores were found to correlate as hypothesized with the Mental Processing Composite. Subtest correlation coefficients with the Nonverbal scale range from .58 to .80 across ages. Although a factor analysis was performed to support division of the scale into type of processing (simultaneous vs. sequential), the Nonverbal Scale is not interpreted according to type of processing.

Use of the Test with Hearing-Impaired Children.   In a survey of 105 U.S. programs serving hearing-impaired children, Powers, Elliot, and Funderburg (1987) found the K-ABC to be the second most frequently used test of intelligence to assess learning disabilities.

Only a few reports have been published, however, in which the K-ABC has been used with hearing-impaired children. The K-ABC manual reports one study (Courtney, Hayes, Watkins, & Frick, 1983; cited in Kaufman & Kaufman, 1983) conducted during K-ABC standardization. Forty hearing-impaired children were given the Nonverbal Scale and the *Adaptation of the WISC-R for the Deaf* (Ray, 1979). Subtest requirements for the Nonverbal Scale were communicated by sign. A correlation coefficient of .63 was found between the two tests. It is important to note that poor performance on two of the Nonverbal Scale subtests (Matrix Analogies and Photo Series) is attributed to poor reasoning ability or difficulty understanding tasks using sign.

Gibbons, Ulissi, and Brice (1984) reported a correlation coefficient of .84 between the Nonverbal Scale and the WISC-R Performance Scale using R. J. Anderson and Sisco's (1977) normative data in a study of 50 hearing-impaired children. Subtests were administered using total communication. Support was found for giving only the subtests of the Nonverbal Scale to hearing-impaired children rather than all K-ABC subtests. In the same study, correlation of the Nonverbal Scale and the *Stanford Achievement Test–Hearing Impaired Edition* resulted in coefficients of .71 for reading and .64 for math.

In a third study, L. J. Porter and Kirby (1986) reported a correlation coefficient of .66 between the Nonverbal Scale and the WISC-R Performance Scale (original norms). In the study, 25 hearing-impaired children were given the Nonverbal Scale using pantomime, whereas 24 additional hearing-impaired children were given the scale using American Sign Language (ASL). No significant differences were found between the scores of the two groups or between either group and the standardization sample. Correlation coefficients of .46 to .69 were found between the Nonverbal Scale and Reading Comprehension and Mathematics subtests of the *Metropolitan Achievement Test*. The authors indicated the suitability of the Nonverbal Scale as a measure of cognitive ability for hearing-impaired children.

Conclusions. Data from use of the Nonverbal Scale with hearing-impaired children indicate that the scale may be of utility with this population. Data are needed, however, to demonstrate the technical adequacy of the scale with these children. Additional data are needed to indicate that norms for hearing children are relevant for hearing-impaired children using methods of communication other than those used in the L. J. Porter and Kirby (1986) study. Furthermore, concurrent validity data from scales other than the WISC-R are needed to further establish concurrent validity.

Despite any future efforts to demonstrate the technical adequacy of the Nonverbal Scale with hearing-impaired children, some obvious difficulties exist. First, the Nonverbal Score is based on only a few subtests at some age levels (e.g., three subtests at age 4, four at age 5). Second, it is stated in the manual that impulsivity may hinder performance on two subtests, Face Recognition and Photo Series. Third, one subtest, Triangles, is a timed test. The performance of some hearing-impaired children may be penalized on these three subtests.

Additional studies supporting the validity of the Nonverbal Scale with hearing-impaired children would greatly aid future use of the scale with these children. Already, the scale has gained popularity with hearing-impaired children due to several factors, including current normative data and test items, sample items for each subtest, concurrent validity data with the WISC-R and achievement measures, and data supporting use of different methods of communicating directions without the need for separate normative data.

Stanford–Binet Intelligence Scale (4th Edition)

Authors: R. L. Thorndike, E. P. Hagen, and J. M. Sattler
Publisher: Riverside Publishing Company
              8420 Bryn Mawr Ave.
              Chicago, IL 60631
Copyright: 1986

General Description. The fourth edition of the *Stanford–Binet* (S-B IV) is for ages 2 to adult and contains 15 tests that assess four areas: Verbal Reasoning, Abstract/Visual Reasoning, Quantitative Reasoning, and Short-term Memory. The number of tests given to a child depends on age and skill level; no child is given all 15 tests. Scores can be reported in terms of Standard Age Scores. Standard Age Scores convert to Area Scores for each of the four areas, and Area Scores yield a Composite Score as an overall test score. Total time to administer the scale is 60 to 90 minutes, with approximately 15 to 25 minutes required for each area. There is one form of the test. Only one test, Pattern Analysis, has time limits. Subtests of the Abstract/Visual Reasoning Area require nonvocal responses; subtests of the Quantitative Reasoning Area require vocal or nonvocal responses. Instructions are primarily verbal, with pointing and gesturing also used with some subtests. Materials consist of the examiner's manual, a record book, multiple booklets for test stimuli, and objects used in testing such as blocks and beads.

Description of Subtests by Area. Subtests requiring nonvocal responses are included in the Abstract/Visual Reasoning Area and the Quantitative Reasoning Area. Four subtests comprise the Abstact/Visual Reasoning Area, and three subtests make up the Quantitative Reasoning Area.

Abstract/Visual Reasoning Area. The Pattern Analysis subtest requires placing pieces into a form board (6 items) and reproducing designs with blocks (36 items). Copying involves reproducing block patterns with blocks (12 items), and copying geometric designs (16 items). Matrices involves choosing an object to complete the relationship expressed by stimulus objects (26 items). Paper Folding and Cutting requires identifying the design produced by the unfolding of a cut paper (18 items). Sample items are provided for Pattern Analysis, Matrices, and Paper Folding and Cutting subtests. Examiners may have difficulty communicating to some hearing-impaired children some aspects of the Copying subtest (e.g., that erasing is permitted) and the Paper Folding and Cutting subtest (e.g., that children are to indicate what the paper would look like when unfolded).

Quantitative Reasoning. The Quantitative subtest involves matching, counting, and adding with numbered blocks, as well as knowledge of math operations and concepts including measurement, fractions, counting, money, and area (40 items). Number Series requires determining the next two numbers in a series (26 items). Equation Building involves using given numbers and mathematical symbols to create true relationships (18 items). Each subtest, except for the Quantitative area, has sample items.

Technical Adequacy

Standardization. The basis for subject selection was inclusion in randomly selected school districts or the meeting of sampling design specifications. A minimum of 195 subjects were included at each age level from 2 to 17. Less than 100 subjects per age level were included at ages 18 and above. The standardization sample closely approximates 1980 U.S. census data percentages for the variables of sex, geographic region, race, and urban/rural residence. Data for socioeconomic status are presented according to parental occupation and were weighted to conform to census percentages.

Most subjects were students in regular classrooms; however, students from "special population groups" were included. The inclusion of hearing impaired students is not specified.

Reliability. Internal consistency reliability coefficients are presented by age level for ages 2 to 17. Coefficients for the Abstract/Visual Reasoning Area range from .85 to .97 across the age levels. Coefficients for the Quantitative Reasoning Area range from .80 to .97 across the age levels, with coefficients less than .85 at ages 2, 3, and 6 years. Each test of the Absract/Visual Reasoning Area has a reliability coefficient of .85 or above, with the exception of Pattern Analysis and Copying at ages 2 and 3. Each test of the Quantitative Reasoning Area has a coefficient of .85 or above, except Quantitative at ages 2 to 3 and 6 to 9.

Test–retest reliability data were collected for two groups of children, 5-year-olds and 8-year-olds. Length of time between testings varied from 2 to 8 months. Correlation coefficients for the Abstract/Visual Reasoning Area and Quantitative Reasoning Area were below .85 for each group.

Validity. Evidence of content validity is presented through item analyses from two field testings, and through review of test items by independent reviewers. Evidence of criterion-related validity is provided through correlation of the S-B IV with an earlier edition, the *Stanford–Binet Form L-M* (1973), as well as with WISC-R, WPPSI, WAIS-R, and K-ABC. Correlation coefficients for overall scores were .81, .83, .80, .91, and .89, respectively. Construct validity data are provided by intercorrelation of subtests with Areas and the Composite, through factor analyses for three age groups, and from studies investigating the ability of the S-B IV to discriminate among groups of exceptional students (i.e., gifted, learning disabled, and mentally retarded).

Use of the Test with Hearing-Impaired Children. The test's standardization does not include hearing-impaired students, and use of the test with such students has yet to be reported.

Conclusions. The standardization and validity of the test are very good, except for the weighting of socioeconomic status data. The test–retest data provided are low and are given for only two age levels. Areas requiring nonvocal responses (Abstract/Visual Reasoning and Quantitative Reasoning) may produce scores with limited value, given that scores are based upon four or fewer subtests each, depending on a child's age and skill level.

The usefulness of the *Stanford–Binet IV* with hearing-impaired children is yet to be determined. Currently, the test lacks instructions standardized on a representative sample of hearing-impaired children, and lacks demonstrated validity and reliability with this population.

Wechsler Preschool and Primary Scale of Intelligence

Author: D. Wechsler
Publisher: The Psychological Corporation
                555 Academic Court
                San Antonio, TX 78204
Copyright: 1967

Note: Although the revised version of *Wechsler Preschool and Primary Scale of Intelligence* was published in 1989, the older version was selected for review because of the work that has been carried out with the older version and hearing-impaired children, and its frequent use with this population. Such work has not been carried out yet with the recent version.

General Description. The *Wechsler Preschool and Primary Scale of Intelligence* (WPPSI) is an intelligence scale for children 4 to 6½ years of age. Although not designed to be a downward extension of the WISC, the WPPSI is similar to the WISC in structure, and includes several subtests and items found on WISC. The WPPSI contains 11 subtests, divided into a Verbal Scale (6 subtests) and a Performance Scale (5 subtests). Scores include scaled scores for each subtest and IQs for the Verbal Scale, Performance Scale, and Full Scale (the overall score). Spoken instructions are given for each subtest. The Performance Scale subtests require nonvocal responses and can be used with hearing-impaired children. Three of the Performance Scale subtests (Animal House, Mazes, and Block Design) have time limits. Materials include a formboard and colored pegs, picture booklet, red pencils, Mazes sheet, Geometric Design sheet, two design booklets, and blocks. Approximately 25 to 40 minutes are required to administer the five Performance Scale subtests.

Description of Performance Scale Subtests

Animal House.   There are 20 possible items on this timed test. The child matches colored pegs with a shape according to the associations demonstrated by the examiner.

Picture Completion.   Twenty-three items involving the identification of a missing essential part from a picture comprise this subtest.

Mazes.   This 10-item subtest requires the child to draw a line through a printed maze.

Geometric Design.   This subtest requires the child to copy a design from a printed card (10 items).

Block Design.   This subtest has 10 items involving the arrangement of two-dimensional blocks to match an examiner model (6 items) or a printed design (4 items).

Technical Adequacy

Standardization.   A stratified sample of 1,200 subjects were included in the standardization group. One hundred boys and 100 girls were included at each half-year level from 4 to 6½ years. Stratification variables and percentages of children included according to each variable were taken from 1960 U.S. census data. The sample closely approximates census data for sex, race (white/nonwhite), geographic region, residence (urban/rural), and father's occupation.

Reliability.   Internal consistency reliability data based on the standardization sample are provided by age level for each subtest (except Animal House) and the three scales. Coefficients for Performance Scale subtests range from .62 to .91, with an average coefficient of .82. Coefficients for the Performance Scale range from .91 to .95 across the age levels, with an average of .93.

Test–retest data for subtests and scales are presented from a study of 50 5-year-olds. The retest interval was from 1½ to 4 months. Corrected coefficients for Performance Scale subtests (including Animal House) range from .62 to .93, and the coefficient for the Performance Scale is .89.

Standard errors of measurement are provided by age level based on the internal consistency reliabilities (or test–retest reliability for Animal House).

Validity.   Initial evidence of content validity of the WPPSI is provided through the overlap of WPPSI and WISC subtests. Eight WPPSI subtests were borrowed from the well-established WISC. Not only were tasks borrowed, but some WISC items also are used on the WPPSI.

Evidence of WPPSI construct validity is provided through subtest intercorrelation. Average intercorrelation coefficients indicate that although Verbal Scale subtests correlate highly with the Verbal Scale, Performance Scale subtests do not correlate as highly with the Performance Scale. In fact, two Verbal Scale subtests are among the five subtests that best correlate with the Performance Scale. Correlation coefficients of the Verbal and Performance Scales range from .62 to .71, with an average coefficient of .66. Correlation coefficients between the Full Scale and Performance Scale that are corrected for common subtest scores are not presented.

Criterion-related validity data are presented in a study of 108 children given the WPPSI, *Stanford–Binet Form L-M, Peabody Picture Vocabulary Test* (PPVT) Form A, and *Pictorial Test of Intelligence* (PTI). The overall correlation coefficient of the WPPSI Performance IQ with the *Stanford–Binet* was .65; with the PPVT, .44; and with the PTI, .60.

Use of the Test with Hearing-Impaired Children.   Levine's (1974) survey of measures used with hearing-impaired children found the WPPSI to be the eleventh most popular measure. Bragman (1982a) also indicated that the the test is commonly used with hearing-impaired children. Boyle (1977) stated that the test may be used with hearing-impaired children when other measures are not available. Sullivan and Vernon (1979) considered the test unsuitable for hearing-impaired children due to difficulty communicating task instructions, regardless of the form of communication used. Thus, it is likely that the WPPSI's popularity is due primarily to that of the WISC-R.

Unfortunately, less data regarding technical adequacy of the WPPSI with hearing-impaired children have been published than for the WISC-R. Boyd and Shapiro (1986) administered the WPPSI Performance Scale and *Leiter International Performance Scale* to 20 hearing-impaired preschool children (ages 52 to 76 months). A correlation coefficient of .65 was obtained.

Conclusions. The standardization of the WPPSI is excellent for hearing children, although the norms are dated. Because the norms are 23 years old, results may be inflated. Internal consistency reliabilities are satisfactory for the subtests and excellent for the scales. Test–retest data are provided only for 5-year-olds. Validity data also are incomplete; however, a number of studies (including a factor analysis) have further established the validity of the WPPSI since its publication. Sattler (1982) provided a review of such studies.

For hearing-impaired children, there are many demonstration items for Performance Scale subtests. All Performance Scale subtests require nonvocal responses; however, all of the subtests are timed in some manner. For example, Picture Completion and Geometric Design have time limits if the child has not started to respond (Picture Completion) or cannot accomplish the task (Geometric Design). Although the WPPSI is similar to the WISC-R, considerably less is known about the validity of the WPPSI with hearing-impaired children than of the WISC-R, and use of its scores is recommended only in a supplemental manner for hearing-impaired children. WPPSI Performance Scale scores should not be used as the sole cognitive measure for eligibility decisions.

Criterion-Referenced Tests and Informal Measures

Arthur Adaptation of the Leiter International Performance Scale

Author:	G. Arthur
Publisher:	Western Psychological Services
	12031 Wilshire Blvd.
	Los Angeles, CA 90025
Copyright:	1950

General Description. The *Arthur Adaptation of the Leiter International Performance Scale* (referred to as *Adaptation*) is a revision of the *Leiter International Performance Scale* (Leiter, 1940). Administration procedures, scoring criteria, and normative data differ from those of the original Leiter. Administration procedures for the *Adaptation* are provided for ages 2 to 12 years; however, normative data are restricted to ages 3 to 7 years. Instructions for the *Adaptation* are given by pantomime; no verbal instructions are required. Scores are reported for the *Adaptation* in terms of an Intelligence Quotient and mental age for overall test scores. Required materials are the *Adaptation* manual and the *Leiter* materials, including trays 1 and 2 (blocks, stimulus strips, and response frame) and record cards.

Description of Items. A total of 60 items comprise the *Adaptation;* however, children are rarely given all items. Subtests require matching colors and forms, completing patterns, determining analogous designs, and classifying objects.

Technical Adequacy

Standardization. Subjects included 289 children; however, the subjects are not described. Because a stated purpose of the *Adaptation* was to include normative data from white, middle-class, midwestern children, it is likely that a high percentage of such children were included in the standardization. It does not appear that hearing-impaired children were included in the sample.

Reliability. Kaplan (1974) reported internal consistency reliability of .89 for the *Adaptation*. Test–retest correlation coefficients for language-impaired samples are reported in the manual. Correlations are from varying retest intervals, and values range from .63 to .92.

Validity. The test manual reports correlation coefficients for the *Adaptation* and *Stanford–Binet,* WISC, PPVT, and ITPA, and with two general achievement tests, the *California Achievement Test* and the *Wide Range Achievement Test.* All coefficients were, as expected, in the moderate to high range.

Ratcliffe and Ratcliffe (1979) provided an overview of validity studies with the *Adaptation* and the *Leiter.* The review indicated that correlation coefficients between the *Adaptation* and the *Stanford–Binet* have ranged from .67 to .79, values somewhat higher than coefficients between the *Leiter* and the *Stanford–Binet.* Both the *Adaptation* and the *Leiter,* however, tend to consistently underestimate *Stanford–Binet* scores, especially for above-average IQs. Correlational data from the *Adaptation* and the WISC Performance Scale has resulted in correlations in the .70s. Again, it appears that *Adaptation* scores underestimate WISC Performance Scale scores. The reviewers cautioned against using the *Adaptation* (or the *Leiter*) as the sole measure of cognitive skills, especially for those of average or above IQs.

Use of the Test with Hearing-Impaired Children. Both the *Leiter* and the *Arthur Adaptation of the Leiter* have been commonly employed with hearing-impaired children, and continue to be used (Bragman, 1982a). Reliability data for the *Adaptation* with hearing-impaired children were reported by Mira (1962), who obtained a test–retest correlation coefficient of .36 for 18 preschool children with "marked" to profound hearing losses. These data do not indicate adequate reliability for eligibility decisions; however, a 1- to 2-year retest interval was used, so the coefficient may best be viewed as one of stability rather than reliability.

Criterion-related validity data for use of the *Adaptation* with hearing-impaired children have been reported in three studies. Musgrove and Counts (1975) found a correlation coefficient of .65 with *Raven's Progressive Matrices* in a study with 13 hearing-impaired children. A coefficient of .77 was obtained with the *Hiskey–Nebraska Test of Learning Aptitude* for 60 hearing-impaired children (Mira, 1962). Ritter (1976) reported a coefficient of .79 with *Raven's Coloured Matrices,* and a coefficient of .78 with the WISC Performance Scale in a study involving 31 children with mild to moderate hearing losses.

Conclusions. Sullivan and Vernon (1979) stated that the *Arthur Adaptation* is not appropriate for preschool hearing-impaired children due to extrapolated norms. Furthermore, they stated that the *Adaptation* does not have the technical adequacy to be used with any hearing-impaired child regardless of age. Werner (1965) recommended that, in its present form, the *Adaptation* should be restricted to research and as a special diagnostic instrument due to unevenness in difficulty levels from item to item, outdated pictures, questions about cultural fairness, and lack of validity data. On a positive note, Sattler (1982) indicated that the *Leiter* format may be less culturally loaded than other cognitive scales. In addition, the *Adaptation* is relatively easy to administer, does not require spoken instructions, and contains some educationally relevant tasks. Given that norms are outdated and not representative, however, and that inadequate information is available on test–retest reliability for hearing-impaired children, use of the *Adaptation* requires caution. It is recommended that scores not be reported and the test be used as an informal measure to assess skills such as matching and classification. Yet, with restandardization, reliability and validity data, and updated materials, scores from the *Adaptation* might be useful for both handicapped and nonhandicapped populations.

Ordinal Scales of Psychological Development

Authors: I. C. Uzgiris and J. McVicor Hunt
Publisher: University of Illinois Press
              Box 5081, Station A
              54 Gregory Dr.
              Champaign, IL 61820
Copyright: 1989

General Description. The *Ordinal Scales of Psychological Development* are designed to measure the cognitive development of children during the Sensorimotor Period (age 0 to 2 years), as described by Piaget. Six scales comprise the *Ordinal Scales,* with items of each scale arranged in a hierarchy according to expected development during the Sensorimotor Period. Approximately 1 to 2 hours are needed to administer all six scales, depending upon the cooperation of the child; however, the *Ordinal Scales* can be given over more than one session, and the number and sequence of scales to be administered can be altered. Not all scales need to be administered. Because of these options, the *Ordinal Scales* are well adapted for handicapped populations, including hearing-impaired children. Materials for the six scales are listed in the text (pp. 147–150). Thirty-four different materials are suggested to elicit behaviors for the *Ordinal Scales,* but, when appropriate, the child's own toys may be substituted in order to establish or maintain interest in an activity. The examiner's manual and a record book also are needed.

Items are scored as behavior that is absent or present. Because items follow a developmental sequence, the number of the highest behavior present in the hierarchy can be used as a score for a scale or portion of a scale. More important is the developmental profile for each scale, indicating the current skill development, the skills that are emerging, and later skills in the developmental sequence. Although ages at which a majority of children exhibit a skill are provided, the ages are not meant to provide normative data.

Description of the Scales

Scale I: The Development of Visual Pursuit and the Permanence of Objects. This scale includes 15 items. Initial items assess a child's ability to visually track an item, and later items concern finding an object that varies in how completely it is hidden (e.g., hidden in more than one place, hidden under more than one object, and hidden without permitting direct observation of the object).

Scale II: The Development of Means for Obtaining Desired Environmental Events. Twelve items are included in this scale, which assesses the child's use of objects to produce an effect (e.g., a noise or movement), obtain another object or produce an effect, or recognize and use object properties to solve problems.

Scale III: The Development of Vocal Imitation and Gestural Imitation. Vocal Imitation assesses the child's ability to produce increasingly complex sounds following examiner or parent vocalization. Gestural imitation includes having the child imitate gestures that the child has been observed to show, and gestures that are new to the child. There are six Vocal Imitation items and four Gestural Imitation items. Only one of the Vocal Imitation items would be appropriate for most hearing-impaired children, because assessment of imitation also requires hearing.

Scale IV: The Development of Operational Causality. This scale is divided into two sections, Efforts to Prolong Interesting Inputs (3 items) and Actions to Reinstate Interesting Spectacles (4 items). These items assess the infant's attempts to cause an event by repeating a body movement, acting directly on an object, or signaling another to repeat the event. For hearing-impaired children, some toys may have to be substituted during the assessment (e.g., those that produce a visual consequence for those producing an auditory one).

Scale V: The Construction of Object Relations in Space. This scale also is divided into two parts, Development in Localization of Objects in Space (5 items) and Development in Appreciation of Spacial Relationships Between Objects (6 items). Scale items assess ability to continually recognize objects as their orientation to the child changes, to combine schemes to act upon these objects (e.g., to locate and grasp), and to act upon objects based on their unchanging properties despite changes in relationship to the child. Some items of this scale may not be appropriate for hearing-impaired children due to their reliance on sound (item 2) or speech (item 11).

Scale VI: The Development of Schemes for Relating to Objects. This scale contains three items that assess the complexity of the child's actions upon familiar objects. For example, critical observations include whether the child repeats actions independent of the specific object, or whether actions vary based on properties of specific objects. Some actions that are assessed are dependent upon speech (e.g., naming objects) and would not be appropriate for many hearing-impaired children.

Technical Adequacy

Field Testing. Three separate field testings were conducted during scale development. Sample sizes included 42, 23, and 84 children ranging in age from 1 to 23 months. Samples were primarily from middle-class, educated

families from the same geographic area. Use of the scale with handicapped and at-risk children has been reported by Dunst (1980).

Reliability.   Data for interobserver agreement were obtained from the
third sample (84 children). The reported mean percentage of agreement
for scales was 96.1, with a range of 93.1 to 96.9 . Only two items were
rated with less than 80% agreement. Agreement may be inflated, however,
due to the second observer's scoring simultaneously with the examiner
rather than in a more controlled situation, such as from a videotape. Interrater reliability data from four studies were presented by Dunst (1980).
Correlation coefficients ranging from .85 to .99 were found. Kahn (1976)
reported interexaminer reliabilities of .78 to .95, with a mean scale coefficient of .86.

Test–retest reliability data also were obtained from the third sample.
Approximately a 48-hour retest interval was used. This interval is more
appropriate for this age group than a 2-week interval, because coefficients
based on a 2-week interval may be depressed due to cognitive development occurring during the interval. A mean value of 79.9 was obtained,
with scale values ranging from 79.0 to 81.9. Half of the items had reliabilities greater than or equal to .80. Reliability values may be lowered
because the examiner conducting the retest was not the original examiner.
Higher test–retest correlation coefficients, ranging from .88 to .96, were
reported by Kahn (1976).

Validity.   Evidence of construct validity is presented through correlation
of scale scores with age (scores were obtained by determining the highest
step or item achieved for each of the six scales). Coefficients range from
.86 to .94, suggesting that the scores, as expected, are highly related to age.
These data, however, were from children from middle-class families. Values may be lower for developmentally delayed children or for children
from families of other socioeconomic status.

Scale intercorrelation coefficients were found to range from .80 to .93.
Dunst (1980) found similar ranges with values from .70 to .92.

Concurrent validity data are provided by Dunst (1980). The *Ordinal
Scales* and the *Griffiths Mental Development Scales* were given to 36 handicapped and at-risk children 0 to 30 months of age. The overall correlation
coefficient, after correction for the influence of chronological age, was .83.
Correlation of the *Ordinal Scales* and *Bayley Scales of Infant Development*
was obtained in a longitudinal study of black, firstborn, male, inner-city
children 14 months of age (W. L. King & Seegmiller, 1973). Coefficients of
the *Bayley Mental Scale* score and the *Ordinal Scale* subtests ranged from
.03 (Vocal Imitation) to .44 (Object Relations in Space). The mean coefficient was .26. The same tests were given to the same children at 18 months
and 22 months of age. Mean coefficients were .11 and .30, respectively.
Wachs (1970) reported a correlation coefficient of .62 for the *Ordinal Scales*

and the *Stanford–Binet* with older retarded children (mean age of 4-10). Wachs and DeRemer (1978) reported correlational data for *Ordinal Scale* subtests and subtests from the *Alpern–Boll Developmental Profile.* Coefficients ranged from –.39 to .64 with a mean of .22.

Use of the Test with Hearing-Impaired Infants. Mavilya (1982) reported use of selected items of the *Ordinal Scales* for educational programming with hearing-impaired children at the Mailman Center for Child Development in Miami and at other programs.

Best and Roberts (1976) found that hearing-impaired children aged 23 to 38 months developed at the same rate as normal children as measured by the *Ordinal Scales,* with the exception of development measured by the Vocal Imitation Scale.

Conclusions. Due to the age range that this test covers, the sequential nature of the items, and the emphasis on skill acquisition rather than normative data, the *Ordinal Scales* can provide useful information for present, emerging, and later skill development for program planning. With slight adaptation, all scales except the Vocal Imitation Scale would be appropriate for hearing-impaired children.

A second manual to use with the *Ordinal Scales* was written by Dunst (1980). The manual expands the six ordinal scales by adding 53 additional "experimental items" to provide continuity and completeness to each scale. Some items from the original scale have been separated so that item progression follows a developmental sequence to a greater degree. Dunst's manual provides scores including an Estimated Developmental Age (EDA) for scales, an average EDA as a total test score, a deviation score (EDA – CA, where CA refers to Chronological Age) for scales, and an average deviation score as a total test score. These four additional scores are not standard scores, but aid interpretation of the child's performance across scales. The Dunst manual also provides a profile for scores and intervention techniques "to facilitate both the acquisition and synthesis of sensorimotor skills" (p. 7). As a supplement, Dunst's manual can be of great utility in administering, scoring, interpreting, and intervening, and is recommended when the *Ordinal Scales* are used with hearing-impaired children and other handicapped populations.

Available Measures of Cognitive Ability for Hearing-Impaired Infants and Preschoolers

Figure 4.1 provides an overview of the measures of cognitive ability according to the ages each measure is designed to include. For children

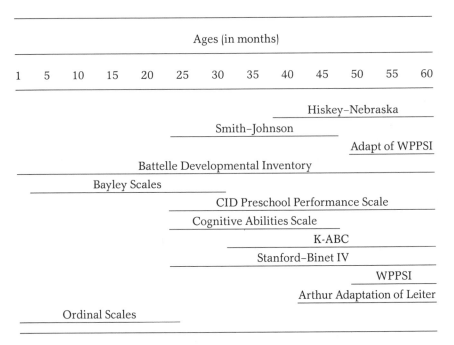

Figure 4.1. Cognitive measures and applicable ages for hearing-impaired infants and preschoolers.

from 0 to 30 months, an overall score can be obtained only from the *Battelle Developmental Inventory* and the *Bayley Scales of Infant Development*. Because neither of these measures is well suited for hearing-impaired infants, examiners requiring an overall score should attempt to give both measures. The *Ordinal Scales* can provide additional programming data for children up to 24 months of age, and the *Smith–Johnson* for children older than 24 months. Data supporting the validity of the *Stanford–Binet IV* and the *Cognitive Abilities Scales* for hearing-impaired children are required before their use can be recommended.

For children of ages 30 to 36 months, the K-ABC can be given; however, due to the small number of subtests given at early age levels and test–retest reliability coefficients, the Nonverbal Scale score requires supplementation. The only other measure providing an overall score is the *Battelle,* and examiners desiring an overall score should attempt to supplement the K-ABC with the *Battelle.* The *Smith–Johnson* may provide additional programming information.

For children of ages 36 to 48 months, the *Hiskey–Nebraska* can be used to supplement the K-ABC. Neither measure should be used alone due to factors such as limited item sample (K-ABC) and dated norms and materials (*Hiskey–Nebraska*). The *Smith–Johnson* and *Arthur Adaptation of the Leiter* can be used to provide programming information.

At ages 48 to 60 months, the *Adaptation of the WPPSI,* WPPSI, K-ABC, and *Hiskey–Nebraska* can provide an overall score. Because none of these measures is considered to provide an overall score with sufficient validity with hearing-impaired children to be used alone, a minimum of two measures should be given. The *Adaptation of the WPPSI* is recommended over the WPPSI, as little is known about administering the WPPSI using a standard method of communicating instructions to hearing-impaired children. A combination of the *Adaptation of the WPPSI* and *Hiskey–Nebraska* would provide a large number of items; however, use of the K-ABC could shorten administration time and provide more current normative data.

5

Cognitive Assessment of School-Age Hearing-Impaired Children and Adolescents

In this chapter, differences between the assessment process for infants and preschoolers and that for school-age children and adolescents are noted. Detailed reviews of available instruments for use with school-age students are presented. As in Chapter 4, the first section of each review provides general information regarding administration of the test and the type of student for whom the test is appropriate. This section is followed by a comprehensive evaluation of the test's technical adequacy. Information regarding use of the test with hearing-impaired students is included when such information is available. The final section of each review addresses the strengths and limitations of the test when it is used with hearing-impaired students.

Assessment Differences: Infants and Preschoolers Versus School-Age Children and Adolescents

Cognitive assessment of a hearing-impaired school-age child is more straightforward than that of an infant or preschooler. More information from other disciplines often is available, and the child's language and communication method(s) generally are more firmly established. Often the child is better adapted to amplification equipment and has less frequent need for earmold changes. Problems during assessment due to the child's fatigue or lack of cooperation are less likely to occur than with younger children. Additionally, older children are less likely to be anxious or to misunderstand test instructions (Furth, 1973). As a result, usually more confidence can be placed in the test results and the interpretation. Also, more services currently are available to the school-age child and adolescent, although under PL 99-457 the distinction should lessen.

Cognitive Measures

Through surveys and reviews, a number of instruments have been identified as useful with school-age hearing-impaired children and adolescents. Additional measures have been used with hearing-impaired students, as indicated in their respective test manuals, or the tests have scores that are obtained by nonvocal means. Table 5.1 presents these measures and the ages for which they are appropriate.

Screening measures, outdated tests (i.e., older than 15 years), or revised tests were excluded from the reviews, except for those tests that continue to be used frequently with hearing-impaired students. In addition, the *Coloured and Standard Progressive Matrices* (Raven & Summers, 1986) have been excluded from review. The new editions of the measures have U.S. norms, but the norms are based on a collection of local norms from U.S. schools. Information regarding representativeness of the norms, use of the norms with hearing-impaired children in the United States, and reliability data are not given; hence, more data are needed before the use of these tests can be recommended.

Table 5.2 presents measures for school-age children and adolescents that are reviewed in this chapter. As can be seen from the table, a number of measures appropriate for school-age children and adolescents also can be used with preschoolers and, thus, were reviewed in Chapter 4. The reviews in Chapter 4 for these instruments pertain to the entire age range of the scale. Although these scales are noted in this chapter, the reviews appear in Chapter 4. The criteria used to evaluate the tests were presented in Chapter 1 under Direct Testing.

TABLE 5.1

Cognitive Ability Measures for Hearing-Impaired School-Age Students

Adaptation of the WISC-R for the Deaf (Ray, 1979)	6-0 to 16-11 years
Adaptation of the WPPSI for the Deaf (Ray & Ulissi, 1982)	4-0 to 6-6 years
Arthur Adaptation of the Leiter International Performance Scale (Arthur, 1950)	3-0 to 7-11 years
Battelle Developmental Inventory (Newborg, Stock, Wnek, Guidubaldi, & Svinicki, 1984)	Birth to 8 years
Coloured Progressive Matrices (Raven & Summers, 1986)	5 to 11 years
Columbia Mental Maturity Scale (Burgemeister, Blum, & Lorge, 1972)	3-6 to 9-6 years
Detroit Tests of Learning Aptitude–2 (Hammill, 1986)	6-0 to 17-11 years
Hiskey–Nebraska Test of Learning Aptitude (Hiskey, 1966)	3-0 to 16-0 years
Kaufman Assessment Battery for Children (Kaufman & Kaufman, 1983)	2-6 to 12-6 years
Leiter International Performance Scale (Leiter, 1969)	3 to 16-11 years
Nonverbal Test of Cognitive Skills (Johnson & Boyd, 1981)	6-0 to 13-0 years
Ontario School Ability Examination (Amoss, 1936)	4 to 10 years
Pictorial Test of Intelligence (French, 1964)	2-6 to 8-6 years
Revised Beta Examination (2nd ed.) (Kellogg & Morton, 1978)	16 years to adult
Slosson Intelligence Test (Armstrong & Jensen, 1981)	2 weeks to adult
Standard Progressive Matrices (Raven & Summers, 1986)	8 years to adult
Standardization of the WISC-R Performance Scale for Deaf Children (R. J. Anderson & Sisco, 1977)	6-0 to 16-11 years
Stanford–Binet Intelligence Scale Form L-M (Terman & Merrill, 1973)	2 years to adult
Stanford–Binet Intelligence Scale (4th ed.) (Thorndike, Hagen, & Sattler, 1986)	2 years to adult
Test of Nonverbal Intelligence–2 (L. Brown, Sherbenou, & Johnsen, 1990)	5 years to adult
Wechsler Adult Intelligence Scale–Revised (Wechsler, 1981)	16-0 to 74-11 years
Wechsler Intelligence Scale for Children–Revised (Wechsler, 1974)	6-0 to 16-11 years
Wechsler Preschool and Primary Scale of Intelligence (Wechsler, 1967)	4-0 to 6-6 years

TABLE 5.2
Reviewed Tests of Cognitive Ability for
Hearing-Impaired School-Age Students

Norm-Referenced Tests with Hearing-Impaired Norms
Hiskey–Nebraska Test of Learning Aptitude (Hiskey, 1966)   3-0 to 16-0 years

Norm-Referenced Tests with Hearing Norms, Nonvocal Instructions, and Nonvocal Responses
Adaptation of the WISC-R for the Deaf (Ray, 1972)   6-0 to 16 years
Adaptation of the WPPSI for the Deaf (Ray & Ulissi, 1982)   4-0 to 6-6 years
Nonverbal Test of Cognitive Skills (Johnson & Boyd, 1981)   6-0 to 13-0 years
Test of Nonverbal Intelligence–2 (Brown, Sherbenou, & Johnsen, 1990)   5 years to adult

Norm-Referenced Tests with Hearing Norms, Verbal Instructions, and Nonvocal Responses
Battelle Developmental Inventory (Newborg, Stock, Wnek, Guidubaldi, & Svinicki, 1984)   Birth to 8 years
Detroit Tests of Learning Aptitude–2 (Hammill, 1986)   6-0 to 17-11 years
Kaufman Assessment Battery for Children (Kaufman & Kaufman, 1983)   2-6 to 12-6 years
Revised Beta Examination (2nd ed.) (Kellogg & Morton, 1978)   16 years to adult
Standardization of the WISC-R Performance for Deaf Children (R. J. Anderson & Sisco, 1977)   6-0 to 16-11 years
Stanford–Binet Intelligence Scale (4th ed.) (Thorndike, Hagen, & Sattler, 1986)   2 years to adult
Wechsler Adult Intelligence Scale–Revised (Wechsler, 1974)   16 years to adult
Wechsler Intelligence Scale for Children–Revised (Wechsler, 1981)   6-0 to 16-11 years
Wechsler Preschool and Primary Scale of Intelligence (Wechsler, 1967)   4-0 to 6-6 years

Informal Measures
Arthur Adaptation of the Leiter (Arthur, 1950)   3-0 to 7-11 years
Leiter International Performance Scale (Leiter, 1969)   3-0 to 16-11 years

Norm-Referenced Test with Hearing-Impaired Norms

Hiskey–Nebraska Test of Learning Aptitude

(See review in Chapter 4.)

Norm-Referenced Tests with Hearing Norms, Nonvocal Instructions, and Nonvocal Responses

An Adaptation of the WPPSI for the Deaf

(See review in Chapter 4.)

An Adaptation of the WISC-R for the Deaf

Author: S. Ray
Publisher: Steven Ray
             Northwestern State University of Louisiana
             P.O. Box 5503
             Natchitoches, LA 71457
Copyright: 1979

General Description.   The *Adaptation of the WISC-R for the Deaf* contains modified WISC-R Performance Scale instructions standardized upon hearing-impaired students. Adapted instructions have been linguistically lowered and include practice items to convey subtest requirements. Based on use of the instructions with the standardization group, Ray found that the original WISC-R normative data could be used with hearing-impaired students given the *Adaptation*. The *Adaptation* contains the same Performance Scale subtests and items as the WISC-R, and is designed for the same ages (6-0 to 16-11). The *Adaptation* was designed for "skilled signers, those with limited ability, and children with minimal standard language"

(p. 4). Two sets of instructions are provided. Alternate Instructions represent linguistically lowered WISC-R instructions and are designed for hearing-impaired students with good language skills. The Alternate Instructions may be presented orally and/or manually. The Supplemental Instructions include practice items designed to communicate subtest instructions to students with limited language skills. The Supplemental Instructions use gestures with speech or sign. The *Adaptation* test manual includes the Alternate and Supplemental Instructions. Reusable practice items for the Picture Arrangement and Block Design subtests are provided, as are consumable practice pages for Coding, Mazes, and Picture Completion subtests. Protocols, Performance Scale materials, and normative tables are those used in the nonadapted WISC-R.

Description of Subtests.   See review of the WISC-R Performance Scale subtests.

Technical Adequacy

Standardization.   Subjects included 127 prelingually hearing-impaired children, having a minimum hearing loss of 70 dB in the better ear and no other handicaps. Further basis for subject selection is not provided. No additional information on hearing loss of the students is given. Few subjects were included at some age levels (e.g., 5 students at age 6½ and 4 students at age 16½). Compared with 1970 U.S. census data, subjects included in the normative group overrepresented students of the Northeast region and underrepresented those of the North Central region. The standardization group approximates census data for the variables of sex, socioeconomic level, race, and urban/rural residence.

Reliability.   No additional reliability data are presented for the *Adaptation*.

Validity.   No additional validity data are presented.

Use of the Test with Hearing-Impaired Students.   The *Adaptation* was designed for and standardized upon hearing-impaired students. Courtney, Hayes, Watkins, and Frick (1983; cited in Kaufman & Kaufman, 1983) reported a correlation of .63 for the *Adaptation* and K-ABC Nonverbal Scale. Evans (1983) administered the *Adaptation* to 33 students, and did not find support for a practice effect from use of the additional example and practice items of the Supplemental Instructions.

Conclusions.   It can be argued that the *Adaptation* comprises two tests, one for each instructional set. Use of either instructional set may not utilize a student's language or communication skills as required by law. It could also be argued that the *Adaptation* does not possess adequate standardization or demonstrated reliability and validity. The standardization group does not adequately represent the hearing-impaired population, as the group excluded the high percentage of hearing-impaired students with additional handicaps. Sullivan (1985) suggested that the standardization group's performance was comparable with that of the hearing children of the original WISC-R standardization due to the exclusion of hearing-impaired students with additional handicaps, rather than the use of modified instructions and practice items.

The subtest scores and Performance IQ may be inflated due to a practice effect from the items included in the Supplemental Instructions (Phelps & Ensor, 1986), although support for a practice effect was not found by Evans (1983). Some subtests contain multiple practice items in addition to those already included in the WISC-R. For example, using the Supplemental Instructions for Coding B requires the examiner to demonstrate a 27-item coding task, followed by the subject completing a 28-item coding task. Neither coding task is identical to that contained on the WISC-R. Following demonstration and practice, the examiner demonstrates the three WISC-R sample items, allowing the subject to do the final four before beginning the subtest.

The appropriateness of the statistical analyses used to determine that the performance of hearing-impaired students on the *Adaptation* is no different from that of hearing children in the original WISC-R sample has been questioned by Sullivan (1985). She argued that the analyses failed to take into account the correlation between subtests, and that more appropriate analyses are available.

Even if the method of analysis were not a question, too few subjects at several age levels were included in the standardization to support use of the WISC-R norms at all age levels. In addition, no data are presented to indicate applicability of WISC-R reliability and validity data to the *Adaptation.*

Based on the data that are available, support for use of the *Adaptation* is not strong. The same criticisms, however, could be applied to other methods of using the WISC-R with hearing-impaired students. Sullivan (1982) recommended using the hearing norms when total communication is used, yet this is not a standardized method with demonstrated technical adequacy. Likewise, R. J. Anderson and Sisco's (1977) hearing-impaired norms do not present a standard administration method, reliability data, or adequate validity data. In view of these issues, the *Adaptation* may be useful in two instances. First, an examiner may choose to use the linguistically lowered Alternate Instructions using total communication when the student does not understand the original WISC-R instructions using total communication. Second, if neither set of instructions can be communicated effectively using total communication, use of the Supplemental Instructions may be employed to communicate subtest directions.

Nonverbal Test of Cognitive Skills

Authors: G. O. Johnson and H. F. Boyd
Publisher: Charles E. Merrill
               Columbus, OH 43216
Copyright: 1981

General Description.   The *Nonverbal Test of Cognitive Skills* (NTCS) is designed for children 6 to 13 years of age. The test was standardized on hearing children, and instructions are communicated by gesture, demonstration, and speech. All responses are nonvocal. Administration time is approximately 30 to 40 minutes. Five subtests include time limits. Scores include a Cognitive Skills Age (similar to a mental age) and a Cognitive Skills Index (similar to an IQ). There is one form of the test. Materials consist of the examiner's manual, a record book, and a set of materials including pictures and blocks.

Description of Subtests.   The NTCS comprises 14 subtests; however, students are not administered the first 3 subtests if performance on the 4th subtest reaches a criterion.

Paper Folding.   This subtest requires the student to reproduce folds in paper squares following the examiner's demonstration. One, two, and three folds are involved.

Cube Building.   This subtest requires the student to copy a block design following demonstration. Five structures are included, ranging from a three-block tower to a four-block cross.

Figure Identification.   This subtest requires matching of geometric figures.

Figure Completion.   This subtest requires the student to form geometric figures using shapes.

Figure Discrimination.   This subtest requires discrimination of the unique geometric figure from a set.

Figure Drawing.   This subtest requires copying of geometric figures using paper and pencil.

Figure Memory.   This subtest involves copying of designs from memory.

Picture Completion I.   This subtest requires identification of missing parts in a drawing.

Picture Completion II.   This subtest requires the identification of a part needed to complete a drawing.

Color Patterns. This subtest has the student assemble colored blocks to match a card pattern.

Knox Cubes. This subtest involves imitation of sequences of taps on blocks.

Dominoes. This subtest requires reproducing patterns of cards from demonstration, modeling, and memory.

Tapping. This subtest requires the imitation of sequences of taps on blocks and the table.

Figure Association. This subtest requires that the student draw symbols to complete paired symbol relationships (coding for matched symbols).

Technical Adequacy

Standardization. The standardization sample included 849 children from grades K to 7. The number of subjects per age level is not specified. Students from each geographic region were included; however, weighting was not done so that percentages conformed to percentages from 1980 U.S. census data. The sample matches the census data for race. Data pertaining to residence, ethnicity, socioeconomic status, and sex are not provided. The authors indicate that normative data should be considered preliminary.

Reliability. Internal consistency data from the entire standardization group yielded a coefficient of .88. Coefficients for individual grades are not specified. Test–retest data are provided for 49 subjects (7 from each grade) with a 1-week to 3-month retest interval. Only an overall coefficient (.95) is provided.

Validity. Criterion-related validity data with achievement tests are presented, with overall coefficients ranging from .41 to .68 for the *Metropolitan Achievement Test, Comprehensive Test of Basic Skills, Stanford Achievement Test,* and *Iowa Test of Basic Skills.* No correlational data with intelligence tests are provided.

Use of the Test with Hearing-Impaired Students. The NTCS was not standardized upon hearing-impaired students, and the manual does not report use of the test with this population. A literature review did not identify use of the test with hearing-impaired students.

Conclusions. It appears that the primary purpose of the test is to predict achievement for students with a language difference or for deprived students, yet the lack of technical adequacy severely limits the test's usefulness for these students. Too few subjects were included at each age level to enable the use of percentile scores (only estimates are given); data are not presented for socioeconomic level, ethnicity, sex, or residence; and only limited reliability and validity data are presented.

With more data regarding the technical adequacy of the test with hearing students, the potential use of the test with hearing-impaired students can be considered. Currently, although instructions are primarily nonvocal and the simple verbal instructions can be omitted or signed, the normative data are preliminary and scores should not be used for eligibility decisions. The test also is limited as a measure to identify strengths and difficulties, because scores are available only for the overall test, not for individual subtests.

Test of Nonverbal Intelligence–2

Authors: L. Brown, R. J. Sherbenou, and S. K. Johnsen
Publisher: PRO-ED
              8700 Shoal Creek Blvd.
              Austin, TX 78758-6897
Copyright: 1990

General Description.   The *Test of Nonverbal Intelligence–2* (TONI-2) is designed to be a language-free measure of cognitive ability for ages 5 to adult. The role of language skills is minimized due to the pantomimed instructions and nonvocal (pointing) responses. Diminished dependence on language also produces a test less culturally biased and more appropriate for handicapped populations, according to the authors. The authors state that TONI-2 is appropriate for hearing-impaired students.

TONI-2 has two equivalent forms of 55 items each. No items are timed, and total test time for each form is about 15 minutes. Scores include an overall IQ and percentile. Required materials include the Picture Book, examiner's manual, and record forms.

Description of Test Items.   Although TONI-2 is not divided into subtests, five classes of nonvocal problems are interspersed throughout the test. The item format is similar for each group of items; a set of stimulus figures is presented with a figure(s) omitted. The subject must select the best figure(s) from four to six alternatives to complete the set. Six training items (nonscored) are given to teach the format. The TONI-2 taps ability "to solve problems by identifying relationships among abstract figures and then solving problems created by the manipulation of these relationships" (p. 3).

The first group of items requires the subject simply to choose the alternative that is the same shape as the stimulus items, that is, to make form discriminations. The second group of items involves analogies, and requires selection of the alternative that completes a relationship. The third group of items involves selection of an alternative completing a classification (e.g., all ellipses). The fourth type requires selection of the alternative that is the result of the combining (intersection) of stimulus figures. The final type of item involves the selection of a figure to complete a progression (e.g., in size).

Technical Adequacy

Standardization. The total number of subjects in the TONI-2 normative sample was 2,764, with 80 to 244 subjects per age level for ages 5 through 19. The sample closely matches 1980 U.S. census data on the variables of sex, race, ethnicity, urban/rural residence, and geographic distribution. Educational attainment of parents of children in the sample was similar to the census data, with a few too many college graduates (21% vs. 16%). The inclusion of hearing-impaired students is not indicated.

Reliability. Internal consistency reliability data from the normative sample are presented for both forms of the TONI-2. Coefficients are above .90 for ages 5 to 19 for both forms (except Form A at age 6, with a correlation of .81).

Alternate-form/test–retest reliability was assessed with only a 7-day interval. A resulting correlation of .85 was obtained for test–retest reliability; for internal consistency, a correlation of .95 for Form A and .96 for Form B was found. A similar study was carried out with 46 students from the Texas School for the Deaf, except only immediate test–retest reliability was assessed. The mean age of the students was 16.1 years. Internal consistency was found to be .90 for Form A and .91 for Form B. Immediate test–retest reliability was .87. Standard errors of measurement are presented, based on internal consistency reliabilities.

Validity. Evidence of the TONI's content validity is provided through a review of items by professionals and from subsequent field testing. Results from the field testing underwent item analysis, including both item discriminating power and item difficulty analyses.

The relationship of the results of the TONI-2 with various achievement measures was examined in eight studies. Low to moderate correlations were found with measures that included the *Diagnostic Achievement Battery,* the *Diagnostic Achievement Test for Adolescents,* the *Formal Reading Inventory,* the *Iowa Test of Basic Skills,* the *SRA Achievement Series,* the *Stanford Achievement Test,* and others. One study involved 16 deaf students from 16.1 to 18.8 years of age, whose performance on the TONI-2 was compared with their performance on the *Stanford Achievement Test*. The term "deaf" was not defined. For Form A, correlations were .80 for Reading Comprehension and .81 for Math Concepts; for Form B, correlations were .68 for Reading Comprehension and .72 for Math Concepts.

For concurrent validity, TONI-2 results were correlated with various measures of aptitude and intelligence in 15 studies. Correlations generally were above .35. Two studies involved deaf students, although the term "deaf" was not defined. One study compared results of the TONI-2 and the *Leiter International Performance Scale* for 30 deaf students from 14.8 to 17.2 years of age. Correlations were .89 for Form A and .83 for Form B. Another study compared TONI-2 results with results of the *Standard Progressive Matrices* for 16 deaf students 16.1 to 18.8 years of age. Correlations were .92 for both Forms A and B.

A factor analysis of TONI-2 results did not result in evidence of any strong subfactors.

Several studies showed that TONI-2 discriminates between groups as hypothesized (e.g., retarded and nonretarded, gifted and normal).

Construct validity information is provided through evidence that scores increase as hypothesized with age.

Use of the Test with Hearing-Impaired Students. The TONI-2 is not standardized upon hearing-impaired students; however, the test manual reports use of the test with hearing-impaired adolescents. These results were described in the section above.

Conclusions. The TONI-2 has good potential as an instrument to be used with hearing-impaired students. Instructions are pantomimed, responses are nonvocal, no time limits are imposed, and two forms are available. It must be kept in mind, however, that TONI-2 "is not intended to replace broad-based tests of intelligence or aptitude" and its content is "limited in scope" (p. 5). Further data on test–retest reliability are needed with at least a 2-week interval and data presented by age level. The immediate retest data for "deaf" students are of little use. Guessing may be a problem with some students. The TONI-2's best use may be as a supplemental measure to other intelligence test data when there is difficulty communicating instructions or gathering responses. Examiners can give both forms of TONI-2 to increase confidence in results, yet this will add to testing time by only a small amount. The fact that the test taps only "abstract/figural problem solving" ability (p. 5) requires cautious interpretation of scores, and supplementation with scores from other measures.

Norm-Referenced Tests with Hearing Norms, Verbal Instructions, and Nonvocal Responses

Battelle Developmental Inventory

(See review in Chapter 4.)

Detroit Tests of Learning Aptitude–2

Author:	D. D. Hammill
Publisher:	PRO-ED
	8700 Shoal Creek Blvd.
	Austin, TX 78758-6897
Copyright:	1986

General Description. The *Detroit Tests of Learning Aptitude–2* (DTLA-2) is a measure of intelligence for students ages 6-0 to 17-11. The DTLA-2 is the second edition of the 1935 DTLA. The 19 subtests of the DTLA have been replaced by the 11 subtests of the DTLA-2: Word Opposites, Sentence Imitation, Oral Directions, Word Sequences, Story Construction, Design Reproduction, Object Sequences, Symbolic Relations, Conceptual Matching, Word Fragments, and Letter Sequences. The 11 subtests can be combined to form nine composites. Of the 11 subtests, 5 subtests—Design Reproduction, Object Sequences, Symbolic Relations, Conceptual Matching, and Letter Sequences—require a nonvocal response, although verbal instructions are provided for each subtest. These 5 subtests form the Nonverbal Aptitude Composite. Scores for the test include standard scores and percentiles for subtests, and quotients for composites. Administration time for the entire test is stated to be 50 to 120 minutes. Approximately half the total time could be expected to give the Nonverbal Aptitude Composite. Materials include the examiner's manual, picture book, response form, and record form.

Description of Nonverbal Aptitude Subtests

Design Reproduction. This subtest requires the student to draw a design exposed for 5 seconds. There are 23 items. Instructions may be adapted to sign, gesture, or pantomime, and there is one practice item.

Object Sequences. This 10-item subtest requires the student to reorder a sequence of pictures to match the initial order that was shown for 5 seconds. The verbal instructions are complex and may be difficult to communicate manually; however, there are practice items.

Symbolic Relations. The 30 items of this subtest are taken from the *Test of Nonverbal Intelligence.* The student chooses a figure(s) to complete the pattern provided by stimulus figures. There are six practice items.

Conceptual Matching. The student points to the 1 of 10 pictures that best expresses the same concept as a stimulus picture. The verbal instructions are complex, yet two practice items are included. There are 30 items.

Letter Sequences. The student is shown a sequence of letters for 5 seconds and is asked to reproduce the letters and sequence. There are 12 test items and 2 practice items. Because hearing-impaired students show delayed development of reading skills, and may be exposed to letters at a later age than hearing students, a hearing-impaired student may be penalized because of the requirement to remember material that is less familiar to hearing-impaired students than to hearing students. Therefore, the score of a hearing-impaired student may underrepresent his or her ability, particularly if the score differs markedly from the score for the Object Sequences subtest.

Technical Adequacy

Standardization. A total of 1,532 subjects were included in the standardization sample. Over 100 were included at each age level except ages 13 (92 subjects) and 15 (91). The standardization sample closely represents the 1980 U.S. population in terms of the demographic variables of sex, residence, race, and geographic area. Data regarding the socioeconomic level of the sample are not provided; however, related data concerning the education of parents is provided. Inclusion of handicapped students in the sample is not specified.

Reliability. Internal consistency reliability data are presented by 2-year age groupings. Coefficients for the subtests comprising the Nonverbal Aptitude Composite range from .61 to .94. Coefficients for the composite are greater than .90 at each age group, with a mean value of .95.

Test–retest reliability data are reported from a study of 33 students using a 2-week retest interval. Coefficients are reported not by age level, but by subtest across all age levels. Coefficients for the subtests of the Nonverbal Aptitude Composite range from .63 to .83. A coefficient of .84 was obtained for the Nonverbal Aptitude Composite.

Standard errors of measurement based on internal consistency reliabilities and on test–retest reliabilities are presented in the manual.

Validity. Evidence of content validity is provided through the selection of items from the original DTLA, selection from other tests (e.g., TONI), indication that the subtest items conform to models of intelligence, and item analysis.

Evidence of criterion-related validity is given through correlation of DTLA-2 with WISC-R, PPVT, and *SRA Achievement Series.* Correlation of the WISC-R Full Scale IQ and DTLA-2 Nonverbal Aptitude Composite resulted in a coefficient of .75, whereas a value of .69 was found between the composite and the PPVT. The correlation of the composite and SRA Reading resulted in a value of .41. Correlation with SRA Math did not produce a significant value, but the coefficient for the Nonverbal Aptitude Composite and the SRA Composite was .45.

Construct validity data are provided by showing that subtest and composite scores increase as hypothesized with age, subtest intercorrelations demonstrate both unique and shared contributions to the test, and test scores differentiate groups expected to differ in intelligence.

Use of the Test with Hearing-Impaired Students. The DTLA-2 was not standardized upon hearing-impaired students, and the test manual does not report use of the test with the population. A review of the literature did not reveal reported use of the test with hearing-impaired students.

Conclusions. The Nonverbal Aptitude Composite has the potential to be used with hearing-impaired students with good language skills. Some subtest instructions may be too complex to give manually, yet there are practice items for each subtest of the composite. With hearing students, the composite correlates well with the overall test score ($r = .80$), and has reliability near the value required for placement decisions. Skills tested by subtests may provide information about specific strengths and difficulties within cognitive skill areas. Research with the DTLA-2 is needed to establish its value for use with hearing-impaired students.

Kaufman Assessment Battery for Children

(See review in Chapter 4.)

Revised Beta Examination (2nd Edition)

Authors: C. E. Kellogg and N. W. Morton
Publisher: The Psychological Corporation
                555 Academic Court
                San Antonio, TX 78204
Copyright: 1978

General Description. The *Revised Beta Examination (2nd ed.)* (Beta-II) is designed as a measure of general intelligence for persons from age 16 to adult "who are relatively illiterate, or non-English speaking, or suspected of having other language difficulties" (p. 3). Approximately 30 minutes are required to give the six tests of the Beta-II. Each test has a time limit of 1½ to 4 minutes. Materials include the examiner's manual and the response booklet. Directions for each test are spoken; however, demonstration may be provided if an examinee does not understand test directions. Practice items are provided for each test. Scores include an overall IQ and percentiles.

Description of Tests

Mazes. The five items of this test require an examinee to draw a line to indicate the shortest path through a maze.

Coding. This test requires completion of a digit and symbol association modeled in a key. Symbols are provided, and the examinee is required to provide the number associated with the symbol (87 items).

Paper Form Boards. The examinee indicates how two to four puzzle pieces would form a square (18 items).

Picture Completion. This 20-item test requires identifying and drawing the missing part of a picture.

Clerical Checking. The 56 items of the test involve determination if two figures or numbers are alike or different.

Picture Absurdities. The test requires selection of one of four pictures that is wrong or "foolish" (21 items). For example, three pictures illustrate proper use of a tool and a fourth shows improper use.

Technical Adequacy

Standardization. Sample selection was stratified according to the variables of age, sex, geographic region, race, and occupation according to 1970 U.S. census data. A total of 1,038 subjects were included in the standardization sample, with 147 to 150 subjects per age group. Seven age groups (16 to 17, 18 to 19, 20 to 24, 25 to 34, 35 to 44, 45 to 54, and 55 to 64 years) were formed. The sample matches census data for the variables of sex, geographic region, and race (white/nonwhite). Data regarding residence and ethnicity are not provided. The inclusion of handicapped subjects is not specified.

Reliability. Test–retest reliability data are presented for 79 students aged 16 to 17 using a 3-week retest interval. A coefficient of .91 is reported.

Validity. Criterion-related validity data are presented for two age groups given the Beta-II and the WAIS. Seventy-four adults in the 18 to 19 age group produced correlation coefficients of .64 with the Full Scale IQ of the WAIS, .68 with the Performance Scale IQ, and .54 with the Verbal Scale IQ. Coefficients for 76 adults in the 35 to 44 age group were .66, .73, and .50, respectively, for the same scales.

Use of the Test with Hearing-Impaired Students. The test manual reports use of earlier editions of the test with hearing-impaired students, but does not report use of the current edition with these students.

Conclusions. The test is designed to be used primarily with adults who cannot read, but who can understand verbal instructions. The number of practice items, however, can be used to ensure understanding for those having difficulty with verbal instructions, such as hearing-impaired students.

Although the test has excellent standardization, additional reliability and validity data are required before the measure should be utilized with hearing or hearing-impaired students.

Standardization of the WISC-R Performance Scale for Deaf Children

Authors: R. J. Anderson and F. H. Sisco
Publisher: Office of Demographic Studies
                Gallaudet College
                Washington, DC 20002
Copyright: 1977

General Description. The standardization group for the WISC-R does not contain hearing-impaired students; however, the *Standardization of the WISC-R Performance Scale for Deaf Children (Standardization)* does provide normative data for hearing-impaired students given the WISC-R. WISC-R instructions and materials are used; the *Standardization* provides only normative tables for hearing-impaired students for the five Performance Scale subtests.

No standardized method of communicating test instructions was used to obtain the normative data. The majority of subjects (77%) were given the WISC-R using total communication. Other methods included speech only (2.2%), finger spelling with speech (4.4%), gestures (1.3%), pantomime (7.3%), and other methods (6.6%). The method used was not reported for 1% of subjects. Instructions were provided by psychologists experienced in testing hearing-impaired students.

The *Standardization* uses WISC-R instructions and materials, except that the normative tables for the *Standardization* replace those of the WISC-R.

Description of Subtests.   See review of the WISC-R.

Technical Adequacy

Standardization.   Subjects included 1,228 congenitally or prelingually hearing-impaired students with a loss of 70 dB or more in the better ear. Subjects ranged in age from 6.5 to 16.5 years and were selected from residential schools for the deaf. Six age levels included 100 or more subjects, and the remaining five age levels contained between 50 and 100 subjects each. Sample characteristics approximate 1970 U.S. census data for the variables of sex and race. Subjects from rural residences were underrepresented (16% of the sample vs. 29% in the U.S. population), as were those from the South (20% vs. 31%). Low socioeconomic level subjects were slightly overrepresented (12% vs. 6%).

Reliability.   No reliability data are presented in the test manual.

Validity.   No validity data are presented.

Use with Hearing-Impaired Students.   The *Standardization* provides normative data for hearing-impaired students based on administration of the WISC-R to hearing-impaired students. Phelps and Ensor (1986) reported a correlation coefficient of .91 for the WISC-R using the *Standardization* and the HNTLA in a study of 49 hearing-impaired students using total communication. Gibbons, Ulissi, and Brice (1984) reported a correlation coefficient of .84 for the WISC-R using the *Standardization* and the K-ABC Nonverbal Scale using total communication.

Conclusions.   An apparent shortcoming of the *Standardization* is the lack of a standardized communication method for test instructions. Because the method used to communicate instructions has been found to affect test performance (Graham & Shapiro, 1953; Sullivan, 1982), the effects of the various methods used in the *Standardization* may confound the normative data. A breakdown of scores and normative data according to method of communicating test instructions would be helpful to determine if students requiring communication of instructions in one method performed differently from those receiving other methods.

Such a breakdown of scores would not necessarily be an indication that different methods of presenting instructions result in different performance means. Students included in the normative sample were from residential schools and were tested by "qualified, experienced psychologists." Hence, it is unlikely that students were tested using an inappropriate method of communication (e.g., pantomime for a student fluent in total communication). Rather, differences in performance related to varying methods of presenting instructions may reflect differences in language acquisition. For example, students may require gestures to communicate instructions because they do not have the cognitive development to learn total communication yet, or they have had only limited exposure to formal education. Both of these factors may produce the need to use gestures and, thus, lower the mean performance on measures of intelligence.

The *Standardization* represents many of the difficulties involved in assessing hearing-impaired students. As a study, the *Standardization* involves a large number of hearing-impaired students. These students require different methods of communicating test instructions, which introduces an additional variable. Use of a single method would exclude a subset of hearing-impaired students, however, limiting the application of the *Standardization.* In the end, the examiner is uncertain about the validity of the obtained scores. Given the uncertainty, it is recommended that examiners use either the *Standardization* or the hearing norms and recognize that their choice may have a 5-point effect on Performance IQ. In cases where the 5 points has an impact upon eligibility decisions, the Performance IQ will require supplementation with another measure of cognitive development. The supplemental measure and results of an adaptive behavior scale can be used to provide additional data to aid in making the decisions.

Stanford-Binet Intelligence Scale (Fourth Edition)

(See review in Chapter 4.)

Wechsler Adult Intelligence Scale–Revised

Author: D. Wechsler
Publisher: The Psychological Corporation
             555 Academic Court
             San Antonio, TX 78204
Copyright: 1981

General Description. The *Wechsler Adult Intelligence Scale–Revised* (WAIS-R) is designed to measure the intelligence of adults 16 to 74 years of age. Like the WISC-R, the scale is divided into a Verbal Scale and a Performance Scale. Performance Scale subtests require nonvocal responses. The five Performance Scale subtests are Digit Symbol, Picture Completion, Block Design, Picture Arrangement, and Object Assembly. Scaled scores are available for each subtest; an IQ can be obtained for the Performance Scale. Approximately 20 to 30 minutes are required to administer the Performance Scale. Sample items are provided for the Digit Symbol subtest. Failure on the initial item of the remaining subtests results in the examiner demonstrating successful performance. All five Performance Scale subtests have time limits. Materials required to administer the Performance Scale include the examiner's manual, record form, picture booklet, picture cards, puzzle pieces, and blocks.

Description of Performance Scale Subtests

Picture Completion. The 20 items of this subtest require the identification (pointing or naming) of an important missing part of a picture.

Picture Arrangement. The 10 subtest items involve the arrangement of three to six pictures in an order that illustrates a story.

Block Design. This subtest includes nine items, requiring the reproduction of a design using four or nine blocks.

Object Assembly. The subtest involves putting six or seven puzzle pieces together to form an object (4 items).

Digit Symbol. This 93-item subtest requires the use of a set of paired relationships (numbers with symbols) expressed in a key as a guide to complete relationships when only the number is provided.

Technical Adequacy

Standardization. A total of 1,880 adults were included in the standardization sample. Subjects were divided into nine groups based on age, with 160 to 300 subjects per age grouping. Two hundred subjects were included in the age groups 16 to 17, 18 to 19, and 20 to 24. Subjects were selected based on, and closely follow, a stratification of 1970 U.S. census data along the variables of sex, race (white/nonwhite), geographic region, socioeconomic level, and residence (urban/rural).

Reliability. Internal consistency reliability data are presented by age group for the Performance Scale and subtests. Coefficients are greater than .85 for the Performance Scale for each age group. Coefficients for 16- to 24-year-olds are less than .85 for all subtests except Block Design.

Test–retest reliability data are provided for only two groups; however, the groups do not contain 16- to 24-year-olds. Standard errors of measurement are provided for Performance Scale IQ and subtests by age group based on internal consistency reliabilities.

Validity. Evidence of construct validity is provided through intercorrelations of subtests. These data are presented by age group. Corrected correlation coefficients of the Performance Scale with its subtests range from .36 to .66 for 16- to 24-year-olds. Intercorrelation of Performance Scale subtests produced coefficients ranging from .19 to .60 for the same ages.

Criterion-related validity data are provided through correlation of the Performance Scale of the WAIS-R with that of the WAIS $(r = .79)$ for a study including 72 adults of ages 35 to 44, and the Performance Scale of the WAIS-R with that of the WISC-R $(r = .76)$ for a group of 80 16-year-olds.

Content validity information is given through the selection of items from the 1955 WAIS. In all, it is indicated that 80% of WAIS-R items are based on the WAIS.

Use of the Test with Hearing-Impaired Students. The WAIS-R was not standardized upon hearing-impaired students, and the test manual does not report use of the scale with hearing impaired persons. A review of the literature did not reveal reported uses of the test with this population.

Comments. Bragman (1982b) indicated that the test is commonly used with deaf and hard-of-hearing persons; however, the technical adequacy of the scale has not been established with hearing-impaired subjects.

Zieziula (1982) stated that the WAIS-R Verbal Scale is not appropriate for hearing-impaired persons because instructions for Verbal Scale subtests rely on speech, and using sign language instead lacks standardization.

Although the Performance Scale may be one of the few scales for hearing-impaired students over 16 years of age, the scale lacks demonstrated technical adequacy and suitability of hearing norms with hearing-impaired students. The WAIS-R Performance Scale would best be used as a supplemental measure (Zieziula, 1982).

Wechsler Intelligence Scale for Children–Revised

Author: D. Wechsler
Publisher: The Psychological Corporation
             555 Academic Court
             San Antonio, TX 78204
Copyright: 1974

General Description. The *Wechsler Intelligence Scale for Children–Revised* (WISC-R) is a general intelligence test for ages 6-0 to 16-11. The test includes 12 subtests, half of which comprise the Verbal Scale, and the other half the Performance Scale. A subtest from each scale is supplementary and can be used in the case of a spoiled or excluded subtest. The Full Scale incorporates scores from the Verbal and Performance Scales. Both the Verbal and Performance Scales are given to hearing-impaired students, although the Performance Scale is given more frequently because the scale requires only nonvocal responses. Each Performance Scale subtest has a time limit and/or timed items. Test scores for the Performance Scale include an IQ and subtest scaled scores. Administration time for the Performance Scale is approximately 25 to 40 minutes. Materials for the Performance Scale include the manual and record forms, two sets of picture cards, blocks, and puzzle pieces. Adaptation of materials is generally not required for students having only a hearing impairment; however, subtest instructions are often adapted to the communication skills of individual students. These instructions often contain demonstration items designed to communicate subtest instructions. Modification of the WISC-R instructions for Performance Scale subtests has been reported by Sullivan (1982), Sattler (1982), and Ray (1979). Sullivan's instructions are pantomime and use an item from the WISC. Sattler's instructions are based on Neuhaus (1967), Reed (1970), and Murphy (1957) and utilize supplemental pictures and written instructions. Ray's modification of instructions is reviewed as a separate scale, the *Adaptation of the WISC-R for the Deaf.* In addition, examiners may adapt WISC-R instructions to a student's communication skills without using additional materials, but by using total communication, finger spelling, gestures, or pantomime (R. J. Anderson & Sisco, 1977).

Description of Performance Scale Subtests

Picture Completion. This subtest contains 26 pictures, each requiring identification (naming or pointing) of an important missing part.

Picture Arrangement. This subtest includes 12 items, each item requiring arrangement of a series of pictures into a logical sequence.

Block Design. This 11-item subtest requires reproduction of designs using up to nine blocks.

Object Assembly. This subtest has 4 items requiring arrangement of puzzle pieces to form an object.

Coding. This subtest contains 43 items (Coding A) or 93 items (Coding B) and requires copying symbols with a pencil to complete pairings of symbols shown in a key.

Mazes. This 9-item subtest involves identifying and drawing an unobstructed path through a printed maze.

Technical Adequacy

Standardization. The sample included 2,200 children of ages 6-0 to 16-11. One hundred males and 100 females were included at each age level. Children were selected from a stratified sample and did not include children with handicaps. The sample closely follows 1970 U.S. census data for the variables of sex, race, geographic region, socioeconomic status, and residence.

Reliability. Internal consistency reliability data are presented for each age level, with Performance Scale coefficients above .85 at each age level. Performance Scale subtest internal consistency reliabilities range from .57 to .90 across age levels.

   Test–retest coefficients are provided for three groups of subjects. Groups contained students from adjacent age levels (6.5 to 7.5, 10.5 to 11.5, and 14.5 to 15.5). Coefficients for the Performance Scale are above .85 for each group; coefficients for Performance Scale subtests range from .50 to .86.

   Standard errors of measurement are presented by age level for subtests and scale scores, and are based on internal consistency reliability or test–retest reliability coefficients (Coding and Digit Span).

Validity. Limited validity data are presented in the WISC-R manual. Correlation coefficients with WPPSI (.82), WAIS (.95), and *Stanford–Binet* (1973; .73) provide evidence of criterion-related validity. Subtest intercorrelation coefficients range from .19 to .69, supplying evidence of construct validity. Since the WISC-R was published, a wealth of additional validity data have been published for hearing children, including factor analysis data (Kaufman, 1975), correlational data with various measures of intelligence, achievement, and adaptive behavior scales, as well as other assessment instruments. Sattler (1982) provided a review of a subset of these studies.

Use of the Test with Hearing-Impaired Students. The WISC-R Performance Scale is the most frequently used intelligence test with hearing-impaired students (McQuaid & Alovisetti, 1981; L. J. Porter & Kirby, 1986), even though hearing-impaired students were not included in the standardization sample, standardized instructions are primarily verbal, and all subtests have time limits. A number of studies have investigated its use with hearing-impaired populations. Normative data have been generated, mean scores and profiles have been compared with those of hearing students, and studies of reliability and validity have been conducted.

Watson, Goldar, and Kroese (1983) suggested that the Wechsler Scales may be more appropriate than the *Hiskey–Nebraska* with hearing-impaired students who may be identified as retarded or gifted. It seems that the *Hiskey–Nebraska* tends to result in an unexpectedly high number of students with extreme performances on the test.

Watson, Goldar, Kroese, and Lotz (1986) found a median correlation of only .24 for hearing-impaired students given the Performance section of either WISC-R or WAIS and various measures of achievement. Hence, it must be noted that the Performance section of the WISC-R is only half of the test, and results must be interpreted in light of the fact that, by itself, the Performance section is not a good predictor of achievement.

Standardization for Hearing-Impaired Students. R. J. Anderson and Sisco (1977) provided normative data for the WISC-R Performance Scale with 1,228 hearing-impaired subjects (see test review of the *Standardization of the WISC-R Performance Scale with Deaf Children*). The *Standardization* does not include the use of a standardized set of instructions, which has resulted in limited acceptance of the normative data. Ray (1979) found that use of instructions designed for hearing-impaired students results in scores no different from hearing children and recommends use of the original norms with the adapted instructions (see test review of *An Adaptation of the WISC-R for the Deaf.*) The small number of subjects (127) upon which Ray's conclusions are based and the statistical analyses used to draw conclusions, however, have been criticized (Sullivan, 1985). Hence, at this time the WISC-R Performance Scale has not been standardized (norms, instructions, scoring, and interpretation) on hearing-impaired subjects. The current use of either original hearing norms or hearing-impaired norms has resulted in problems in interpreting individual student performance, the performance of hearing-impaired students as a group, and the interpretation of studies involving the WISC-R Performance Scale.

Mean performance of hearing-impaired students on the WISC-R Performance Scale has been reported by R. J. Anderson and Sisco (1977), Courtney, Hayes, Couch, and Frick (1983; cited in Kaufman & Kaufman, 1983), Hirshoren, Hurley, and Kavale (1979), Phelps and Ensor (1986), Ray (1979), and Sullivan (1982). Reported values have ranged from 74 to 115.

Standard deviations have ranged from 17.6 to 19.4. Similar hearing-impaired profiles for the WISC-R Performance Scale were found by R. J. Anderson and Sisco (1977) and Ray (1979) and are characterized by Object Assembly scores significantly higher than those of hearing students, Picture Arrangement and Coding scores below that of the hearing, and Picture Completion and Block Design scores similar to those of hearing students. Hirshoren et al. (1979) found a similar profile for 59 hearing-impaired students; however, all mean subtest scores were lower, and no mean was higher than that of hearing students. Figure 3.1 presents a comparison of the three profiles.

Reliability for Hearing-Impaired Students.   Hirshoren et al. (1979), in a study of 59 hearing-impaired subjects, found that internal consistency reliability coefficients did not differ significantly from original (hearing) values for the Performance Scale and each performance subtest (except Coding, whose coefficient was not calculated). The reliability coefficient for the Performance Scale was found to be .90; subtest coefficients ranged from .62 (Object Assembly) to .84 (Picture Arrangement).

Validity for Hearing-Impaired Students.   Two studies have investigated the criterion-related validity of the WISC-R Performance Scale and the *Hiskey–Nebraska.* Hirshoren et al. (1979) found a correlation coefficient of .89 for overall scores (Performance IQ and Learning Quotient) using total communication and hearing norms. Similar results were obtained by Phelps and Ensor (1986) in a study of 49 hearing-impaired students using total communication and norms for hearing-impaired. A coefficient of .91 was obtained.

Three studies have reported correlational data for the WISC-R Performance Scale and K-ABC Nonverbal Scale. Courtney, Hayes, Watkins, and Frick (1983; cited in Kaufman & Kaufman, 1983) found an overall coefficient of .63 between the scales. L. J. Porter and Kirby (1986) reported similar coefficients of .68 and .64. A coefficient of .84 was found by Gibbons et al. (1984) using total communication and hearing-impaired norms.

James (1984) reported correlational data for the WISC-R Performance Scale and the *Raven Progressive Matrices.* A value of .87 was found between the WISC-R Performance Scale and the *Coloured Progressive Matrices* in a study of 34 students; a value of .78 was obtained between the WISC-R Performance Scale and the *Standard Progressive Matrices* in a second study involving 50 students. A variety of communication methods were used, and hearing norms were used for the WISC-R Performance Scale.

Studies of the WISC-R Performance Scale and achievement tests with hearing-impaired students have been reported by several researchers. Hirshoren et al. (1979) found correlation coefficients with *Stanford Achievement Scales* subtests and the WISC-R Performance Scale ranging from .09 (Language) to .34 (Word Meaning). Correlation with an average grade score resulted in a coefficient of .35. In a study of 25 hearing-impaired students, Watson, Sullivan, Moeller, and Jensen (1982) investigated correlational data from the WISC-R Performance Scale and two language measures, the *Test of Language Development* (TOLD) and the *Reynell Developmental Language Tests*. The coefficient for the WISC-R Performance Scale and TOLD overall scores was .54; coefficients for the WISC-R Performance Scale and *Reynell Scales* were .49 for the Expressive Scale and .30 for the Receptive Scale.

Conclusions. Just as the WISC-R Performance Scale is the most popular measure of cognitive ability for hearing-impaired students, the scale has generated the most data as an assessment instrument for the population. Standardization data are not in complete agreement in terms of the mean and standard deviation; however, as long as scores are interpreted using a range based on the standard error of measurement, rather than a single value, the discrepancies are reduced. Reliability data for the scale are similar for those of hearing children, although test–retest data for hearing-impaired students would be welcome. Validity data from correlating with measures of intelligence and achievement provide evidence of the scale's validity with hearing-impaired students.

Use of the WISC-R Verbal Scale has been suggested for some hearing-impaired students. Sattler (1982) pointed out that comparison of Verbal IQ to Performance IQ "provides an estimate of the degree to which the child has mastered verbal concepts" (p. 418). Miller (1985) gave the Verbal Scale to 30 profoundly hearing-impaired students by translating instructions into sign language. The mean IQ was found to be 97.8; however, this value may be inflated because initial incorrect responses were assumed to be due to failure to comprehend instructions. Zieziula (1982) stated, however, that the Verbal Scale "appears" to be inappropriate for most hearing-impaired students, thereby recommending caution in interpreting the Performance Scale IQ as a measure of overall intelligence due to the limited range of assessed skills.

Informal Measures

Arthur Adaptation of the Leiter International Performance Scale

(See review in Chapter 4.)

Leiter International Performance Scale

Author: R. G. Leiter
Publisher: Stoelting Company
             620 Wheat Lane
             Wood Dale, IL 60191
Copyright: 1969

General Description. The *Leiter International Performance Scale* contains items with age levels ranging from 2 to 18 years. The norm tables, however, range only from 3 to 16-11 years. In this nonvocal test, the examiner conveys directions through demonstration, and the student responds by manipulating blocks that are placed below picture strips held in a wooden tray. Administration time is about 30 to 45 minutes. There is one form of the test. Results for overall performance are expressed in terms of a mental age or an IQ. Materials consist of the examiner's manual, a record book, a wooden tray, and three large boxes of picture strips and blocks with pictures on them.

Description of Items. Items are grouped by 1-year age levels, each consisting of from four to six items. The examiner secures a picture strip to the wooden tray and the student manipulates blocks into slots in the tray to indicate answers. Tasks are varied and involve matching colors and objects at the beginning levels and then become more complex so as to require sequencing, seriation, and analogy skills, for example. Four items have time limits. The timed items first appear at age level 10.

Technical Adequacy

Standardization. The *Leiter Scale* was published in 1948. Although manuals have been published subsequent to this time, the data have not been updated. The "norm group" comprised Chinese and Japanese children who lived in Hawaii. When the test was later administered to children in the continental United States, it was found that the "norms" were 5 points too low. Hence, 5 points were added to the overall intelligence score. No information is available to describe the other demographic characteristics of the sample. Thus, this cannot be considered a norm-referenced measure.

Reliability. In a review of the research with the *Leiter Scale,* Ratcliffe and Ratcliffe (1979) indicated that studies of the split-half reliability of the scale range from .91 to .94.

A study by Sharp (1958) examined the test–retest reliability of the test with 48 mentally retarded children. A 6-month interval was used, and a correction of .91 was obtained.

Validity. Over the years, numerous studies have examined the relationship of the *Leiter Scale* with other measures of intelligence. In reviewing these studies, Ratcliffe and Ratcliffe (1979) found a median correlation of .77 for 10 studies that compared results of the *Leiter Scale* and the *Stanford–Binet*. They found correlations ranging from .75 to .85 for five studies with the *Leiter Scale* and the Wechsler Performance Scales.

Use of the Test with Hearing-Impaired Students. In a study with 25 deaf children, J. R. Birch, Stuckless, and Birch (1963) examined the relationship of the *Leiter Scale* results with teacher ratings of achievement and performance on the *Stanford Achievement Test.* A correlation of .60 was obtained with teacher ratings and low to moderate correlations were found between the *Leiter Scale* and *Stanford* Paragraph Meaning, Word Meaning, and Reading.

Conclusions. Ratcliffe and Ratcliffe (1979) found that, in reviewing studies comparing *Leiter Scale* results and results from the *Stanford-Binet* and the Wechsler Scales, scores on the *Leiter Scale* often were lower than those on the other tests. Ratcliffe and Ratcliffe concluded that, although Leiter tried to correct the test for being scaled too low, the 5-point correction does not appear to have solved the problem.

Results from the *Leiter Scale* should not be used to make important educational decisions about hearing-impaired students. Although the materials are interesting and the test is nonvocal, the test lacks necessary information on standardization, reliability, and validity. Despite its popularity and long-standing use, this test has not been shown to meet minimal requirements for technically adequate tests.

Results from the *Leiter Scale* may provide some information useful to planning educational programs in terms of skills such as matching, sequencing, and classifying, for example. Even in this respect, there is not a good sample of each of these skills. Salvia and Ysseldyke (1985) suggested that the test be used only to obtain qualitative information about a student, and then only by examiners with a great deal of experience.

As noted in Chapter 1, a number of hearing-impaired students have visual problems. This test requires good visual discrimination because many items require attention to considerable detail. If a student has a visual problem, this is likely to interfere with performance on the test.

As has been noted in the literature since the *Leiter Scale* was published, this test is "promising," but, until further data on technical adequacy are available, should not be used as a norm-referenced measure for normally hearing or hearing-impaired students.

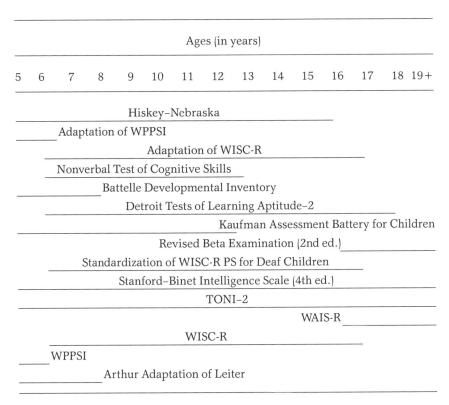

Figure 5.1. Tests for school-age hearing-impaired children according to applicable age.

Available Measures for Hearing-Impaired Students

Figure 5.1 provides an overview of the reviewed measures for school-age students, and the ages each is designed to include. The most adequate instruments for students from 5 to 6 years include the *Hiskey–Nebraska,* WPPSI and WPPSI Adaptation, and K-ABC, as these measures have the greatest amount of data supporting their use with hearing-impaired children at this age level. Because each test has weaknesses when used with hearing-impaired students, two of the three measures should be given. The Cognitive Scale of the BDI and the Abstract/Visual Reasoning Area and Quantitative Reasoning Area of the *Stanford–Binet* are best used with students having good receptive speech and language skills, but do not contain a sufficient number of items to yield an overall IQ score. Programming information might be gained by using the *Arthur Adaptation of the Leiter Scale.*

For students of ages 6-0 to 16-11 years, WISC-R possesses the most data to support its use with hearing-impaired students. Additional measures should be used because usually only the Performance subtests can be used with hearing-impaired students. Results from the WISC-R Performance subtests only are not good predictors of achievement. WISC-R results are best supplemented with the *Hiskey–Nebraska* (to age 16-0) or the K-ABC (to age 12½). Again, examiners may wish to give the TONI-2 to help resolve questions arising from use of WISC-R and *Hiskey–Nebraska* or K-ABC. Once an overall level of functioning has been determined, additional supplemental and programming information may be gained from the DTLA-2.

Assessment of students 16 years and older should include the WAIS-R Performance Scale, with supplementary data obtained from TONI-2, *Revised Beta,* or DTLA-2. None of the scales has demonstrated validity with hearing-impaired students in the United States; however, the WAIS-R Performance Scale contains a larger number of tasks than the other measures.

6

Assessment of Achievement

This chapter provides background on the achievement of hearing-impaired students and addresses special issues that require consideration for assessment of their achievement. The areas of reading, mathematics, written expression, and oral and manual communication are discussed. Norm- and criterion-referenced tests that have been standardized on, or designed for, hearing-impaired students are reviewed in detail. The use of curriculum-based assessment is considered as well. Also noted are tests that have been standardized on normally hearing samples, but that do not require vocal responses or reading (unless reading is being assessed). Finally, directions for future research on achievement testing for hearing-impaired students are discussed.

Reading and Hearing-Impaired Students

When assessing reading skills of hearing-impaired students, it is critical to consider several issues. As noted by Madison (1985), learning to read is a particularly difficult task for deaf children, and the intelligence and general ability of deaf students are not different from the rest of the population. Because these issues may seem obvious, it is easy to lose sight of them when interpreting test results. The issues apply to deaf students as a group, but have implications for interpretation of results of reading tests for individual students.

As examiners, we tend to focus on deficits and assume that low scores on tests reflect a learning disability of the student. Instead, low scores on reading tests for hearing-impaired students may reflect professionals' lack of knowledge regarding effective methods for teaching reading to these students. Wood, Wood, Griffiths, and Howarth (1986) indicated that, to their knowledge, there are no "well-designed evaluations demonstrating the effectiveness of any reading scheme being used with deaf children. The field abounds in opinion but is noticeably lacking in evidence" (p. 104). Clarke, Rogers, and Booth (1982) also described current instructional methods as being in a state of "confused eclecticism" because of "the remarkable lack of empirical data in this critical area" (p. 65). Although a great deal of research has been carried out on the reading process for deaf persons, considerably more research is needed to clarify which methods are effective for teaching reading to deaf students.

Low scores on tests also may reflect problems with the construction of reading tests for students with a hearing loss. No comprehensive tests of reading have been designed specifically for deaf students; hence, tests used with these students have been designed for, and standardized on, hearing students. Quigley and Paul (1984) noted that these tests may not be sensitive to the linguistic skills and problems of deaf children and, therefore, are probably of little use in determining strengths and needs of deaf students.

Hence, low scores on reading tests may reflect a lack of effective procedures for teaching reading, inappropriate construction and standardization of the reading tests for students with a hearing loss, a learning problem of the student tested, or any combination of these variables. Therefore, cautious interpretation of test results is necessary.

Achievement in reading is much lower for deaf students than for their hearing peers. Numerous studies, beginning as early as 1918 with a study by Pintner, have found very low achievement in reading for deaf students. In summarizing various surveys carried out since 1969 by the Center for Assessment and Demographic Studies of Gallaudet University, Quigley and Paul (1986) noted that the mean rate of growth per school year for deaf students is less than .3 of a grade level, and the median reading level was found to be less than fourth grade. (A fourth-grade level of reading is considered the level of functional literacy.) Upon completing a secondary education program, the average deaf student performs at a level similar to that of the average 9- or 10-year old hearing student. In response to these survey results, Gjerdingen (1987) commented that these data demonstrate that "the major failure of deaf education in America is in teaching deaf students to read. . . . Over half of deaf students graduating from high school in America are functionally illiterate" (p. 3).

Exceptions to these low achievement levels do exist for some deaf students who have attended comprehensive, private oral programs; those who have been integrated into regular education classrooms; and those in some well-organized total communication programs (Quigley & Paul, 1989). Some of these students have achieved at levels commensurate with their hearing peers. Most of them, however, have had relatively high intelligence and socioeconomic status. These two factors necessarily affect the development of communication skills and the use of residual hearing, and are related to having well-educated, involved parents. Quigley and Paul noted that "highly-trained dedicated instructors and administrators, and well-developed educational programs" (p. 16) also were important factors in the achievement of these students.

Despite the low achievement levels found for these students, it is not valid to conclude that low performance in reading necessarily must exist for deaf students. Such a conclusion could result in professionals and parents setting unnecessarily low expectations for these students and in accepting a student's minimal efforts in the classroom. This situation would not be conducive to deaf students learning the reading skills that they are capable of learning. It is critical that examiners perceive deaf children as potentially competent to learn, rather than as necessarily lacking in skills.

One factor that contributes to making the reading process particularly difficult for deaf students involves the problems encountered in recoding written material. When recoding written material, deaf students may "a) use a visual code (how the word looks), b) a manual code (how the word is signed or finger spelled), or c) a speech-based code (how the word is pronounced)" (Madison, 1985, p. 129). Research suggests that deaf children without internal speech do not change words they see into speech sounds. Instead, they employ memorized associations between the shapes of the words and the objects to which they refer (Wood et al., 1986). "For profoundly hearing-impaired readers, however, the translation of print into sound is generally difficult if not impossible. Hearing-impaired people typically do not use phonetic recoding in the way that hearing readers do" (Hirsh-Pasek & Treiman, 1982, p. 72). Conrad (1979) found that good deaf readers primarily used a speech-based code in recoding print. Why speech recoding is superior to visual or sign recoding is not clear. Perhaps it is more efficient to represent English grammatical structures in memory using speech recoding than using visual or sign recoding (Lake, 1980; Lichtenstein, 1984). Current research suggests, however, that the majority of deaf students recode print most effectively using a nonspeech-based code, that is, visual, sign, or both (Quigley & Paul, 1984). At this time, it is not clear whether the use of a speech-based code is critical for efficient reading. Considerably more research is needed regarding this issue.

Signing while reading may be analogous to vocal and subvocal reading used by hearing students when they encounter reading material that is difficult (Robbins & Hatcher, 1981). Robbins and Hatcher found that many of the children they tested signed sentences they read, although they were not told to do so, whereas others signed only when sentences were particularly confusing. Hence, a student's signing while reading is important to note during testing. It may indicate that the material is too difficult or confusing for the student, may indicate that signing facilitates the student's reading, or both.

In describing the difficulties deaf students encounter in learning to read, Quigley and Paul (1984) stated, "In short, deaf children are likely to have problems with every aspect of the reading process" (p. 115). This difficulty is not surprising, because an adequate language system is necessary to understand what is read. Although the intellectual level of deaf students is not different from that of their hearing peers, the considerable delay in development of a language system interferes with learning to read. For example, by age 6, hearing children have learned most rules of syntax and have a vocabulary of 8,000 to 14,000 words (Carey, 1977), whereas most deaf children have difficulty constructing complete sentences and have a sign language vocabulary that ranges from several words to approximately 493 words (Griswold & Commings, 1974). This problem with vocabulary continues well beyond age 6, as numerous studies have found that, regardless of the age levels investigated, deaf students comprehend fewer vocabulary words than hearing students (Quigley & Paul, 1986). In addition, their knowledge of various classes of words (e.g., nouns, verbs) is quantitatively less than their hearing peers (Quigley & Paul, 1989). Thus, vocabulary development for deaf students is similar to, but slower than, that of their hearing peers (Paul, 1984). The result is the same for Spanish deaf students for whom English is a second language (C. King, 1981) and for other language-impaired students learning English as a first or second language (Paul, 1985).

In a number of studies, Quigley and his associates (summarized in Quigley & Kretschmer, 1982) found that even when the researchers ensured that the deaf students understood the vocabulary and concepts in the material to be read, the students still had problems understanding simple declarative sentences. Hence, difficulty understanding syntax interferes with deaf students' learning to read successfully. Kretschmer (1982) also noted that the problems deaf students experience in reading are not simply a difficulty in recoding printed words, but also a result of problems with higher order processing, such as with syntax. Most profoundly hearing-impaired students acquire the major syntactic structures in a manner similar to, but slower than, that of their hearing counterparts (Quigley & Paul, 1984). To further investigate syntactic difficulties, Robbins and Hatcher (1981) conducted a study with deaf children in which they taught one group of children to recognize and understand the words used in sentences to be read. Another group did not receive this training, yet no differences were found between the groups in their ability to comprehend sentences. These results provide additional support for the fact that problems exist with syntax. The authors also noted a hierarchy of syntactic problems, with passives (e.g., He is being chased by her) being the most difficult for deaf students to understand. The remainder of the hierarchy (from most to least difficult) was: relative clauses (e.g., The boy who is running is being chased by the policeman), conjunctions and pronoun substitutions (e.g., He is chasing her and she is running away), indirect objects (e.g., He is giving the book to the girl), and simple active sentences (e.g., The boy is chasing the girl).

The literature indicates that children for whom American Sign Language (ASL) is their native language (i.e., hearing-impaired children with hearing-impaired parents) "may approach print as a second language" (Kretschmer, 1982, p. 112). This has contributed to some researchers (e.g., Schlesinger, 1986) suggesting that a bilingual approach to education may be helpful. These children are likely to have a strong, but different language base as a background for reading. Madison (1985) noted that it is unfortunate that curricula rarely focus on the unique needs of these children. He further commented that it is understandable why this lack of attention to the needs of these children occurs, given that so few deaf children have deaf parents. Less than 10% of deaf children have a deaf parent, and only about 3 to 4% have two deaf parents (Rawlings & Jensema, 1977). In planning educational programs, however, it would seem to be helpful to take advantage of the language base of children whose native language is ASL.

Kretschmer (1982) suggested that, in general, hearing-impaired students not raised in an ASL environment (i.e., those whose native language is not ASL) approach reading "with a faulty or at least altered English-language base" (p. 112). ASL is a language system with grammar that differs from that used in English (Lane & Grosjean, 1980; Wilber, 1987). The differences that exist between the English language system and ASL may make learning to read more difficult for some ASL users than for those who use some form of oral English (Quigley & Paul, 1984).

Thus, as noted by Quigley and Paul (1986),

> It has been shown that the most marked deficits of deaf students are those associated with the Sentence (paragraph) Meaning (that is reading comprehension) and Word Meaning (that is reading vocabulary) subtests. These skills may be considered the foundations of all other phases of reading and are heavily influenced by language comprehension ability. (p. 61)

Quigley and Paul (1989) further suggested that, "In essence, it is shown that the poor reading skills of most deaf students are inextricably related to their inadequate primary English language development" (p. 7).

In addition to these difficulties, several other problems may interfere with the reading process and negatively affect the performance of deaf students on reading tests. These students appear to have more difficulty than their hearing peers in drawing inferences from material they read. This was demonstrated in a study by Wilson (1979). Despite Wilson's controlling for specific syntax, deaf students had much greater difficulty drawing inferences than hearing students.

Another problem has to do with memory. Deaf students seem to have more difficulty on memory tasks, especially those involving sequential memory, than do hearing students (Quigley & Paul, 1984). Deaf persons' difficulties with memory tasks seem to be a function of the memory strategies they employ, rather than a deficiency in memory (Karchmer & Belmont, 1976). Regardless of the reason for the difficulty, memory tasks are more difficult for hearing-impaired students then for hearing students. Hence, if reading comprehension tests involve numerous inference questions, and require students to answer questions from memory (rather than by locating the answer in material before them), deaf students will be likely to receive very low scores. When selecting tests of reading comprehension, and when interpreting results of these tests, examiners should review the structure of tests to determine whether, because of their construction, the tests may be especially difficult for deaf students.

In summary, as suggested by Quigley and Paul (1989), the problems that deaf students have with reading are similar to problems of many students for whom English is a second language. These problems may be a function of deficits in their experience (e.g., knowledge about the world), cognitive skills (e.g., memory, drawing inferences), and linguistic skills (e.g., knowledge of vocabulary and syntax). Quigley and Paul noted that other educational and socioeconomic variables also influence the development of reading skills. They suggested, however, that these deficiencies are quantitative, not qualitative, in comparison to those of hearing students.

Issues in Testing Reading Skills

Given the many problems deaf students have with reading, it is important not to assume that, for example, a fourth-grade reading level for a deaf student means the same thing as a fourth-grade reading level for a hearing student. Quigley and Kretschmer (1982) suggested that, despite the low levels of reading achievement that have been found for deaf students, these results may overestimate their skills because of their difficulties in reading comprehension. When deaf students take reading tests, they tend to attempt more items than hearing students and they make more errors (Quigley & Paul, 1984).

The following cautions are warranted in interpreting reading test results for any student, and are particularly important when testing students who have as much trouble with reading as deaf students have. First, most reading comprehension tests do not have reading levels given for the passages students are asked to read. Hence, low scores on these tests could be due to comprehension difficulties, due to a student's inability to decode the material, or both. One would not be able to determine if the student had a problem with comprehension unless further testing were carried out on decoding skills only, or on comprehension using materials that are known to be written at a level the student can decode successfully.

A second caution is that results of norm-referenced reading tests are unlikely to correspond to the level in a basal reading series where a student can benefit from instruction. There is often quite a range of reading levels for any book in a basal series, and the various reading series are quite different from each other (Lesiak & Bradley-Johnson, 1983). Because of this variability in reading series, results of a norm-referenced test may serve only as an "estimate" as to where the student should begin in the series used for instruction. Unfortunately, the informal inventories that come with some reading series to aid in instructional placement may not provide a sufficient sample of skills taught and, therefore, may not result in accurate placement within the series. To determine appropriate placement in a basal series, an informal inventory should be prepared from the series used for instruction, using procedures that research has shown to be fairly reliable. These procedures are described in detail in Lesiak and Bradley-Johnson (1983).

A third caution is that norm-referenced tests for reading vocabulary are not prescriptive. It is difficult to determine which vocabulary words students need to be able to understand to be successful in reading. Furthermore, research on the efficacy of teaching vocabulary in order to improve comprehension has resulted in contradictory findings (Lesiak & Bradley-Johnson, 1983). Hence, in terms of instructional planning for students who receive low scores on vocabulary, it would not be possible to determine which words should be taught. Instead, it would seem beneficial to suggest that the teacher go over reading assignments prior to having the student read them, and explain any potentially troublesome vocabulary words to the student. Once the meaning of these words has been clarified, then the student could read the assignment independently.

Ewoldt (1982) advocated the use of miscue analysis for assessing reading skills for hearing-impaired students. Such an approach would require a student to read material, while allowing the examiner to obtain information regarding how the student approaches the task of reading. Although such observation certainly has merit, until further research is available on miscue analysis, and more sophisticated procedures are developed, conclusions drawn from the use of miscue analysis must be interpreted carefully. Results could vary considerably as a function of the difficulty of the reading material selected for the assessment as well as the examiner's skill in noting miscues. The ambiguity of the procedures used for analyzing the student's retelling of the story could yield unreliable, and therefore invalid, conclusions. We agree with C. M. King and Quigley (1985) that observation of a student's reading in context should complement results from administration of standardized measures and, thus, provide a good data base for drawing conclusions about a student's skills.

Arithmetic and Mathematics Skills for Hearing-Impaired Students

The mathematics reasoning process is similar for hearing-impaired and hearing students, except that the skills typically are delayed for hearing-impaired students (Wood et al., 1986). Fortunately, the delay is not as great as it is for reading. According to the 1983 survey of achievement of deaf students by the Center for Assessment and Demographic Studies of Gallaudet University, the median achievement level for 14-year-old deaf students was sixth grade for math computation (Harkins, 1985).

The reason for the delay in development of these skills is unclear. Wood et al. (1986) suggested, however, that the way in which the skills are taught may be a factor, rather than the limited abilities of deaf students. The authors suspected that the lower performance of hearing-impaired students in math might be due to deaf students being taught fewer skills than their hearing peers. As in reading, a low score on a test of arithmetic/mathematics must be interpreted cautiously, because it may be more likely to reflect lack of effective teaching techniques for hearing-impaired students than it would for hearing students. Low scores may be indicative of a learning problem for a student, a problem with techniques for teaching, or both.

Issues in Testing Arithmetic and Mathematics

In terms of their approach to arithmetic/mathematics tests, deaf students attempt a similar number of items as do students with normal hearing, and they make similar errors (Wood et al., 1986).

Written Expression and Hearing-Impaired Students

Although deaf students clearly have serious problems with written expression, no reliable and valid techniques exist to assess written expression for these students (Quigley & Paul, 1984). Nevertheless, it is critical that deaf students develop expertise in written expression, if for no other reason than to enable them to use writing to communicate with others in situations where oral and sign communication fail.

Given the low levels of achievement found for hearing-impaired students in reading, it is not surprising that their written expression skills are low as well. Quigley and Kretschmer (1982) suggested that writing skills depend on reading skills, which, in turn, are based on adequate development of a primary language.

Hearing-impaired students have a very limited vocabulary for use in written expression (Hamp, 1972). Also, studies have shown that deaf students have difficulty using correct syntax in writing (Kretschmer & Kretschmer, 1978; Quigley, Wilbur, Power, Montanelli, & Steinkamp, 1976). Other difficulties encountered by hearing-impaired writers include omission of verbs and subjects, failure to clarify pronoun reference, and errors on or omission of articles, possessives, and derivational and inflectional endings (Sarachan-Deily & Love, 1974). Taylor (1969) found that deaf students use very few complex sentence structures in their writing. When deaf students did use complex sentence structures, they were usually incorrect. In a study with 20 hearing-impaired students enrolled in a public high school who used total communication, Gormley and Sarachan-Deily (1987) found that few attempted to revise their written compositions. It seems the students felt that drafting and copying without revising was sufficient for their writing efforts. This may not be a motivational problem, but may be due, at least in part, to the way in which written expression is taught to these students.

Issues in Testing Written Expression

Whether a contrived or a spontaneous format is used to assess written expression makes a difference in the results obtained. Typically, a contrived format involves having a student correct written material; for example, given a passage without capitalization and punctuation, a student is to add what is needed. A spontaneous format involves having a student write in response to a story starter such as a picture or a beginning sentence. This sample is then scored for various aspects of writing. A contrived format allows one to determine what discrete elements of written language a student knows, whereas a spontaneous format allows the assessment of a student's ability to apply skills in a passage generated by the student. If only a contrived format is employed, results may not describe the skills that a student uses in his or her own writing. If only a spontaneous format is used, it is unlikely that a student would use all of the rules that an examiner would want to assess. Hence, ideally, both formats should be employed to obtain a comprehensive assessment.

The low levels of reading typically achieved by hearing-impaired students present problems for assessing their written expression. Most tests of written language that employ a contrived format do not include reading levels for the material used. Hence, hearing-impaired students may receive extremely low scores because they could not read the material; for example, a student may not use a capital letter because he or she did not recognize a word as a proper name. When contrived formats are used to assess written language skills, examiners should ask students to read each item on which an error was made to determine whether the student could read the material. If this is not done, the results will be of questionable validity.

Some tests such as the *Peabody Individual Achievement Test–Revised* (Markwardt, 1989) assess spelling by having students point to the correct spelling of a word, rather than write the word. Although a pointing task might seem to be an appropriate format for hearing-impaired students, this format taps word recognition rather than spelling. Such a test could identify a good reader who is a poor speller as a good speller (Bradley-Johnson & Lesiak, 1989). Spelling involves writing words. Writing a word provides visual and kinesthetic feedback and allows a student to check the correctness of a response. Hence, to obtain valid results for spelling, it is best to select tests that require students to write words (Bradley-Johnson & Lesiak, 1989).

For students with problems in handwriting, none of the current norm- or criterion-referenced tests provides an adequate sample of handwriting. To assess this area comprehensively, legibility, fluency, and the subskills of handwriting need to be considered using samples taken on three different days. A detailed checklist designed for this purpose can be found in Bradley-Johnson and Lesiak (1989).

Oral and Sign Language and Students with a Hearing Loss

As noted by Thompson, Biro, Vethivelu, Pious, and Hatfield (1987), "The greatest deficit sustained by hearing impaired persons occurs in language development and use" (p. 3). The age at onset of the hearing loss appears to be a critical factor in students' learning language. Those who have hearing, even during their first year or two, are able to learn language more easily than those who have not heard language (Rogers & Soper, 1982). Age 2 seems to be a critical age at onset for hearing loss, in terms of affecting language development (Quigley & Paul, 1984).

As noted earlier, vocabulary development often is very delayed (Griswold & Commings, 1974; Quigley & Paul, 1989). Meadow (1980) found that hearing-impaired subjects acquire concepts in the same order as hearing subjects, but acquisition is delayed. This is consistent with Furth's (1964) suggestion that hearing-impaired students have difficulty discovering concepts, rather than difficulty understanding or using them.

Deaf students also learn syntactic skills later than their hearing peers (Quigley & Paul, 1986). Babbini and Quigley (1970) noted large differences in syntactic abilities not only between deaf and hearing students, but also between deaf students and students with less severe hearing losses. Besides having problems learning syntactic skills, it seems that deaf persons use some rules that are not part of standard English (Quigley & Paul, 1984). The important point regarding the syntactic skills of deaf students is that their skills are qualitatively similar to, but slower to develop than the syntactic skills of their hearing peers.

Hearing parents of deaf children tend to give more directive statements and provide fewer explanations than parents who share their child's hearing status (i.e., deaf–deaf or hearing–hearing) (Hyde, Power, & Elias, 1980; Schlesinger & Meadow, 1972). This finding led Day and Meadow-Orlans (1985) to suggest that hearing parents of deaf children model a functional language system that could be "structurally different from that to which hearing children are exposed" (p. 34). The difficulties in communicating may interfere with parents' ability to become as involved with their child as parents with shared hearing status, affecting their ability to display the more typical interaction patterns of parents and children. If these parents do model a different functional language system, this could contribute to the difficulties these children face in learning language.

Differences of opinion remain in the literature regarding the form of communication (e.g., oral vs. manual) that is most helpful to deaf students. We agree with Quigley and Paul (1984) that "each language approach and each communication form probably has a place in the education of deaf children" (p. 161). Further research should eventually lead to a better understanding of the variables that are critical in learning language for these students. Until these issues are clarified, flexibility in working with students with a hearing loss is needed to best meet students' individual needs. If teaching is to be effective, however, decisions regarding instruction need to be based on sound research, whenever possible.

Issues in Testing Oral and Sign Language

The examiner who assesses a student's communication skills must be skilled in the form of communication used by the student if comprehensive and valid results are to be obtained. Just to establish rapport requires easy and frequent communication between the examiner and the student.

Whatever type of communication the student uses, both receptive and expressive aspects should be assessed. Futhermore, semantics and syntax should each be assessed in both the receptive and expressive modes. In addition, it may be necessary to assess more than one language, such as American Sign Language and Spanish. Thus, assessment of oral language, sign language, or some combination of communication forms will be time-consuming.

Longhurst and Grubb (1974) found that deaf subjects used more language and more complex language in less structured, more natural settings than in structured situations with specified tasks or in which they were asked to describe pictures. Hence, Thompson et al. (1987) suggested that the use of spontaneous language samples is "a critical part of any test battery" (p. 96). Detailed guidelines for obtaining and analyzing language samples, including recoding forms, can be found in Thompson et al. (1987).

Undoubtedly, spontaneous language samples can provide important information on a student's use of language in the natural setting, but, as with miscue analysis, reliable procedures have yet to be determined. Hence, because results obtained from such assessments have not been shown to be reliable, results necessarily have questionable validity. In addition, these language samples include only a small sample of a student's language skills, and many skills that a child is able to use may not be observed when the samples are taken (Moog & Kozak, 1983). This does not mean that such procedures are of no use. It does mean that conclusions based on such methods must be questioned unless they are supported by information from several other reliable sources.

The use of formal tests can provide information on specific components of language that may not be evident from language samples. These results reflect the skills a student has learned, not necessarily the skills a student typically uses. Therefore, given the diversity of language skills within the population of hearing-impaired students, it is incumbent that examiners are aware of the many published tests, as well as the less formal procedures, so that a battery of measures can be compiled to best meet the needs of individual students. Procedures that work well for one student may be inappropriate for another. Both language samples and formal tests should be considered in planning a language assessment for any student with a hearing loss.

Review of Tests and Procedures

Tests reviewed in this chapter were evaluated using the same criteria employed in Chapters 4 and 5 for evaluating tests of cognitive development. These criteria are described in Chapter 1. Tests were selected for review if they had been published within the past 15 years and were either standardized on, or designed for, hearing-impaired students.

In addition to reviewing norm- and criterion-referenced tests, the use of curriculum-based measurement is addressed. This relatively new method of assessment is receiving increasing amounts of attention. The primary purpose of curriculum-based measurement (CBM) is to evaluate a student's progress within a particular curriculum, rather than the effect of intervention after a portion of a program or an entire program has been completed, as is usually the case with norm-referenced assessment. Results of CBM can be used to determine whether modifications are needed within an instructional program for a particular student. The material used for assessment is prepared from the material that is used for instruction. Unlike norm-referenced assessment, the procedure can be used frequently (even several times a week) without practice effects. Thus, it is ideally suited for use in the classroom.

The results obtained can be used to compare an individual student's performance with his or her prior scores to evaluate the progress that has been made within the curriculum. Results for a particular student also can be compared with results of other "average" students in the classroom on the same tasks. For hearing-impaired students, comparisons could be made for a particular student with the performance of both "average" hearing-impaired students and "average" normally hearing students. Up to this point, research with CBM seems to have involved only normally hearing students. Other types of comparisons with larger groups of students can be made also, but require a great deal of preparation and require further research to establish the technical adequacy of such procedures.

Although different procedures can be employed to carry out CBM, those that seem to be the most well researched were described by Shinn (1989). The procedures described by Shinn have been shown to be reliable for assessing progress in reading, some arithmetic operations, and spelling. When used as a measure of overall written language, however, the reliability coefficients usually fall below .85.

Details on how to use CBM for reading, arithmetic, and spelling are included under Reading and Written Language in the material that follows. The reliability and validity of these procedures are discussed also.

General Achievement Measures

Although some group-administered tests have been standardized on the hearing-impaired population, individually administered tests are needed for making decisions regarding eligibility for special education services. However, one group-administered test, the *Stanford Achievement Test* (SAT;

Psychological Corp., 1989), deserves special consideration because of its exemplary technical adequacy for this population of students. Several editions of this test have been published over the years and standardized on hearing-impaired students by the Center for Assessment and Demographic Studies (CADS) of Gallaudet University.

The following information is based on communication with Judith Holt (1990) of CADS. The latest version of the SAT, the eighth edition, is currently being standardized on 8,000 to 10,000 hearing-impaired students across the nation. The eighth edition of the SAT will be kept in its original form for the standardization. For the sixth edition, some sections of the test had been reorganized for hearing-impaired students, but this does not appear to be necessary. Nationally representative samples of hearing-impaired students have been obtained by CADS for prior editions of the SAT, which have taken the important demographic characteristics into consideration. The reliability and validity information on the SAT is extensive. Hence, it is likely that standardization of the eighth edition of the SAT will result in a very technically adequate measure.

The eighth edition has 16 screening tests, 8 for reading and 8 for math. There is a screener for each level of the test. The screeners are used to determine the appropriate levels of the test to administer. Performance on the math screeners is used to determine where to begin tests for Math Computation and Concepts of Number. Performance on the reading screeners is used to determine where to begin testing for all other subtests, except Math Application, to ensure that a student can read the material tested. For Math Application, results of either the reading or the math screener are used, whichever is lower. Some of the subtests are dictated, and CADS recommends that these subtests not be used with hearing-impaired students. If they are given, the communication mode the student uses in the classroom should be employed. The subtests for the eighth version of the SAT include Sounds & Letters/Word Study Skills, Word Reading/Reading Vocabulary, Sentence Reading/Reading Comprehension, Language Mechanics, Language Expression, Study Skills, Spelling, Listening, Concepts of Number, Computation, Mathematics Applications, Environment, Science, and Social Science. Which subtests are appropriate for a particular student varies with the level of the test employed.

With the norms for hearing-impaired students, it will be possible to compare a student's performance on the SAT with a nationally representative sample of hearing peers and with a nationally representative sample of hearing-impaired peers. Base norms will be available by age and by hearing loss: profound, severe, and less than severe. Norms for the eighth edition for hearing-impaired students should be available in the 1990–1991 academic year. Given the limited number of individually administered tests appropriate for hearing-impaired students, and the problems that exist with technical adequacy with many of the available measures, the SAT provides a useful alternative, despite the fact that it is group administered.

Preschool/Kindergarten Skills

Uniform Performance Assessment System

Authors: O. R. White, N. G. Haring, E. B. Edgar, J. Q. Affleck, & A. H. Hayden
Publisher: The Psychological Corporation
555 Academic Court
San Antonio, TX 78204
Copyright: 1981

General Description. The *Uniform Performance Assessment System* (UPAS) assesses skills typically learned by normal children between birth and 6 years of age. It is designed for use with handicapped children to obtain information for planning instruction. Five areas are assessed: Preacademic/Fine Motor Development, Communication, Social/Self-help Skills, Gross Motor Development, and Inappropriate Behaviors. Many items can be scored by observing the child during regular activities, whereas other items are administered to the child. Items are not timed. Although there are no practice items, many items are demonstrated by the examiner and procedures can be adapted to meet the needs of individual children. To take the individual needs of children into account, and to obtain information useful to planning instruction, items are scored using the following categories: not applicable (item cannot be adapted for child), support (e.g., special positioning required), prosthetic device (e.g., use of hearing aid to respond to sound), general adaptation (support other than physical devices needed, such as use of signing), upgraded task to make age appropriate (e.g., use of pictures of appropriate content for older children rather than pictures of balloons), or no chance/no test (if it is obvious without testing that the child has or does not have the skill). Although age levels at which normal children acquire the skills are indicated for each item, no norm-referenced interpretations should be made. These levels are age estimates based on information from other measures. Instead, results should be interpreted as skills mastered and those to be taught. Results also may be described as percentage of items passed. Materials consist of the examiner's manual, an administration manual, a record book, stimulus cards, and a number of common toys or objects that do not come with the test kit. These objects are listed in the manual's appendix.

Subtest Description. The two subtests that are relevant to achievement are the Preacademic/Fine Motor subtest and the Communication subtest.

Preacademic/Fine Motor. This subtest consists of 76 items ranging from fixating eyes on red yarn to demonstrating knowledge of the concepts "right" and "left." Eight of these items require the child to use either speech or sign. These items involve naming colors, shapes, letters, and numbers; reading words; answering questions involving "How many"; indicating "What number comes after _____"; and counting by rote. Three additional items must be scored as not applicable for many hearing-impaired children as the items cannot be adapted. These involve identifying rhyming words, discriminating consonants, and discriminating vowels. Other than these 11 items, the items for this section do not require speech. Directions can be given by modeling plus the use of manual communication. A number of items that tap fine motor skills are not prerequisite to academic performance, but involve skills used in some classrooms. Examples include cutting with scissors, using puzzles and pegboards, and building with blocks. Examples of more educationally important skills include gripping a pencil, copying with a pencil, printing one's name, and writing numbers.

Communication. This subtest consists of 69 items ranging from indicating an awareness of sound to understanding the concepts of "same" and "different." Eight of the items on this subtest are not adaptable for most hearing-impaired students (e.g., turns to sound, responds to "Come here" without the use of gesture). Ten additional items require speech. Most of the remaining items require sign if the child does not use speech. Hence, this subtest is unlikely to be as useful with hearing-impaired children as with hearing children. Both receptive and expressive skills are tapped, but the majority of items involve expression.

Technical Adequacy

Field Testing. Six versions of the test were drafted over a 6-year period and field tested. The testing apparently took place at the University of Washington in the Experimental Education Unit, although this is not specifically stated in the manual.

Reliability. Three studies were carried out to investigate the test–retest reliability of the UPAS. Twenty-five children from 3.7 to 21.3 years participated in the first study, and the retest interval was 4 months. The correlation was .98 for the Preacademic/Fine Motor subtest and .96 for the Communication subtest. The second study involved 24 children from 4.2 to 14 years of age, also with a 4-month retest interval. The correlation for the Preacademic/Fine Motor subtest was .94 and for the Communication subtest was .98. The third study involved 50 children from 7 months to 4.5

years and employed a 16-month retest interval. The correlation was .86 for the Preacademic/Fine Motor subtest and .76 for the Communication subtest. This also reflects the predictive validity of the results.

Validity.   In terms of content validity, the UPAS items were based on feedback from teachers in the Experimental Education Unit at the University of Washington. The age ranges for the items are based on analysis of items from other unspecified scales. A Guttman Scalability analysis for data obtained with 101 handicapped preschoolers on 37 of the skill sequences resulted in reproducibility coefficients ranging from .9 to 1.0. Thus, the skills appear to be in the sequence in which they usually are learned. No other information on validity is given.

Conclusions.   The adaptability of the scoring system is a strength of the UPAS. How useful the information is for planning educational programs depends upon how closely the skills tested correspond to the curricula used with the child being assessed. This is noted by the authors in the manual. Further evidence is needed to support the educational importance of the skills tested and references for the age levels used. For the assessment of communication skills, other more comprehensive tests that contain more appropriate items for hearing-impaired children, are described under the Oral and Manual Communication section of this chapter.

Reading

Test of Early Reading Ability–Deaf or Hard of Hearing

Authors: D. K. Reid, W. P. Hresko, D. D. Hammill, & S. Wiltshire
Publisher: PRO-ED
             8700 Shoal Creek Blvd.
             Austin, TX 78758
Copyright: 1991

General Description.   The *Test of Early Reading Ability–Deaf or Hard of Hearing* (TERA-D/HH) is presently being standardized on hearing-impaired students from 3 to 13 years of age and taps a variety of skills associated with reading. TERA-D/HH is individually administered, and there are two forms of the test (A and B). It is not timed. Materials consist of an examiner's manual, a one-page protocol, and a picture book.

Description of Test Items.   The test provides one overall score; that is, there are no subtests. Skills tested include items involving letter names, number recognition, recognition of symbols (e.g., wrapper for a chocolate bar, logo for a local restaurant), knowledge of homonyms, word recognition, book handling skills (e.g., recognition of the top of a book, being able to follow along with words as the examiner reads them), and reciting the alphabet. Items were selected to address three areas: construction of meaning (e.g., recognition of signs and logos), knowledge of the alphabet and its functions (e.g., letter naming and word recognition), and conventions of written language (e.g., book handling skills and ability to recognize when material read does not make sense).

Technical Adequacy.   Because the test is currently being standardized, it is not possible to evaluate its technical adequacy. Preliminary information indicates that a geographically representative sample will be obtained that also is representative in terms of race and ethnicity. The authors have indicated that they will try to include an extensive description of the sample, including such factors as degree of hearing loss, age at onset, and etiology.

Conclusions.   This test should have considerable potential as a useful norm-referenced measure of reading skills for hearing-impaired students, especially young children. If a nationally representative sample of children is obtained, and detailed demographic data are provided on the background of the children, particularly on their hearing status, this test will be an important contribution. Adequate data on reliability and validity will be needed as well.

Test of Syntactic Abilities

Authors: S. P. Quigley, M. W. Steinkamp, D. J. Power, & B. W. Jones
Publisher: PRO-ED
               8700 Shoal Creek Blvd.
               Austin, TX 78758-6897
Copyright: 1982

General Description.   The *Test of Syntactic Abilities* (TSA) was designed for deaf students 10 through 18 years of age, and hearing students 8 through 10 years, to assess the ability to recognize correct syntax in material that is read. The test may be group or individually administered. Administration time for the Survey Test is 1 hour, and there are two forms of the survey. Each Diagnostic Battery (for in-depth assessment of a particular area) takes approximately 30 minutes. Practice items are included in TSA. Results can be expressed as percentile ranks or age equivalents. Materials consist of the examiner's manual and student record books for the Survey and each Diagnostic Battery.

Description of Survey Test and Diagnostic Batteries

Screening Test.   The 120-item Screening Test provides an overall assessment of syntactic skills. Scores are obtained for each of the nine structures assessed: negation, conjunction, determiners, question formation, verb processes, pronominalization, relativization, complementation, and nominalization. Based on the profile from the Screening Test, examiners can determine which Diagnostic Batteries to administer in order to obtain detailed information for instructional planning.

Diagnostic Batteries.   There are 20 Diagnostic Batteries, each made up of 70 items. Some of the nine syntactic structures assessed have more than one Diagnostic Battery.

Students must read the material and mark their choice on the record book for each item. A four-choice, multiple-choice format is used for the TSA. Scores were not corrected for guessing because it was found that, when students were given enough time, and instructed to answer all items, the correlation of corrected and uncorrected scores was perfect.

The TSA was designed primarily for use with deaf students. The distractors for the items were selected from written language samples of deaf students. Because the reading level of most deaf students is low, the authors tried to select vocabulary at or near the first-grade level.

To minimize cultural bias, the material includes varied interests and experiences. Descriptions of boys and girls in nontraditional sex roles are included. Teachers in Australia and England reviewed the items for their appropriateness for English-speaking students with different dialects.

It is noted in the manual that the TSA is not likely to discriminate well for students 14 years old or older with IQs of 130 or higher. Also, students with reading ability above sixth or seventh grade probably would have mastered skills covered by the TSA. These students may still have language problems, but the TSA is not designed to assess these more advanced skills.

Technical Adequacy

Standardization.   There were 411 students in the sample of deaf students, with approximately 23 boys and 23 girls at each age level 10 through 18 years. Students were randomly selected from schools for the deaf with 100 or more students throughout the United States. Nine geographic regions were represented, with one day and one residential program from each region. This may be a nationally representative sample, but it is difficult to determine because the data are not presented so as to correspond to the regions used in the census data. All students had sensorineural losses of at least 90 dB in the better ear, hearing loss prior to age 2, IQs of at least 80, and no other apparent disabilities other than corrected vision. No data are provided on race, ethnicity, socioeconomic level, or urban/rural residence.

For comparison purposes, limited data are presented on a sample of 66 hearing children ages 8 through 10. Some data are presented on several other samples as well, including hearing students with achievement levels above national norms ($n = 320$), deaf Australian students ($n = 69$), deaf college students ($n = 50$), and hearing-impaired Canadian students ages 8 to 18 ($n = 157$).

Reliability. For the Screening Test, the internal consistency (KR-20s) for both forms was .98. Item difficulty levels were 53% and 54% for the forms, suggesting the similarity of the forms.

For the Diagnostic Batteries, internal consistency reliability coefficients (KR-20s) range from .93 to .98.

Test–retest reliability was examined with a 6-month interval. Correlations ranged from .62 to .87 for the subtests. Only one subtest, Relative Pronouns and Adverbs, reached the .85 criterion for acceptable reliability.

Standard errors of measurement are provided for each subtest by age groupings.

Validity. In terms of content validity, items were selected based on the authors' 10 years of research, collection of language samples, and pilot work with the TSA. The authors suggested that this work showed that these language structures were important for deaf students, and aspects of syntax on which deaf students tend to make errors are covered by the items.

It is stated in the manual that "the reading requirement was maintained at an elementary level throughout the TSA" (p. 73). Also, vocabulary close to first-grade level was selected. A reading level on the material would have been informative. Hobbs (1980) found that students 14 years of age and older, who are reading below a 2.5 grade level, tend to guess randomly on TSA items.

As noted previously, material was selected to try to minimize sex role or cultural bias.

Item difficulty ranges were from 36 to 72%.

To demonstrate construct validity, correlations of TSA results and language-related subtests of the *Stanford Achievement Test* were obtained and ranged from .26 to .89. Correlations with the TSA and nonverbal IQ ranged from .29 to .42. Age correlated .37 with the TSA total score. Item–total correlations were greater than .40 for 88% of TSA items. Subtest intercorrelations ranged from .50 to .85.

Conclusions.   In terms of standardization, it would be helpful to have more subjects per age level and demographic information on race, ethnicity, socioeconomic level, and urban/rural residence of the students. Internal consistency reliability data are very good, but test–retest data are too low. The low test–retest correlations may well be due to learning that took place over the 6-month interval. Test–retest data by age level over about a 2-week interval would be more informative and would likely result in higher correlations. Information on the reading level of the material is needed. The TSA is a very well thought out, comprehensive test that appears to have good validity. The manual is well written, and results are carefully interpreted and clearly explained. TSA's strength is in its use as a domain-referenced measure for planning instructional programs. It is difficult to imagine a more comprehensive measure in this area. With more data on standardization and reliability, the TSA could be a very technically adequate measure as well.

Curriculum-Based Measurement

Marston (1989) described the technical adequacy of CBM when used for assessing progress in reading for students with normal hearing. In terms of test–retest reliability, correlations range from .92 to .97. The retest intervals varied from 2 to 10 weeks. Reliability estimates for parallel form range from .84 to .96. Interrater agreement was found to be .99.

In terms of validity, several studies have examined the relationship of CBM results and performance on published measures of reading, criterion-referenced mastery tests in basal readers, and teachers' ratings. Results of CBM correlated well with these measures. Results of CBM also were found to discriminate among learning disabled students, students in Chapter I, and regular education students.

The following procedures are based on material described by Shinn (1989), except that use of the procedures with students who sign was not addressed by Shinn. The first step is to select passages to be used for assessment from the material used for reading instruction. Two copies should be made of each passage. One copy is used by the examiner, and the student reads from the other. Next, the student should be asked to read the passage aloud (or students who use manual communication can sign) as the examiner marks words read incorrectly. The student should read for 1 minute. If a student signs the material, a 2- or 3-minute sample would seem to be more appropriate. A vertical line should be placed after the last word read to indicate where the student stopped reading. Then, the number of words read correctly should be counted. Repetitions and self-corrections within 3 seconds are not considered errors. If signing is used, more than 3 seconds may need to be allowed for self-corrections. Errors include substitutions, omissions, mispronunciations, and words not read within 3 seconds. Again, the 3-second limit may need to be extended for students who sign.

Unfortunately, research on the use of CBM with hearing-impaired students is not available; hence, the changes suggested for students using manual communication are only estimates. A critical factor in using CBM for assessing progress is to use the same procedures each time the student is assessed so that meaningful comparisons can be made. The most useful length for a reading sample for hearing-impaired students needs research. An additional concern in using CBM with hearing-impaired students that also requires research has to do with the effect on results for students who sign and encounter words for which there is no sign. In this case, the word would have to be finger spelled. Another issue to consider if CBM is to be used, is that the examiner needs to understand the student's signs well.

Although research to determine the most effective procedures to use for CBM with hearing-impaired students has yet to be carried out, the potential usefulness of CBM warrants its use at this time as an informal measure to aid in planning instruction. It can be used frequently and has content validity, given that the material used for assessment also is used for instruction.

Arithmetic

No published, individually administered arithmetic tests have been developed for hearing-impaired students.

Curriculum-Based Measurement

Marston (1989) described the technical adequacy of CBM when used for assessing progress in arithmetic for students with normal hearing. In terms of test–retest reliability, correlations were .93 for addition, .87 for subtraction, .79 for multiplication, .78 for division, and .93 for mixed problems. Use of CBM for addition, subtraction, and mixed problems seems to provide sufficiently reliable data, although only a 1-week retest interval was employed. Correlations on parallel form reliability ranged from .48 to .72. Interrater reliability was reported as .90 or higher.

In terms of validity, studies have found a relationship between CBM results and performance on published norm-referenced math tests, but the median correlation was only .42.

The following procedures are based on material described by Shinn (1989). If single-skill probes are to be used, the examiner should indicate to the student that the problems are all, for example, subtraction. If mixed probes are to be used, the examiner should instruct the student that several different types of problems appear on the sheet and that he or she should look carefully at each problem before answering. The examiner allows the student to work the problems for 2 minutes. To score the probe, the examiner counts the number of correct digits, not the number of correct problems.

Written Language

Written Language Syntax Test

Author:	S. R. Berry
Publisher:	Gallaudet College Press
	800 Florida Ave., NE
	Washington, DC 20002
Copyright:	1981

General Description. The *Written Language Syntax Test* (WLST) was designed to assess the ability of 10- to 17-year-old students to write using correct syntax. It is a group or individually administered test. A Screening Level test, which indicates what level of the WLST to administer, requires less than 20 minutes for administration. Levels I, II, and III of the WLST require less than 1 hour. Practice items are included, and the test is not timed. Results are in terms of mastery of objectives for instructional planning. Materials consist of the examiner's manual and student record books.

Description of Screening Level and Levels I, II, and III

Screening Level. This level consists of 10 items. The student is shown a picture and then reads a list of words presented randomly. The student's task is to put the words in the correct order and write a sentence using the words.

Levels I, II, and III. Level I begins with 34 items on which the student looks at a picture and reads a list of randomly presented words. The student is then to write a declarative sentence using these words. This section is followed by 6 items of the same format, except the student must use the words to write a question. On the last section of the test, the student is to look at several pictures and write a story about them. This section is scored based on the number of syntactically correct sentences the student writes.

Level II utilizes the same formats and includes 36 declarative sentences, 9 questions, and the free-write story.

Level III also utilizes the same formats and includes 36 declarative sentences, 12 questions, and the free-write story.

Each item is scored as correct or incorrect and compared with a list of the 69 objectives that are covered on the test. Each syntactically correct sentence on the free-write section of the test is also compared with this list of objectives. Results from the contrived and the free-write sections can be compared, and this information is used for instructional planning. Every objective is assessed at least three times on the contrived section.

Technical Adequacy

Field Testing. The sample consisted of 209 hearing-impaired students from four unspecified states. There were from 12 to 64 students per age level. There were 105 boys and 104 girls. Fifty-one of the students attended day programs and 158 were in residential programs; 65 were hard-of-hearing and 144 deaf; 194 used total communication and 15 used oral methods. No information was provided on race, ethnicity, socioeconomic level, or urban/rural residence.

Reliability. Internal consistency reliability coefficients (Spearman–Brown) ranged from .87 to .93 for the three levels of the test. KR-21 for the total test resulted in a correlation of .90.

Validity. With regard to content validity, it is stated in the manual that items were reviewed by linguists and teachers of hearing-impaired students. How many professionals participated and how they were selected are not indicated. It is stated that the skills tested are "common to a variety of curriculum guides and programs" (p. 7), but the curricula and programs reviewed are not given. No other information is given on validity.

Although the students must read the words, no reading level for the material is given. Reading level could confound results for the screener and the first section of each of the three levels of the test.

No information is given in the manual regarding how results from this test correlate with samples of students' spontaneous writing.

Conclusions. Because each objective is assessed at least three times on each level, results should be reliable for instructional planning. Whether the items (objectives) are educationally important requires more documentation, such as a list of the curricula from which they were selected. Teacher ratings might also be employed to provide further evidence of validity. Readability levels for each of the levels of the test should be given as well. With these limitations in mind, the results could be used to provide some general information for instructional planning.

Curriculum-Based Measurement

Marston (1989) summarized research with CBM for spelling for students with normal hearing. Test–retest reliability correlations range from .85 to .94. The retest intervals varied from 2 to 20 weeks. For parallel form reliability, correlations range from .72 to .96. The interscorer reliability coefficient was .91.

In terms of validity, results of CBM were found to correlate well with results of norm-referenced tests. CBM results also discriminated among learning disabled students, students in Chapter I, and regular education students. CBM assessment results for spelling were shown to increase throughout the school year as well.

The following procedures were described by Shinn (1989), except that use of the procedures with hearing-impaired students was not addressed. First, a list of words should be selected from those being used for instruction. The examiner should present the first word and then begin timing. Each word should be presented twice, and homonyms need to be given in a sentence. New words should be presented every 10 seconds for students in grades 1 through 3, and every 7 seconds for older students. Words are presented for a 2-minute period. For the last 3 seconds, the student is allowed to finish the last word; that is, no new words are presented. The number of words spelled correctly within the 2-minute period are then counted.

Fortunately, the use of CBM with hearing-impaired students to assess spelling does not require as many modifications as CBM for reading does. It may be, however, that more than a 2-minute sample may provide a better measure of spelling for hearing-impaired students, particularly if the words are presented using sign. Research is needed on this issue.

Oral and Manual Communication

Battelle Developmental Inventory (Communication Domain)

Because a review of this measure appears in Chapter 4, only a description of the Communication Domain is presented here.

Description of Test Items.   Although it is suggested in the manual that this test can be adapted for handicapped children, a number of items on the Communication Domain have no adaptations for hearing-impaired children, and some adaptations that are given seem inappropriate. The first 27 items tap receptive skills, 8 of which are not appropriate for hearing-impaired children and have no adaptations. For example, an item at the 3- to 4-year level requires the child to clap loudly and to clap softly. On another item, the child is asked to indicate which word in a word pair is a real word. The adaptation suggested is to make sure the child is looking at the examiner when the stimuli are presented. One word pair is "apple-abble." This would be difficult for a good speech reader to discriminate. If a child did not read speech, would the items be finger spelled? If so, this would change the task. The remaining 32 items tap expressive skills. If a student knows sign well, these items may be appropriate. The directions, however, are lengthy and confusing on some items. The number of items per age level for receptive skills ranges from 2 to 5; the number of items per age level for expressive skills ranges from 2 to 6. Hence, having to eliminate items that are inappropriate for hearing-impaired children would not leave many items on which to base a score.

Conclusions. Given the limited number of items on the Communication Domain, and the fact that a number of items cannot be used with hearing-impaired students without changing the task, this does not seem to be a very useful measure for use with hearing-impaired students. The expressive skills section could provide some useful information for programming for children who can communicate well.

Carolina Picture Vocabulary Test

Authors:	T. L. Layton & D. W. Holmes
Publisher:	PRO-ED
	8700 Shoal Creek Blvd.
	Austin, TX 78758-6897
Copyright:	1985

General Description. The *Carolina Picture Vocabulary Test* (CPVT) was designed for hearing-impaired students ages 2-8 to 18 who use sign as their primary method of communication. The test does not discriminate, however, beyond 12 years of age, and it is suggested in the manual that because few children below age 5 were in the standardization sample, results are tentative for these children. The CPVT assesses receptive vocabulary and must be individually administered. The single form of the test takes about 10 to 15 minutes to administer. There are no practice items. Results can be expressed as age equivalents, percentiles, or standard scores (mean = 50, SD = 10). Materials consist of the examiner's manual, the score sheet, and a flip book of illustrations.

Description of the CPVT. The test consists of 130 items. The examiner presents a sign, and the student is to point to one of four pictures to indicate an answer. The CPVT was standardized with examiners who used only sign, not simultaneous sign and vocalization. Hence, norm-referenced results are meaningful only if the items are presented using sign alone. Examples of early items include "hat" and "insect" and later items include "noon" and "curious."

On the examiner's page of the illustration book, a black-and-white stop-action photo shows how to produce each sign. In the manual (p. 23), it is suggested that "the CPVT requires no special training on the part of the examiner." This does not appear to be the case; even with considerable practice, an examiner who is unfamiliar with sign language is apt to be awkward. This situation could confound results, especially because reliability data were collected using only examiners experienced in signing. Also, it is stated in the manual (p. 23) that the "examiner should not reveal any tension or uncertainty about the testing procedure, otherwise he may encounter resistance and negativism from the child." This appearance of comfort would be difficult to achieve if the examiner did not have experience signing.

Technical Adequacy

Standardization. The standardization sample consisted of children 2-8 to 18 years of age. The number of subjects per age level ranged from 18 to 75. (Because the CPVT did not discriminate among children above the age of 12, the norm tables do not go above age 12.) The sample was fairly representative in terms of geographic region, with the Southern region somewhat overrepresented and the Northeast somewhat underrepresented. Data are presented on occupational level for parents, but factory workers and farmers were overrepresented. Approximately half of the sample was girls. The sample seemed to be representative in terms of race, but data on ethnicity were not given. All students were receiving sign training; 53.3% were in residential schools and 46.6% were in day schools.

In terms of hearing loss, most had a loss greater than 70 dB in the better ear and 97.3% had acquired the loss prior to 24 months of age. Also, 70.6% had been signing for more than 4 years.

Reliability. For one test–retest study, the mean retest interval was 31 days ($n = 30$), and the correlation was .86. For a second study ($n = 11$), the retest interval was at least 2 weeks, and the correlation was .99.

Internal consistency reliability coefficients by age were greater than .85, except at ages 6, 8, 10, and 11.

Standard error of measurement data are given by age level.

Validity. Items were selected that had accepted ASL or Signing Exact English sign equivalents and that could be represented in pictures. Nouns, verbs, and adjectives were included. The pictures represent multiethnic backgrounds and represent the sexes equally. Item analysis was carried out on a field test version and the data used to rank the items.

The CPVT correlated .05 to .50 with the WISC-R Performance Scale and –.03 to .83 with the *Hiskey–Nebraska Test of Learning Aptitude.* The CPVT correlated .75 with the *Test of Auditory Comprehension of Language* for oral hearing-impaired students, and .81 for a sample of hearing-impaired students using total communication.

In terms of construct validity, scores were shown to increase with age to age 12.

Conclusions. The authors should be commended for addressing most of the important aspects of technical adequacy. Nonetheless, the CPVT could be improved by including a larger number of students at each age level and by giving data on urban/rural residence and ethnicity of the sample. A more geographically representative sample would be useful. Because most hearing-impaired students are in regular education programs, a larger number of these children in the sample would be better, or separate norm tables added if necessary. Norm tables for children using total communication would be helpful as well.

The reliability information presented for the CPVT is impressive, although test–retest data by age level would be preferable.

In future work with the scale, additional studies on validity would seem to be beneficial.

If the concerns noted in the review are considered, the CPVT would seem to provide useful norm-referenced information on the overall development of receptive sign vocabulary, especially if administered by an examiner having at least some familiarity with the use of sign language.

Central Institute for the Deaf Phonetic Inventory

Author:	J. S. Moog
Publisher:	Central Institute for the Deaf
	818 South Euclid
	St. Louis, MO 63110
Copyright:	1988

General Description. The *Central Institute for the Deaf Phonetic Inventory* was designed to measure speech skills of students with severe and profound hearing impairments for the purpose of measuring progress and as an aid in program planning. No age limits are noted in the manual. The individually administered inventory takes about 30 minutes. No practice items are needed, and there is one form of the inventory. Results are expressed in terms of the percentage correct for each of the six phonetic areas assessed and for overall performance. Materials consist of the examiner's manual, a set of 165 cue cards, and a rating form.

Description of the Inventory. On the *Phonetic Inventory,* the examinee's ability to produce phonemes is assessed at the syllable level to lessen confounding results by factors such as context and familiarity of speaker with the material spoken. Both the suprasegmental aspects of speech (e.g., voice quality and intensity) and the ability to produce phonemes are assessed. One section covers the suprasegmental aspects of speech and five tap phonetic aspects.

Each stimulus is modeled by the examiner, and the student is to imitate. The written cue cards are used as needed to provide additional help to the student in determining what he or she is to produce. Under the Suprasegmental section, vocal duration, intensity, pitch, quality, and breath control are considered. The Vowels and Diphthongs section contains 16 items that are assessed in terms of single syllable, repetitive syllable, and alternating syllable production. Initial Consonants has two sections: Single and Repetitive, and Alternating Vowels. This subtest is made up of 22 items assessed in terms of single syllables, repetitive syllables, and alternating syllable production. The Final Consonants section has 27 items assessed in terms of single and repetitive syllable production. Alternating Consonants has 20 items assessed in terms of single and repetitive syllable production.

Detailed instructions are given for scoring each item to aid the examiner in knowing what to consider for scoring the productions.

In the manual, the author cautions that if results are used to establish instructional objectives, it should be kept in mind that the *Phonetic Inventory* assesses skills only at the syllable level. Instruction is needed that includes production of words, sentences, and connected speech. Also, it is suggested that results may be useful for assessing effects of assistive devices (e.g., hearing aids, tactile aids), as well as for assessing progress in speech acquisition.

Technical Adequacy

Reliability. A correlation of .93 is reported for test–retest reliability ($n = 20$), but no interval is reported.

Validity. The *Phonetic Inventory* sequence corresponds to that described by Ling (1976).

Conclusions. The *Phonetic Inventory* could be improved by the addition of the interval used to assess test–retest reliability and the provision of additional information on validity. For example, it would be interesting to know how well performance on this measure corresponds to performance on the *CID Picture SPINE* and other procedures used to assess intelligibility. Use of the *Phonetic Inventory* could be useful in program planning as it is quite comprehensive. Each skill could be assessed three times to ensure reliability of the results.

Central Institute for the Deaf Picture SPINE

Authors:	R. Monsen, J. S. Moog, & A. E. Geers
Publisher:	Central Institute for the Deaf
	818 South Euclid
	St. Louis, MO 63110
Copyright:	1988

General Description.   The *Central Institute for the Deaf Picture SPINE* was designed to assess how well the speech of a severely or profoundly hearing-impaired child or adolescent can be understood by a listener when verbal context is not presented. The individually administered test takes about 20 to 30 minutes. There are practice items to ensure that the student knows the desired label for each picture. Results are expressed in terms of a global rating of intelligibility based on percentage correct. The materials consist of the examiner's manual, a response form, and 300 picture cards.

Description of SPINE Items.   Speech intelligibility is assessed without confounding results with reading, as skills are assessed by having a student label pictures. The student selects a picture card from a deck of cards and labels it. The examiner writes the word that he or she thinks the student said on the response form. The student must label the picture without signing.

Three hundred cards (three copies of 100 different pictures) are organized into four sets. One set of cards assesses production of bilabial initial consonants, another set taps lingua-velar initial sounds, another taps lingua-alveolar initial consonants, and the fourth taps lingua-palatal and w initial sounds. Each set has two parts. One part of a set is light colored on the back; these are the practice cards used to ensure that the student can label the picture correctly. The other part of the set is dark colored on the back and consists of two copies of pictures of each word to be tested. Each set taps "phonemically confusable words" (p. 11). The cards are presented randomly, with the deck of cards face down on the table, so that the examiner is unaware of the picture the student is labeling. When using the practice set of cards, if a student is unable to label more than five cards, the test should be discontinued as it will not yield valid results.

Technical Adequacy

Standardization. In the manual, it is stated that norms for the *Picture SPINE* are not yet available, suggesting that norms will be developed.

Reliability. Interrater reliability was evaluated using 20 profoundly hearing-impaired children from 6 to 13 years of age. Each child was tested by one examiner and retested by another. The resulting correlation was .96. Within 4 weeks, the children were videotaped producing 10 simple sentences. Monsen's (1981) procedure was used, and 12 listeners wrote down what they thought the children said. An average intelligibility score was computed for each child and correlated with results of the *Picture SPINE.* The correlation with scores was .96 for Examiner A and .91 for Examiner B. Neither test–retest reliability nor standard error of measurement was addressed.

Validity. Words were selected for *Picture SPINE* that could be dipicted so as to elicit consistently the desired response. Only words that were within the vocabulary of young hearing-impaired students were used. The *Picture SPINE* was field tested with students from the Central Institute for the Deaf and St. Joseph Institute. Results indicated that the words were known by most students as young as age 7. Also, the words were tested at the Illinois School for the Deaf and found to be appropriate for children in programs using total communication. All words exemplified phonemic contrasts shown by Monsen (1978) to be good predictors of speech intelligibility.

Conclusions. Normative data are needed to support the global ratings that result. Without this information, the results are questionable. Test–retest information is needed also. Further references would be helpful to support the importance of the phonemic contrasts assessed. Also, correlation of performance on the *Picture SPINE* with degree of hearing loss would be useful validity information. If adequate data were available on the technical adequacy of this measure, *Picture SPINE* would seem to be a useful norm-referenced test for assessing speech intelligibility. It appears to be well conceived and carefully structured.

Grammatical Analysis of Elicited Language

Pre-Sentence Level (P), Simple Sentence Level (S), and Complex Sentence Level (C)

Authors: (P) J. S. Moog, V. J. Kozak, & A. E. Geers
                (S) J. S. Moog & A. E. Geers
                (C) J. S. Moog & A. E. Geers
Publisher: Central Institute for the Deaf
                818 South Euclid Ave.
                St. Louis, MO 63110
Copyright: (P) 1983; (S) 1985; (C) 1980

General Description. The three levels of the *Grammatical Analysis of Elicited Language* (GAEL) were designed to test receptive and expressive grammar skills for either spoken or signed English. The GAEL Pre-Sentence Level (GAEL-P) was designed for hearing-impaired students from 3 to 6 years of age; the GAEL Simple Sentence Level (GAEL-S) was designed for hearing-impaired students from 5 to 9 years of age and normally hearing students from 2½ to 5 years of age; the GAEL Complex Sentence Level (GAEL-C) was designed for hearing-impaired students 8 to 12 years of age and normally hearing children from 3 to 6 years old. The tests are individually administered and take approximately 2½ hours to administer. The GAEL-P, however, may take considerably less time, especially for children who are not yet understanding or producing words, and for whom only the Readiness Section would be appropriate. Several practice items are included for each section as the task requirements change. There is one form for each test.

Results for GAEL-P are expressed in terms of percentiles for overall performance and for each of the three sections of the test. For program planning, each skill is evaluated in terms of the student's ability to comprehend the task, demonstrate the task with a prompt, and imitate the task. For the GAEL-S, overall performance can be described as a percentile or Language Quotient (mean = 100, *SD* = 15). For program planning, mastery points are given for each grammatical category to evaluate skills in terms of mastery, emerging skill level, or barely developed skill. For the GAEL-C, overall performance can be described in terms of a percentile or a standard score (mean = 100, *SD* = 15). Results for each grammatical category can be described in terms of percentiles or standard scores (mean = 10, *SD* = 3). For accurate scoring, and to obtain comprehensive information from the test, the testing session should be audiotaped (if the child uses oral communication) or videotaped (if the child uses manual communication). Materials for each test include an examiner's manual, a score sheet, numerous toys, and a sheet for transcribing the child's deviant responses from the tape of the session.

Description of the Tests. For all levels of the test, games and activities are used to elicit target responses. Activities include playing with the toys, opening boxes, labeling and describing objects, and telling stories. First, a "prompted production" (prompted by the use of toys and the examiner's activity) of a phrase or sentence is attempted. The examiner then says or signs the target response, and the child is to imitate for the "imitated production." The imitated production is included whether or not the "prompted production" is correct. For the GAEL-P, a child's comprehension skills also are assessed for each item.

The GAEL-P is made up of three sections: Readiness, Single Words, and Word Combinations. Each skill is assessed in terms of comprehension, prompted production, and imitated production in order to aid in program planning. The Readiness Section has 6 items to tap attention and readiness for learning. Examples include response to speech and imitation of some sounds, syllables, or words. Single Words has 30 items ranging from "ball" to "horse." Word Combinations consists of 13 items for which one to three critical elements are scored. Examples include (for comprehension) "Make Mommy walk" and (for expression) "Mommy walked." Both receptive and expressive skills are included.

GAEL-S items are scored for prompted production and imitated production, as well as for mastered, emerging, or barely developed skill. Ninety-four items assess expressive skills using simple sentence structures. Components assessed are 56 articles, 59 modifiers, 47 pronouns, 58 subject nouns, 56 object nouns, 15 wh- questions, 54 verbs, 50 verb inflections, 42 copula inflections, 29 prepositions, and 14 negations.

GAEL-C items are scored for both prompted production and imitated production. Sixteen grammatical categories are assessed. Included are 96 articles, 29 noun modifiers, 44 subject nouns, 109 object nouns, 28 noun plurals, 87 personal pronouns, 20 indefinite and reflexive pronouns, 33 conjunctions, 58 auxiliary verbs, 88 first clause verbs, 27 "other" verbs, 31 verb inflections, 25 infinitives and participles, 46 prepositions, 21 negations, and 21 wh- questions. Also included are 88 sentence point items, which are those responses that are grammatically correct and complete sentences, but that differ from the target sentence. Even though a grammatical element may have been left out, the sentence is given credit.

Technical Adequacy

Standardization. The GAEL-P was standardized on 150 hearing-impaired children enrolled in oral programs for hearing-impaired students. The age range was 3-0 to 5-11. The programs were from "across the country" (p. 59) and all used an oral approach. The 17 programs were from the four geographic areas used in the U.S. census data, but, without percentages of students by region, it is not possible to determine whether the sample was geographically representative. No audiometric data were provided, as reliable audiograms had not been obtained for some of the sample. No additional information regarding the hearing status of the children is provided (e.g., age at onset or etiology). There were 25 children at each 6-month age level. No data are given for race, ethnicity, sex, socioeconomic level, or urban/rural residence.

Currently, no norms are available for hearing-impaired children in programs using a form of manual communication. It is suggested in the manual that the test can be used with children in total communication programs, and responses recorded as signed, spoken, or a combination. The comparison group for norm-referenced interpretation, however, consists only of children from oral programs. It is suggested that the test could be administered twice, once to assess spoken skills and once for signs. For instructional planning, the results could be useful with these children, but norm-referenced interpretation seems inappropriate without further data to clarify whether children using manual communication would perform differently from those in oral programs.

The GAEL-S was standardized on three groups of hearing-impaired children and a group of normally hearing children. All hearing-impaired children had hearing losses that were congenital or acquired in infancy, had received early intervention since age 3, and had no additional handicaps. One of the hearing-impaired groups was made up of 163 severely hearing-impaired children in oral programs. Their ages ranged from 4-0 to 8-11, and hearing levels were between 70 and 95 dB HL. Some children were mainstreamed, whereas others were in special classes. A second group consisted of 160 children between 5-0 and 9-11. Their hearing levels were greater than 95 dB, and they were enrolled in oral programs. The third group consisted of 177 children from 5-0 to 8-11. Their better ear speech frequency averages equaled or exceeded 90 dB HL. These children were enrolled in total communication programs. The three samples were selected from programs around the country. The percentages of children from each geographic region were not given, making it impossible to determine whether the samples were geographically representative. The number of children per age level group ranged from 30 to 49. No information was provided on sex, race, ethnicity, socioeconomic level, or urban/rural residence of the children.

The normally hearing group consisted of 200 children from preschools and day care centers in St. Louis, Missouri. Their ages ranged from 2-6 to 4-11, and there were 40 children per level. It is stated in the manual that "a wide diversity of economic communities" (p. 95) were represented. No other demographic information is given.

The GAEL-C was standardized on one hearing-impaired and one normally hearing group. The first group consisted of 270 hearing-impaired students from programs throughout the country. Their age range was 8-0 to 11-11, with from 25 to 45 students per age level. The hearing level of the severely hearing-impaired students was from 70 to 95 dB HL, and for profoundly deaf students was greater than 95 dB HL. All were educated using oral methods of communication and acquired their hearing loss before age 2. They did not have additional handicaps. No additional demographic information is provided. The normally hearing group included 240 children ranging in age from 3-0 to 5-11. They attended preschools or day care centers in St. Louis and "represented a wide diversity of economic communities" (p. 79). There were 40 students per age level. No additional demographic information was provided.

Reliability. For the GAEL-P, test–retest reliability correlations for 20 hearing-impaired students (ages 3-0 to 5-11) with a 1-month interval were .97 (comprehension), .95 (prompted production), and .93 (imitated production). No other reliability data are given.

For the GAEL-S, interrater reliability on transcriptions from tapes was evaluated. Correlations for students using total communication ranged from .77 to .99. For students in oral programs, correlations ranged from .69 to 1.00. Test–retest reliability was evaluated using a 2-month interval. The correlations for a normally hearing group were .88 (prompted) and .93 (imitated); for oral hearing-impaired students, correlations were .96 (prompted) and .96 (imitated); and for students using total communication, the correlations were .94 (prompted) and .91 (imitated).

For the GAEL-C, test–retest reliability correlations for 26 normally hearing students (ages 3-5 to 5-8) were .82 (prompted) and .81 (imitated) with a 1-month interval. For 20 hearing-impaired students (ages 8-2 to 11-11), correlations were .96 (prompted) and .95 (imitated) with a 2-month interval. No other reliability data are given.

Validity. The appealing nature of the test materials should aid in obtaining good cooperation and performance from children. This is an important consideration when attempting to elicit language and should aid in obtaining valid results.

GAEL-P scores were shown to increase with age. Results were correlated with results from the *Scales of Early Communication Skills for Hearing Impaired,* rated by the teachers of 20 hearing-impaired children. The correlation was .87 for comprehension, .85 for prompted production, and .80 for imitated production. No information is given to justify item selection, and no further validity data are provided.

For the GAEL-S, scores generally show an increasing trend with age. In terms of difficulty of grammatical structures assessed, the three groups of hearing-impaired children showed a similar performance profile on the grammatical categories. This profile was different from that of hearing children.

Concurrent validity was examined with 37 hearing-impaired children educated in an oral program. When compared with results of the *Scales of Early Communication Skills for Hearing Impaired Children,* a correlation of .81 was obtained for prompted and .83 for imitated production; with the

Northwestern Syntax Screening Test–Expressive, correlations were .83 for prompted and .81 for imitated productions; and with GAEL-C, correlations were .87 for prompted and .84 for imitated productions.

The language structures employed were based mainly on those included in the *Lee Developmental Sentence Scoring* (Lee, 1974) and the *Language Sampling and Analysis* (Tyack & Gottsleben, 1974). No further information on item selection is given.

In terms of diagnostic validity, a study was carried out with 15 hearing children diagnosed as having a language delay and placed in a language development preschool program. These children scored below average on both prompted and imitated productions of the test.

For the GAEL-C, the structures also were based on those used by Lee (1974) and Tyack and Gottsleben (1974). In terms of relative difficulty of the structures assessed, it was found that the structures were much more homogeneous in difficulty for hearing children than for hearing-impaired children.

Percentage correct scores show an increase with age for normally hearing children and for severely and profoundly hearing-impaired children.

To examine concurrent validity, 22 normally hearing children (learning disabled first graders) were given the GAEL-C and the *Carrow Elicited Language Inventory.* Correlations were .81 for prompted and .83 for imitated productions. In addition, 37 profoundly hearing-impaired children were used to compare the GAEL-C with several other measures. Correlations for receptive skills were as follows: *Assessment of Children's Language Comprehension* .46 (prompted), .43 (imitated); *Vocabulary Comprehension Scale* .68 (prompted), .65 (imitated); *Illinois Test of Psycholinguistic Ability* .56 (prompted), .49 (imitated); *Northwestern Syntax Screening Test* .45 (prompted), .47 (imitated); and *Peabody Picture Vocabulary Test* .57 (prompted), .56 (imitated). For expressive skills, correlations were as follows: *Northwestern Syntax Screening Test* .84 (prompted), .83 (imitated); and GAEL-S .87 (prompted), .84 (imitated).

Conclusions.   In terms of standardization, all three levels of the GAEL need more children at the various age levels, as well as descriptions of the representativeness of the samples according to sex, geographic distribution, socioeconomic level, race, ethnicity, and urban/rural residence. More information on hearing loss of the children for the GAEL-P and age at onset for the GAEL-S is desirable. Norms for children educated in programs using manual forms of communication are needed for the GAEL-P and the GAEL-C.

For reliability for the GAEL-P, data are needed for test–retest by age with a 2- to 4-week interval, internal consistency, and standard error of measurement. For the GAEL-S and GAEL-C, data on test–retest would be more useful if provided by age level. Data on internal consistency and standard error of measurement are needed as well.

All of the GAEL tests could be improved by the addition of more detailed information on item selection, comparisons with results of intelligence and achievement tests for construct validity, and studies on diagnostic validity. Predictive validity for the GAEL-P would be useful as well.

The GAEL tests certainly are comprehensive and seem to cover critical elements of grammar. The appealing nature of the tests is another strong feature. Sample reports at the ends of the manuals are carefully written and provide useful examples of how to interpret the results. The sample reports do not interpret results beyond what the the GAEL tests assess, and they avoid the use of jargon. At least at some age levels, the GAEL tests allow for comparisons between hearing students and hearing-impaired students. The provision of norms for hearing-impaired students using manual communication for the GAEL-S test definitely is advantageous. Further research on the technical adequacy aspects of the GAEL tests could make them very strong measures for norm-referenced interpretation, as well as for program planning.

Rhode Island Test of Language Structure

Authors: E. Engen and T. Engen
Publisher: PRO-ED
              8700 Shoal Creek Blvd.
              Austin, TX 78758-6897
Copyright: 1983

General Description. The *Rhode Island Test of Language Structure* (RITLS) is designed to assess comprehension of syntax for normally hearing children ages 3½ to 6, and hearing-impaired students ages 5 to 17+. The test is individually administered and takes about 25 to 35 minutes. If the stimulus sentences are signed, approximately 50 to 70 minutes are needed for administration. There is one form of the test. There are four practice items. For norm-referenced interpretation, results are expressed as either a percentile or a standard score (mean = 50, *SD* = 10). For instructional planning, results are examined for performance on the various sentence types assessed. The materials consist of the examiner's manual, a record book, a sheet for analysis of performance on the various sentence types, and an illustration book.

Description of Test Items. The RITLS consists of 100 items, with five examples of each of the 20 sentence types assessed. Sentence types include 5 simple sentence patterns, imperatives, negatives, passives (reversible and nonreversible), dative sentences, expanded simple sentences, adverbial clauses (main and subordinate), relative clauses (medial and final), conjunctions, deleted sentences, noninitial subjects, embedded imperatives, and complements (subject and object). The stimulus sentences are presented either orally or by using simultaneous signed and spoken English. The child responds by pointing to one of three black-and-white pictures. The pictures are multiracial and multiethnic. They represent opposing interpretations of the stimulus sentence, when possible, using the same figures, so as to more accurately assess knowledge of syntax.

The authors caution that interpretation for program planning should not be done in terms of mastery, "but in terms of development along a continuum" (p. 51), because a precise sequence of development for these skills has not been determined at this point.

Technical Adequacy

Standardization. There were 364 hearing-impaired children in the sample. Although audiometric information was lacking for 3% of the children, hearing losses for the remaining were moderate (3%), moderate–severe (7%), severe (13%), severe–profound (31%), and profound (43%). Information was missing on the type of loss for 40% of the children, but for the remaining children the loss was usually sensorineural. Etiology was not available for almost half of the children. For those for whom etiology was known, loss was due to genetic causes (16%), rubella (13%), infectious disease including meningitis (14%), and birth complications (8%). Age at onset was uncertain for 28% and was usually congenital for the remaining children. For 70% of the children, no other family member suffered hearing impairment. Of the sample, 51% were boys. All children attended schools for hearing-impaired students, and RITLS was administered to these children using simultaneous signed and spoken English. The sample was not geographically representative: 15% were from Massachusetts, 25% from Rhode Island, 13% from New Jersey, and 47% from North Carolina. No information is given to describe the sample in terms of race, ethnicity, socioeconomic level, or urban/rural residence. The number of subjects per age groupings, used in developing the tables, ranged from 27 to 107.

The sample of hearing children consisted of 283 subjects from Rhode Island. They were about half boys and were from public and private rural, urban, and suburban schools. No percentages were given for the categories. It is stated in the manual that they represented "all ethnic groups in the state and a range of socioeconomic groups" (p. 33). Again, no percentages were given to provide a precise description of the demographic characteristics of the children.

Reliability. Internal consistency on an earlier version of RITLS resulted in a correlation of .91. Test–retest reliability on the earlier version ($n = 49$) was .62. This correlation is too low, and the length of the retest interval was not given. No standard error of measurement information is given.

Validity. In terms of rationale for item selection, the vocabulary was selected so as not to confound the assessment of syntax. Vocabulary was selected that would "be appropriate for the youngest group of hearing-impaired children who were to be tested" (p. 12). This was accomplished by compiling a list of words that was evaluated by the Lower School teachers at Rhode Island School for the Deaf. The teachers evaluated the words for their appropriateness and ease in signing. Those words judged appropriate were compared to Guilfoyle and Silverman's (1975) list of vocabulary norms for deaf children, and norms appropriate for 8-year-olds were used. Vocabulary was used only if the word had a commonly understood sign and could be illustrated in an unambiguous drawing. The sentence structures were selected primarily based on R. Brown's (1973) major processes of English sentence construction and Clark and Clark's (1977) description of sentence structure.

Based on results of pilot testing, item analysis was carried out to aid in item selection. Item difficulties, children's age related to item difficulty, content of the domain tested, and the ability of items to discriminate among children were considered. No detailed data on the item analysis are presented in the manual, however.

Because the authors felt that language comprehension is not measured by aptitude and achievement tests, they did not evaluate construct validity by comparing RITLS results with these tests. They also felt that no other tests measured skills assessed by RITLS, so they provided no information on concurrent validity.

The authors suggest that the following results support the construct validity of RITLS. Hearing-impaired children have difficulty with passive sentence structures on RITLS, a finding consistent with research on hearing-impaired children. Hearing-impaired children do less well on RITLS than hearing children. The mean number of errors by normally hearing children decreases with age. The difficulty of the sentences is consistent with theoretical predictions of research in linguistics.

Conclusions. Quite an extensive description of the hearing problems of the hearing-impaired children in the sample is provided. Unfortunately, this is not the case with many other tests standardized on hearing-impaired children. More children per age are needed for the test, however, as is more detail on the demographic characteristics of the hearing-impaired children (e.g., socioeconomic status, urban/rural residence, race, and ethnicity). A geographically representative sample would be more useful.

Insufficient information is given on the hearing sample, and a geographically representative sample is needed with a sufficient number of children per age level.

Test–retest data by age, with about a 2- to 4-week interval, also are needed on the current version of the test, along with information on standard error of measurement by age.

The validity information is the most impressive psychometric property of the RITLS. Studies should be carried out to examine concurrent validity (e.g., with the GAEL) and to compare results with aptitude and achievement measures. It seems that some relationship should exist between the RITLS and these measures.

The RITLS was carefully designed and would seem to provide useful general information for program planning. Having five items for each sentence structure assessed should result in reliable information for this purpose. The test seems to warrant further research in order to establish its technical adequacy.

Scales of Early Communication Skills

Authors: J. S. Moog & A. E. Geers
Publisher: Central Institute for the Deaf
              818 South Euclid Ave.
              St. Louis, MO 63110
Copyright: 1975

General Description. The *Scales of Early Communication Skills* (SECS) were designed to assess receptive and expressive language skills for children from 2 to 9 years of age. The SECS is completed by the classroom teacher. Results are expressed as percentiles or standard scores (mean = 50, *SD* = 10). Materials consist of the examiner's manual and a record book.

Description of the SECS Items. The SECS is made up of general statements to describe receptive and expressive skills. Each item is rated in terms of whether the child demonstrates the skill, demonstrates that the skill is emerging, or does not demonstrate the skill. The SECS has four sections. The Receptive Language Skills section consists of 10 items, ranging from responding to verbalization to engaging in a conversation on a topic. The Expressive Language Skills section consists of 18 items, ranging from "Vocalizing when expected to imitate speech" to spontaneously using sentences of eight or more words. For these first two sections, each item is rated for demonstration during a structured teaching situation and also for use in more naturally occurring situations. The final two sections, Nonverbal Receptive Skills and Nonverbal Expressive Skills, each has 3 items. Skills on these last two sections range from responding to simple gesture to using gestures to relate sequential events.

Technical Adequacy

Standardization.   The SECS was standardized on 372 children ages 2-0 to 8-11. The children were from 14 oral programs, and 35 to 66 children were tested per age level. The children did not have other handicaps of educational significance. The mean hearing level in the better ear ranged from 90.86 to 98.51. No information is given on socioeconomic level, geographic distribution, sex, race, or ethnicity.

Reliability.   Interrater reliability was assessed for 31 children, ages 4 to 8, from the Central Institute for the Deaf. The following correlations were obtained: Receptive (structured) .76, Receptive (natural setting) .81, Expressive (structured) .91, and Expressive (natural setting) .86. No data are presented on test–retest reliability or standard error of measurement.

Validity.   Validity is not addressed in the manual.

Conclusions.   A more representative and larger sample of children is needed for standardization. Test–retest reliability needs to be examined, and various types of validity should be addressed. Given the data currently available on SECS, the GAEL and the *Teacher Assessment of Grammatical Structures* seem to be much more useful than the SECS.

Teacher Assessment of Grammatical Structures

Authors: J. S. Moog & V. J. Kozak
Publisher: Central Institute for the Deaf
               818 South Euclid
               St. Louis, MO 63110
Copyright: 1983

General Description.   The *Teacher Assessment of Grammatical Structures* (TAGS) is a criterion-referenced measure designed to assess receptive and expressive syntax of hearing-impaired children who use signed or spoken English, or children with normal hearing who have difficulty in this area. The TAGS is a rating form completed by the child's teacher for the purpose of planning individual programs. There is one form of the test. Results for each syntactic structure are expressed in terms of the skill's being acquired, emerging, or not demonstrated. Furthermore, each syntactic structure is assessed at four levels: comprehension (child demonstrates understanding of the structure), imitated production (teacher models structure and child imitates), prompted production (a situation or the teacher prompts child to use the structure), and spontaneous production (child independently produces the structure). The TAGS does not cover all possible syntactic structures and, hence, should serve as a guide for instruction rather than as a criterion-referenced test indicating all skills to be taught. This is noted in the manual. Materials consist of the examiner's manual and a rating form. The TAGS is considered the teacher counterpart to the GAEL tests.

Description of TAGS Tests.   A child's understanding and use of grammar can be assessed using speech, sign, finger spelling, or any combination. TAGS was designed to be used in place of recording spontaneous language samples. The authors felt that observing a child's use of language was "more efficient and more practical than the formal procedures of sampling, recording, and laboriously analyzing a spontaneous language sample containing a sufficient number of utterances to make judgments about a child's language skills" (p. 14). There are three levels of the TAGS. The level of the test used should be based primarily on the child's syntactic development.

The TAGS-P is the pre-sentence level designed for a child who uses words, phrases, or three-word sentences. This is the only level of TAGS at which comprehension of the syntactic structures is rated. The authors suggest that this level is most appropriate for children who are younger than 5 years of age. The TAGS-P consists of 6 items to assess single words (ranging from any 3 words to 5 prepositions), 10 items for 2-word combinations, 16 items for 3-word combinations, 5 types of wh- questions, 13 items for pronouns, and 4 items to assess tense markers (e.g., simple past).

The TAGS-S is the simple sentence level designed for children using sentences of 4 or more words. The authors have found that this level seems to be appropriate for children 5 to 9 years old. The TAG-S consists of 23 items to assess use of noun modifiers, 17 for pronouns, 9 for prepositions, 8 for adverbs, 19 for verbs, and 12 for questions.

The TAGS-C is designed for children using complex sentences and seems to be appropriate for children over 8 years of age. The TAGS-C consists of 5 items that assess use of nouns, 16 for pronouns, 19 for verb inflections, 11 for secondary verbs, 18 for conjunctions, and 13 for questions.

The TAGS recording form can be used repeatedly to record a child's progress over time if different colored pencils are used.

Technical Adequacy

Field Testing.   No information is presented on field test trials.

Reliability.   To aid the teacher in obtaining reliable information for program planning, each skill could be observed by the teacher three or more times prior to rating. The number of observations to be used prior to rating is not addressed in the manual, but it is suggested that the first ratings may be estimates that should be refined through further observations.

Validity. The only information presented regarding item selection is that the TAGS was developed out of 10 years of experience with test development at the Central Institute for the Deaf. The first instrument the staff developed was the *Scales of Early Communication Skills for Hearing-Impaired Children.* Based on this experience, and use of other standardized language tests, they listed the skills in what they thought would be the order of development. They correctly note that the exact sequence for development of these skills is yet to be determined.

Conclusions. The TAGS seems to have been carefully developed and interpreted. It is a comprehensive measure and should provide reliable results if teachers use at least three observations for rating skills. It would require a considerable amount of a teacher's time to reliably complete the measure, but appears to be worth the effort in order to systematically plan instruction in this area. Teachers not familiar with the various grammatical structures assessed need to read the manual carefully. Each skill is clearly explained in detail, and examples are given. In some cases, especially if the TAGS-C is used, this reading could be rather time-consuming.

It would have been helpful for the authors to describe how information from teachers who used the scale was used in the development of the TAGS. Further information to justify item selection is needed, such as references to the literature on syntax development, the relationship of the TAGS to curricula or procedures used in classrooms, and perhaps even a comparison with the results of the corresponding GAEL test.

Test of Expressive Language Ability

Author: G. O. Bunch
Publisher: G. B. Services, Ltd.
                100 Waterton Rd.
                Weston, Ontario
                Canada M9P 2R3
Copyright: 1981

General Description. The *Test of Expressive Language Ability* (TEXLA) was designed to assess expressive grammar skills in hearing-impaired students ages 7 through 12. The long or short form of the test is individually administered, and the long form takes about 30 minutes. There are two practice items and no timed items. Normative results are expressed as either percentiles or stanines. For program planning, performance on items can be examined to determine whether students recognize when particular grammatical rules are needed (e.g., plural noun) and then apply them. Materials consist of a record sheet and the examiner's manual, which contains the illustrations.

Description of the Items. The long form of TEXLA is made up of 90 items and the short form of 60. For each item, a student is shown one to three illustrations, followed by one or two descriptive sentences. A word is missing from one sentence, and the student's task is to write in the missing word. Each grammatical principle is tested by 4 to 10 items on the long form, and by 3 to 6 items on the short form. Spelling errors are not considered errors as long as the examiner can determine that the student understood the principle tested. The number of items and principles tested follow. (The first number is for the long form and the number in parentheses for the short form.) There are 5 (4) plural nouns /s/, 5 (4) plural nouns /es/, 10 (6) pronouns, 10 (6) descriptive adjectives, 5 (4) comparative adjectives, 5 (4) superlative adjectives, 10 (6) pronouns, 10 (6) past tenses, 10 (6) future tenses, 5 (3) present progressive singulars, 5 (3) present progressive plurals, 6 (4) items for "to be," and 4 (4) items for "to have."

Technical Adequacy

Standardization. The hearing-impaired sample consisted of 65 Canadian students ages 7 through 12. There were from 7 to 14 students per age level. All students were attending residential schools. No data are presented for sex, geographic distribution, race, ethnicity, socioeconomic level, or urban/rural residence. All children were prelingually deaf, and none had additional handicaps. One student had a hearing loss of 36 to 55 dB, 2 of 56 to 70 dB, 13 of 71 to 90 dB, and 49 of 91 dB or more.

For comparison purposes, a normal hearing sample was included. This sample was made up of 17 Canadian children in first grade. They were from a middle-class district in a major city. No additional demographic information is presented.

Reliability. The only reliability data presented pertain to internal consistency. The correlations were .99 for the long form and .98 for the short form. No information is given for test–retest reliability or standard error of measurement.

Validity. The principles tested were evaluated by teachers of hearing-impaired students and were determined to be principles that hearing-impaired students would be able to use expressively after the first 2 or 3 years of primary school. The vocabulary words were considered by these teachers to be words that severely and profoundly hearing-impaired children would encounter soon after entering school.

Although it is stated in the manual that "high levels of reading and writing ability are not necessary for the child" (p. 5), it is not clear what this general statement means. Because no reading level is given, results on some items could be confounded for some students.

In terms of concurrent validity, the TEXLA correlated .64 with Form A of the *Peabody Picture Vocabulary Test,* and .74 with Form B. The TEXLA long form correlated .99 with the TEXLA short form and .52 with the *Test of Receptive Language Ability* (TERLA). The TEXLA short form correlated .56 with the TERLA.

Although the scores show a tendency to increase with age, there are many exceptions.

For discriminate validity, 9 children considered "language capable" scored at least 1 standard deviation above the mean score for their age group, whereas a "language problem" group (n = 8) all scored below the mean score for their age group.

Conclusions. Given the small number of students in the sample, and the lack of descriptive data on many demographic characteristics, the meaning of the TEXLA results are questionable. Furthermore, without comparative data, it is unclear whether Canadian children are an appropriate comparison group for children from the United States.

Information on test–retest reliability and standard error of measurement are needed. If a student could read the material, the information might be useful for program planning in terms of determining which principles of grammar to teach. With each principle tested at least four times, the information for planning programs should be reliable.

More detailed justification of the educational importance of the items is needed (e.g., correspondence with curricula or the literature). Concurrent validity with newer tests, and correlation of results of the TEXLA with results of intelligence tests and other achievement measures would be helpful as well. The reading level of the material on the test should be provided.

Test of Receptive Language Ability

Author: G. O. Bunch
Publisher: G. B. Services, Ltd.
               100 Waterton Rd.
               Weston, Ontario
               Canada M9P 2R3
Copyright: 1981

General Description. The *Test of Receptive Language Ability* (TERLA) was designed to be used by the classroom teacher to assess receptive grammar for hearing-impaired children ages 6 to 12. The test is individually administered and takes about 10 to 15 minutes for the long form. Results are expressed as percentiles or stanines. For program planning, performance on items can be examined to determine whether students recognize when particular grammatical rules are needed. Materials consist of the examiner's manual, which includes the illustrations, and a record sheet.

Description of the Items. The test has both a long and a short form. The long form consists of 90 items and the short form of 58 items.

The child's task is to read the word at the bottom of a page and then point to one of three pictures that corresponds to the word. Each grammatical principle is tested by 5 to 10 items on the long form and by 3 to 6 items on the short form. The skills tested and number of items used follow. (The first number is for the long form and the number in parentheses for the short form.) There are 10 (6) singular nouns, 5 (4) plural nouns /s/, 5 (4) plural nouns /es/, 10 (6) pronouns, 10 (6) descriptive adjectives, 5 (4) comparative adjectives, 5 (4) superlative adjectives, 10 (6) prepositions, 10 (6) past tense, 10 (6) future tense, 5 (3) present progressive singular, and 5 (3) present progressive plural items.

Technical Adequacy

Standardization. In the process of development, the TERLA was field tested with 35 hearing-impaired children from 6-11 to 11-8 years of age attending residential schools. The students had hearing losses in the better ear of 82 dB or greater. The current version was standardized on 92 hearing-impaired children from 6 to 12 years of age from two Canadian residential schools for hearing-impaired students. The students did not have additional handicaps and were all prelingually hearing impaired. Three students had hearing losses of 36 to 55 dB, 2 of 36 to 70 dB, 24 of 71 to 90 dB, and 63 of 91 dB or more. No data are given on socioeconomic level, sex, race, ethnicity, or urban/rural residence.

For comparison purposes, an additional sample of 27 Canadian children with normal hearing was included. These children were in first grade and from a middle-class area. No other demographic data are provided.

Reliability. The internal consistency reliability coefficient was .96 for the long form and .92 for the short form for hearing-impaired students. For the normally hearing first graders, the correlations were .84 for the long form and .85 for the short form. No information on test–retest reliability or standard error of measurement is given.

Validity. Words were selected from first-grade vocabulary lists and evaluated by teachers of primary hearing-impaired children as being among the first printed words to which children were exposed. Reading skills may still confound results for some children, because a child must be able to read the stimulus words to obtain valid results.

The TERLA results were compared with results for the *Peabody Picture Vocabulary Test* with 31 hearing-impaired children. The correlation was .67 with Form A and .71 with Form B. The correlation for hearing-impaired students was .98 for the TERLA long form and TERLA short form, .89 for the TERLA and TEXLA long forms, and .90 for the TERLA and TEXLA short forms.

The mean scores show a trend for increasing with age, but this is not consistent.

In terms of discriminate validity, a group of 8 hearing-impaired children considered "language capable" all scored at least 1 standard deviation above the mean for their age group. Eight other hearing-impaired children considered to have other language problems all scored below average, with 6 scoring more than 1 standard deviation below the mean for their age group.

Conclusions. To be technically adequate, the TERLA needs a larger sample of children from various types of programs, rather than only from residential schools. Additional demographic information on sex, race, ethnicity, and urban/rural residence is needed. Whether Canadian children are an appropriate comparison group for hearing-impaired children in the United States remains to be investigated.

Test–retest reliability and standard error of measurement information is needed. If a student could read the material, the test may provide some useful information for program planning. With each principle tested at least five times for the long form, the information obtained for program planning should be reliable.

Additional validity information would be helpful as well (e.g., the correlation of TERLA results with intelligence tests and more recent achievement measures). Including multiracial/multiethnic pictures would be helpful as well. The reading level of the material should be presented.

Total Communication Receptive Vocabulary Test

Author: P. Scherer
Publisher: Mental Health & Deafness Resources, Inc.
             P.O. Box 1083
             Northbrook, IL 60062
Copyright: 1981

General Description. The *Total Communication Receptive Vocabulary Test* (TCRVT) was designed to assess receptive vocabulary for students ages 3 through 12 who use total communication. The test is individually administered and takes about 20 minutes. There are three practice items and one form of the test. Results are expressed in terms of age levels. Materials consist of the examiner's manual, which includes the pictures, and a record sheet.

Description of Test Items. TCRVT consists of 75 items. The examiner presents an item using total communication, and the student points to one of four black-and-white drawings to indicate a response. The items consist of 40 nouns, 19 verbs, 9 adjectives, 5 prepositions, and 2 pronouns.

Technical Adequacy

Standardization. The TCRVT was standardized on children who did not have additional handicaps that would interfere with learning and who were not bilingual. The children attended residential and day schools in urban and suburban areas. No specific data are provided on these characteristics. The sample was not geographically representative, as the children were selected from programs in Illinois, Wisconsin, Pennsylvania, New Jersey, and Ohio. No information is provided on the sex, socioeconomic status, race, or ethnicity of the sample. The sample consisted of three subgroups: deaf, hard-of-hearing, and hearing children. The number per age level for deaf students ranged from 15 to 42, for hard-of-hearing 8 to 19, and for hearing 20 to 36.

All of the deaf and hard-of-hearing children were prelingually hearing impaired and had been exposed to total communication for 2 or more years. Preschoolers were an exception, however, but were included if they had started preschool with total communication. Hard-of-hearing children had hearing losses of 35 to 58 dB and were in classes for hard-of-hearing students. Deaf students had hearing losses of 85 dB or more and were in classrooms for the deaf. The age range for deaf children was 3 through 12 years, for hard-of-hearing 4 through 11 years, and for hearing 3 through 5 years.

Separate tables are included for children having one parent who used total communication and for those whose parents had fair or poor signing skills.

Reliability. Reliability is not addressed in the manual.

Validity. Items were selected that "all appear in a variety of curriculum guides for language in schools for the deaf across the country" (p. 5). None of the guides reviewed are listed. All words on the test also appear in the list of the 500 most common English words as indicated in the *Word Fre-*

quency Book. These reviews resulted in a list of 150 words. From this list, 75 were selected that could be clearly pictured and had standard signs. No additional information on other types of validity is presented.

Conclusions. A larger and more geographically representative sample is needed, along with data describing the socioeconomic level, race, sex, ethnicity, and urban/rural residence of the children. Information on test–retest reliability, internal consistency, and standard error of measurement are needed as well. Comparison of results of the TCRVT with children's performance on intelligence and achievement tests, including other measures of language, would be beneficial.

The test seems to have potential for providing an overall measure of a child's acquisition of vocabulary using total communication, if further data were provided to ensure the technical adequacy of the results obtained. Without this information, it is difficult to interpret results.

Additional Tests

The following achievement tests were not reviewed because they were neither designed for nor standardized upon hearing-impaired students. Because they do not require reading (unless designed to assess reading) or a vocal response, they may provide some useful supplemental information for some hearing-impaired students having good receptive skills, but problems with expression.

If these tests are given to hearing-impaired students, a great deal of caution is required in interpreting the results for several reasons. First, because the tests were not designed for hearing-impaired students, a number of the stimulus words on the vocabulary tests do not have signed equivalents. In this case, the examiner would have to either finger spell the word or use several sign descriptors to convey the concept (e.g., poinsettia–red Christmas flower). Such modifications change the task, often making it more difficult for a hearing-impaired student than for a student with normal hearing. A second concern is whether the sign itself, because of its form, may serve as more of a cue for the correct response for deaf students than the auditory presentation of the word would for hearing students. It seems that for some words (e.g., house), there would be more shared characteristics between the sign (i.e., an outline of the roof and sides of a house) and a house, than there would be for the auditory presentation of the word. Although some research on iconicity suggests that this may not be an issue (Orlansky & Bonvillian, 1984), until further research is available, whether this is an issue is open to question. Third, for those tests where the student must read the items, no reading level is reported for the material. Given the problems hearing-impaired students have with reading, this could confound the results. Also, if the directions were not written for hearing-impaired students, they may be confusing and lead to invalid results. All of these tests utilize a multiple-choice format (i.e., pointing to or circling an item), which could affect the accuracy of the results obtained.

A listing of these measures follows:

Oral and/or Signed Language

Bracken Basic Concept Scale (Bracken, 1984).   For ages 2-4 to 7-11. The test assesses 12 categories of receptive vocabulary using pictures.

Peabody Picture Vocabulary Test–Revised (Dunn & Dunn, 1981).   For ages 2-6 to 40-11. The test assesses receptive vocabulary using pictures.

Test of Adolescent Language–2 (Hammill, Brown, Larsen, & Wiederholt, 1987).   For ages 12-0 to 18-5. The subtests that do not require a vocal response are Listening Vocabulary and Listening Grammar.

Test of Language Development–2P (Newcomer & Hammill, 1988).   For ages 4-0 to 8-11. The subtests that do not require a vocal response are Picture Vocabulary and Grammatic Understanding.

Vocabulary Comprehension Scale (Bangs, 1975).   For ages 2 to 6. The test assesses receptive vocabulary using toys.

Reading Comprehension

Test of Adolescent Language–2 (Hammill, Brown, Larsen, & Wiederholt, 1987).   For ages 12-0 to 18-5. Potential subtests are Reading Vocabulary and Reading Grammar.

Test of Reading Comprehension (L. Brown, Hammill, & Wiederholt, 1978). For ages 6-6 to 17-11. The entire test utilizes a multiple-choice format.

(*Note:* Both of these tests assess vocabulary by having a student find two words that go with three stimulus words. Paul (1984) found that deaf students performed significantly less well than hearing students when asked to select two meanings for multimeaning words. Hence, in interpreting results for these tests, it should be kept in mind that this task is particularly difficult for deaf students.)

Written Language

All spelling tests and tests of written language that employ a pictorial story starter would not require reading. Tests using pictorial story starters to elicit a spontaneous writing sample include the *Diagnostic Achievement*

Battery–2 (Newcomer, 1990), the *Diagnostic Achievement Test for Adolescents* (Newcomer & Bryant, 1986), and the Spontaneous section of the *Test of Written Language–2* (Hammill & Larsen, 1988).

In Summary

To be accurate and useful, the information that follows should be applied only in the context of the previous discussion of the issues and the reviews of the tests that appear above.

Preschool/Kindergarten Skills. The Preacademic/Fine Motor subtest of the *Uniform Performance Assessment Scale* (Haring, White, Edgar, Affleck, & Hayden, 1981) could be employed to assess various skills from use of puzzles and blocks to paper-and-pencil tasks. The information obtained is for use in setting instructional objectives for children functioning at or below the level of a normal 6-year-old.

Reading. The planning of a reading assessment, as well as the interpretation of results, needs to be carried out in light of the following information if valid conclusions are to be drawn.

For hearing-impaired students, learning to read is very difficult. Research has shown that delays in development of vocabulary and syntax contribute to reading problems for these students (Quigley & Kretschmer, 1982) and, thus, these areas should be addressed in an assessment. Students whose primary language is American Sign Language may need to learn English as a second language (Schlesinger, 1986) to aid in comprehending what they read.

Most hearing-impaired students do not achieve above the fourth-grade level in reading (Gjerdingen, 1987), but low scores may reflect a lack of knowledge regarding effective methods of instruction for use with hearing-impaired students, problems with test construction, a learning disability, or any combination of these factors. Low achievement should not be assumed to occur for hearing-impaired students, particularly because their general intellectual ability does not differ from that of hearing students.

It is useful to note whether a student signs while reading. Signing may facilitate reading, indicate that the material is particularly difficult, or both (Robbins & Hatcher, 1981).

Tests of reading comprehension that consist of numerous inferential questions and that require answering questions from memory, are likely to be particularly difficult for hearing-impaired students (Quigley & Paul, 1984; Wilson, 1979).

Reading levels from norm-referenced tests are unlikely to be useful for determining where to place a student in a basal reader (Lesiak & Bradley-Johnson, 1983). Results from norm-referenced vocabulary tests are not designed to be used to determine which vocabulary words to teach (Lesiak & Bradley-Johnson, 1983).

The use of miscue analysis may provide useful supportive evidence regarding a student's strengths and difficulties in reading. Currently, however, this procedure lacks sufficient technical adequacy to be used alone as the basis for planning programs.

Tests and procedures to consider for assessing reading for hearing-impaired students include those listed in the upper portion of Table 6.1.

Arithmetic.   Unlike reading, for hearing-impaired students, mathematics reasoning develops in a similar fashion as for hearing students, but skills often are delayed (Wood et al., 1986). Again, low achievement may be more likely to reflect lack of knowledge of effective teaching techniques for these students. Low scores also may reflect learning disabilities.

As shown in Table 6.1, the only test of arithmetic standardized on hearing-impaired students is the *Stanford Achievement Test.*

Written Expression.   Skills in written expression are especially important for hearing-impaired students as another means of communication, but typically these students have serious problems in this area. Problems with vocabulary and syntax frequently are evident. Because reading achievement levels often are low, it is important to check that students could read the material for items missed on tests that employ a contrived format (e.g., where students are required to correct written material). Ideally, both a contrived and a spontaneous format should be employed to comprehensively assess written expression skills. To obtain valid results for spelling, tests that require students to write words should be employed.

Measures for hearing-impaired students for this area include those listed in the final section of Table 6.1.

Oral and Manual Communication.   Age at onset of hearing loss seems critical to language development, and a loss prior to age 2 appears to result in much greater difficulty in learning language than a loss that occurs after that age (Rogers & Soper, 1982). Hearing-impaired students have serious delays in vocabulary and syntax development. Furthermore, for those students who use American Sign Language, the grammar differs from that of English (Quigley & Paul, 1989).

The ability to meet individual needs of a hearing-impaired student seems the best basis on which to select a method of communication for a particular student. Regardless of the test, the examiner should be competent

TABLE 6.1
Tests for Assessing Achievement

Test	Age/grade	Skills tested	Type of information
		Reading	
Stanford Achievement Test (Psychological Corporation, 1989)	Grades K–12	Varies with level, includes letter sounds, vocabulary, and comprehension	Norm-referenced scores
Test of Early Reading Ability–Deaf and Hard of Hearing (Reid, Hresko, Hammill, & Wiltshire, 1991)	Ages 3–12	Various reading skills	Norm-referenced scores
Test of Syntactic Ability (Quigley, Steinkamp, Power, & Jones, 1978)	Ages 10–18	Syntax	Norm-referenced scores and program planning[a]
		Arithmetic	
Stanford Achievement Test (Psychological Corporation, 1989)	Grades K–12	Computation and application	Norm-referenced scores
		Written Expression	
Stanford Achievement Test (Psychological Corporation, 1989)	Grades K–12	Varies with level; includes mechanics, expression, syntax, and spelling	Norm-referenced scores
Written Language Syntax Test (Berry, 1981)	Ages 10–17	Syntax	Program planning
Curriculum-based measurement	Any age	Spelling	Progress within a curriculum

[a]The use of the term *program planning* indicates that detailed criterion-referenced information or informal information is provided that may be useful in designing individual instructional programs.

TABLE 6.2
Tests for Assessing Communication Skills

Test	Age/grade	Skill	Receptive/ Expressive	Type of information
Manual Communication Skills				
Carolina Picture Vocabulary Test (Layton & Holmes, 1985)	5–12 years	Vocabulary	Receptive	Norm-referenced scores
Teacher Assessment of Grammatical Structures (Moog & Kozak, 1983)	Any age	Grammar	Receptive/ expressive	Program planning[a]
Uniform Performance Assessment Scale (Haring, White, Edgar, Affleck, & Hayden, 1981)	Any age	Communication in general	Receptive/ expressive	Program planning
Simultaneous Communication				
Grammatical Analysis of Elicited Language–S (Moog & Geers, 1985)	5–9 years	Grammar	Expressive	Norm-referenced scores and program planning
Rhode Island Test of Language Structure (Engen & Engen, 1983)	5–17 years	Syntax	Receptive	Norm-referenced scores and program planning
Teacher Assessment of Grammatical Structures (Moog & Kozak, 1983)	Any age	Grammar	Receptive/ expressive	Program planning
Test of Expressive Language Ability (Bunch, 1981)	7–12 years	Grammar	Expressive	Norm-referenced scores and program planning
Test of Receptive Language Ability (Bunch, 1981)	6–12 years	Grammar	Receptive	Norm-referenced scores and program planning
Total Communication Receptive Vocabulary Test (Scherer, 1981)	3–12 years	Vocabulary	Receptive	Norm-referenced scores

Test	Age	Skill area	Receptive/expressive	Program planning
Uniform Performance Assessment Scale (Haring, White, Edgar, Affleck, & Hayden, 1981)	Any age	Communication in general	Receptive/expressive	Program planning
Oral Communication				
CID Phonetic Inventory (Moog, 1988)	Any age	Ability to produce phonemes	Expressive	Program planning
CID Picture SPINE (Monsen, Moog, & Geers, 1988)	Any age	Speech intelligibility	Expressive	Program planning
Grammatical Analysis of Elicited Language P, S, C (P: Moog, Kozak, & Geers; 1983; S: Moog & Geers, 1985; C: Moog & Geers, 1980)	P: 3–6 years S: 5–9 years C: 8–12 years	Grammar	P: Receptive/expressive S: Expressive C: Expressive	Norm-referenced scores and program planning
Scales of Early Communication Skills (Moog & Geers, 1975)	2–9 years	Communication in general	Receptive/expressive	Norm-referenced scores
Teacher Assessment of Grammatical Structures (Moog & Kozak, 1983)	Any age	Grammar	Receptive/expressive	Program planning
Test of Expressive Language Ability (Bunch, 1981)	7–12 years	Grammar	Expressive	Norm-referenced scores and program planning
Test of Receptive Language Ability (Bunch, 1981)	6–12 years	Grammar	Receptive	Norm-referenced scores and program planning
Uniform Performance Assessment Scale (Haring, White, Edgar, Affleck, & Hayden, 1981)	Any age	Communication in general	Receptive/expressive	Program planning

[a]The use of the term *program planning* indicates that the test provides detailed criterion-referenced or informal information that may be useful in planning individual educational programs.

in using a student's primary method of communication. Receptive and expressive skills, as well as vocabulary and syntax, need to be addressed.

Analysis of spontaneous language samples may provide useful supplementary information, but these procedures currently lack the technical adequacy needed to be used alone for making important decisions regarding eligibility and program planning.

The numerous measures available for assessing oral and manual skills are outlined in Table 6.2.

The tests noted in this summary section include only those standardized on or developed for hearing-impaired students. Results of these measures might be supplemented with results of tests that are standardized on hearing students, but that do not require vocal responses or reading (unless reading is being assessed). A list of these measures was presented earlier in the section of this chapter called Additional Tests, along with a discussion of considerations that are necessary if such tests are employed.

Future Directions

A number of well thought out measures of academic achievement have been developed for hearing-impaired students. Although these tests measure educationally important skills, many lack sufficient technical adequacy. The standards set for norm-referenced tests for hearing students should be applied to tests for hearing-impaired students as well. These students should be assessed on measures that have been shown to be reliable and valid, and their scores compared with scores of groups of hearing-impaired students who adequately represent the population of hearing-impaired students. Standardization information on the following demographic characteristics should be provided: sex, socioeconomic status, race, ethnicity, geographic distribution, and urban/rural residence. Furthermore, a sufficient number of students per age level is needed, for example, approximately 100 (especially when percentiles are used). Data on test–retest reliability, internal consistency, and standard error of measurement should be given. Concurrent, construct, and content validity also need to be addressed.

For tests standardized on hearing-impaired students, detailed information needs to be provided on the hearing status of the sample. In the literature, variables such as degree of loss, age at onset, communication mode, hearing status of parents, presence of additional handicaps, etiology, type of hearing impairment, and type of educational program have been found to affect the performance of these students. Hence, to determine whether the sample is an appropriate comparison group for a particular hearing-impaired student, this information must be available. For students using total communication, the form of total communication (e.g., speech + Signing Exact English) needs to be described as well. This information was not included in the manuals of the tests that were reviewed. Without this information, errors in interpretation of test results are likely because of the possible lack of similarity of the background of the student tested and the standardization sample with which the student is compared.

Furthermore, with the current trend toward placing handicapped students in regular education classrooms, additional norm tables are needed on normally hearing students as well as on hearing-impaired students in all types of programs. With these additional norms, a hearing-impaired student's performance could be compared with that of his or her hearing peers and to hearing-impaired peers. Such information could be very useful to aid in decisions regarding educational placements.

Research on the use of curriculum-based measurement with hearing-impaired students could provide important information for assessment and instruction. Which procedures are most useful, and how to best employ these procedures with students who use some form of manual communication, need to be determined.

The optimistic aspects of academic assessment of hearing-impaired students are that there is quite a large body of literature from which to draw for future work and many educationally important measures have been developed. Refinement of these measures would be very helpful. Development of new measures, especially in reading, certainly is needed also.

7

Concluding Remarks and Future Directions

Concluding Remarks

In the preceding chapters, several guidelines for the psychoeducational assessment of hearing-impaired students were suggested. The first guideline pertains to obtaining sufficient background information for planning an assessment. This includes obtaining information regarding the child's educational and medical history, as well as the characteristics of the hearing-impaired child or adolescent, and ascertaining how these characteristics might impact assessment. Just as no one communication method, such as total communication, can be recommended for all hearing-impaired students, no one set of tests and procedures can be deemed appropriate for use with all hearing-impaired students. Instead, flexibility is required to tailor assessment to a particular student's needs. To plan assessment procedures requires obtaining information about the student from a variety of sources, including the parents, physician, audiologist, speech–language therapist, social worker, teachers, and perhaps the student himself or herself. When planning an assessment, failure to take into account information from these sources could be detrimental to the performance of a student, and would thereby affect the relevance of assessment results for determining educational objectives.

The second guideline pertains to acquiring a knowledge of the issues that relate to procedures involved in the psychoeducational assessment of hearing-impaired students. General issues have been identified in reviews by Vernon and Brown (1964), Levine (1971), and Sullivan and Vernon (1979). Again, however, the heterogeneous nature of the hearing-impaired population does not permit issue resolution. Tests considered verbal may be appropriate for some hearing-impaired students. No one method of presenting instructions is optimal for all students. An examiner needs to be aware of the issues as they relate to a particular student and the assessment instruments selected. For example, if there are no better alternatives than to use an interpreter, an examiner should be aware of how this procedure may compromise the validity of results.

A third guideline pertains to the available assessment instruments for hearing-impaired students. Independent of what instructions, items, and normative data should be used with a student, an examiner is constrained by the instruments that are available. Unfortunately, despite the work that has been carried out with hearing-impaired students, relatively few instruments have been developed specifically for hearing-impaired students. Many of the measures used to assess hearing-impaired students are adaptations of measures used with normally hearing students. These adaptations often include a change in instructions, test items, and test procedures. Such changes affect the normative data and have unknown effects upon the assessment results obtained. Unfortunately, no widely accepted comprehensive measures of general intelligence or individually administered achievement measures are available for these students, and there are no such measures that could be recommended as a component for most assessments. Knowledge of the available instruments and their strengths and limitations is needed to devise the most appropriate test battery for a hearing-impaired student. Selecting appropriate instruments for a student requires a great deal of information gathering and planning before any direct assessment takes place. Individualization is the key to obtaining valid results. This will necessarily be time-consuming, but it will be time well spent.

A fourth guideline, which has been noted incidentally in previous chapters, pertains to making assessment results relevant to the individual student through consultation with service providers, primarily the teacher. Because the goal of assessment is intervention, it is critical that assessment results provide as much information for intervention as possible. This can be accomplished most effectively through ongoing contact before, during, and after assessment with those involved in providing services to a student.

Future Directions

Additional data related to the relevance of some characteristics of hearing-impaired students to assessment would be welcome. For example, more specific information that could be used to set guidelines for appropriate procedures based on a student's degree of hearing loss would be helpful. Information relevant to assessing students who have the type, degree, and age at onset of hearing loss typical of those impaired due to rubella would be useful. Based on etiology, assessment considerations could be made in a more efficient manner, given that many other characterisitics of hearing-impaired students are related to etiology.

Many issues that pertain to assessment of hearing-impaired students require further research. The impact of various methods of presenting instructions, applicability of hearing norms, and comparability of reliability and validity data need to be explored for nearly all of the measures reviewed. Likewise, the effects of impulsivity need to be determined on a test-by-test basis.

Similarly, more research with test instruments is needed to establish their validity with hearing-impaired students. As mentioned, applicability of technical data obtained from hearing students to hearing-impaired students needs to be provided if the measure is to be used with confidence for hearing-impaired students. Tests designed for hearing students may not result in similar score distribution, reliability data, and validity data when used with hearing-impaired students, and they may not permit a measure to be interpreted in the same manner for hearing and for hearing-impaired students.

A number of available measures designed for assessing intelligence and achievement of hearing-impaired students appear to be made up of appropriate and useful items. These tests, however, lack much of the data necessary to make the instruments technically adequate. Further research on the technical adequacy of these measures is sorely needed.

Evaluation of the social validity of assessments that have been carried out with hearing-impaired students could provide valuable information regarding how to improve psychoeducational assessments. Teacher or parent satisfaction ratings, or measures of student performance, could be used to compare assessment methods in order to increase relevance of assessment results. Archival achievement data may provide one source of comparison.

In closing, Levine (1974) referred to the 30 years prior to the 1970s by stating that they "have produced little if any significant progress in the state of the art of psychological evaluation of the deaf" (p. 298). Data from the 1970s and 1980s have begun to provide information that can aid in obtaining valid assessment results for hearing-impaired students. As the responsibility for conducting assessment has shifted toward examiners with limited experience and skills in assessment of hearing-impaired students, surveys of the manner in which psychoeducational assessments are conducted do not indicate consistent improvement with regard to the valid assessment of hearing-impaired students (McQuaid & Alovisetti, 1981; Trott, 1984).

Thus, the problem is twofold: Valid procedures and instruments are needed for hearing-impaired students, and skill acquisition is needed by those conducting assessments. Given the problem, examiners currently can provide assessment results that are educationally relevant; however, considerable effort is required to determine the most appropriate procedures and instruments for a particular student. One purpose of this text has been to reduce the effort by providing a single, comprehensive source of information regarding assessment procedures and assessment instruments for hearing-impaired students.

A second purpose of the book has been to stimulate further research in this area. It is hoped that significant improvements will be made in the psychoeducational assessment of hearing-impaired students so that it will be possible to make a more helpful contribution to the education of these students.

References

Aiken, L. R. (1985). *Psychological testing and assessment.* Boston: Allyn & Bacon.

Alessi, G., & Kaye, J. H. (1983). *Behavior assessment for school psychologists.* Stratford, CT: NASP.

Allen, T., White, C., & Karchmer, M. (1983). Issues in the development of a special edition for hearing-impaired students of the 7th edition of the SAT. *American Annals of the Deaf, 128,* 34–39.

Altshuler, K. (1974). The social and psychological development of the deaf child: Problems, their treatment, and prevention. *American Annals of the Deaf, 121,* 365–367.

Altshuler, K. Z., Deming, W. E., Vollenweider, J., Rainer, J. D., & Tendler, R. (1976). Impulsivity and profound early deafness: A cross cultural inquiry. *American Annals of the Deaf, 121,* 331–345.

American Psychological Association. (1981). Ethical principles of psychologists (revised). *American Psychologist, 36,* 633–638.

American Speech–Language–Hearing Association. (1987). *Governmental Affairs Review, 7,* 2.

Amoss, H. (1936). *Ontario School Ability Examination.* Toronto: Ryerson.

Anastasi, A. (1982). *Psychological testing* (5th ed.). New York: Macmillan.

Anderson, K. L. (1989). *Screening Instrument for Targeting Educational Risk.* Austin, TX: PRO-ED.

Anderson, R. J., & Sisco, F. H. (1977). *Standardization of the WISC-R Performance Scale for deaf children* (Office of Demographic Studies Publication Series T, No. 1). Washington, DC: Gallaudet College Press.

Armstrong, R. J., & Jensen, J. A. (1981). *Slosson Intelligence Test.* East Aurora, NY: Slosson Educational Publishing.

Arthur, G. (1950). *Arthur Adaptation of the Leiter International Performance Scale.* Los Angeles: Western Psychological Services.

Babbini, B., & Quigley, S. P. (1970). *A study of the growth patterns in language, communication, and educational achievement in six residential schools for deaf students.* Urbana: University of Illinois, Institute for Research on Exceptional Children. (ERIC Document Reproduction Service No. ED 046 208)

Bangs, T. (1975). *Vocabulary Comprehension Scale.* Allen, TX: DLM Teaching Resources.

Baum, V. (1981). Counseling families of deaf children. *Journal of the Rehabilitation of the Deaf, 15,* 16–19.

Bayley, N. (1969). *Bayley Scales of Infant Development.* San Antonio, TX: Psychological Corp.

Berdine, W. H., & Meyer, S. A. (1987). *Assessment in special education.* Boston: Little, Brown.

Bernero, R. J., & Bothwell, H. (1966). *Relationship of hearing impairment to educational needs.* Illinois Department of Public Health and Office of the Superintendent of Public Instruction.

Berry, S. R. (1981). *Written Language Syntax Test.* Washington, DC: Gallaudet College Press.

Best, B., & Roberts, G. (1976). Early cognitive development in hearing impaired children. *American Annals of the Deaf, 121,* 560–564.

Birch, J. R., Stuckless, E. R., & Birch, J. W. (1963). An eleven year study of predicting school achievement in deaf children. *American Annals of the Deaf, 108,* 236–240.

Birch, J. W. (1975). *Hearing impaired children in the mainstream.* St. Paul, MN: University of Minnesota, Leadership Training Institute/Special Education.

Blennerhassett, L., & Spragins, A. (1983, March). *Evaluating deaf students: What the school psychologist needs to know.* Paper presented at the National Association of School Psychologists, Detroit, MI.

Boothroyd, A. (1978). Speech perception and sensorineural hearing loss. In M. Ross & T. G. Gidas (Eds.), *Auditory management of hearing-impaired children: Principles and prerequisites for intervention* (pp. 117–144). Baltimore, MD: University Park Press.

Boothroyd, A. (1987). Technology and science in the management of deafness. *American Annals of the Deaf, 132,* 326–329.

Bornstein, H. (1973). A description of some current sign systems designed to represent English. *American Annals of the Deaf, 118,* 454–463.

Boyd, J., & Shapiro, A. H. (1986). A comparison of the Leiter International Performance Scale to WPPSI Performance with preschool deaf and hearing impaired children. *Journal of the Rehabilitation of the Deaf, 20,* 23–26.

Boyle, P. (1977). Psychology. In B. F. Jaffe (Ed.), *Hearing loss in children: A comprehensive text* (pp. 266–282). Baltimore, MD: University Park Press.

Bracken, B. A. (1984). *Bracken Basic Concept Scale.* San Antonio, TX: Psychological Corp.

Brackett, D. (1981). Assessment: Adaptations, interpretations, and implications. In M. Ross & L. W. Nober (Eds.), *Special education in transition: Educating hard of hearing children* (pp. 47–66). Washington, DC: Alexander Graham Bell Assoc.

Braden, J. P. (1985a). Futile gestures: A reply to Courtney, Hayes, Crouch, and Frick regarding pantomimed administration of the WISC-R Performance Scale. *Journal of Psychoeducational Assessment, 3,* 181–185.

Braden, J. P. (1985b). WISC-R deaf norms reconsidered. *Journal of School Psychology, 23,* 375–382.

Bradley-Johnson, S. (1986). *Psychoeducational assessment of visually impaired and blind students: Infancy through high school.* Austin, TX: PRO-ED.

Bradley-Johnson, S. (1987). *Cognitive Abilities Scale.* Austin, TX: PRO-ED.

Bradley-Johnson, S., & Lesiak, J. (1989). *Problems in written expression: Assessment and remediation.* New York: Guilford Press.

Bragman, R. (1982a). Effects of different methods of conveying test instructions on deaf children's performance on pattern recognition tasks. *Journal of the Rehabilitation of the Deaf, 16,* 17–26.

Bragman, R. (1982b). Review of research on test instructions for deaf children. *American Annals of the Deaf, 127,* 337–346.

Brill, R. G., MacNeil, B., & Newman, L. R. (1986). Framework for appropriate programs for deaf children: Conference of educational administrators serving the deaf. *American Annals of the Deaf, 131,* 65–77.

Brown, L., Hammill, D. D., & Wiederholt, J. L. (1978). *Test of Reading Comprehension.* Austin, TX: PRO-ED.

Brown, L., Sherbenou, R. J., & Johnsen, S. K. (1990). *Test of Nonverbal Intelligence–2.* Austin, TX: PRO-ED.

Brown, R. (1973). *A first language: The early stages.* Cambridge, MA: Harvard University Press.

Bunch, G. O. (1981a). *Test of Expressive Language Ability.* Weston, Ontario: G. B. Services.

Bunch, G. O. (1981b). *Test of Receptive Language Ability.* Weston, Ontario: G. B. Services.

Burgemeister, B. B., Blum, L. H., & Lorge, I. (1972). *Columbia Mental Maturity Scale.* New York: Harcourt Brace Jovanovich.

Busenbark, L., & Jenison, V. (1986). Assessing hearing aid function by listening check. *Volta Review, 88,* 263–268.

Butterfield, S. A. (1986). Gross motor profiles of deaf children. *Perceptual and Motor Skills, 62,* 68–70.

Byrne, B. (1986). Recent advances in acoustic hearing aids. *Volta Review, 88,* 31–43.

Caccamise, F., Meath-Lang, B., & Johnson, D. D. (1981). Assessment and use of vision: Critical needs of hearing impaired students. *American Annals of the Deaf, 126,* 361–369.

Carey, S. (1977). The child as word learner. In M. Halle, J. Bresnan, & G. Miller (Eds.), *Linguistic theory and psychological reality.* Cambridge, MA: MIT Press.

Carlsson, P., Hakansson, B., Rosenhall, U., & Tjellstrom, A. (1986). A speech-to-noise ratio test with the bone-anchored hearing aid: A comparative study. *Otolarngology–Head and Neck Surgery, 94,* 421–426.

Cattell, P. (1960). *The measurement of intelligence of infants and young children.* San Antonio, TX: Psychological Corp.

Clark, H. H., & Clark, E. V. (1977). *Psychology and language.* New York: Harcourt Brace Jovanovich.

Clarke, B., Rogers, W., & Booth, J. (1982). How hearing-impaired children learn to read: Theoretical and practical issues. In R. W. Kretschmer (Ed.), Reading and the hearing-impaired individual [Special issue]. *Volta Review, 84,* 57–69.

Clements, A. H., & Prickett, H. T. (1986). American sign language in the education of the deaf. *American Annals of the Deaf, 131,* 218–219.

Conrad, R. (1979). *The deaf school child: Language and cognitive function.* London: Harper & Row.

Craig, H. B. (1983). Parent–infant education in schools for deaf children: Results of a CEASD survey. *American Annals of the Deaf, 128,* 82–98.

Craig, W. N., & Craig, H. B. (1987). Tabular summary of schools and classes in the United States: October 1, 1986. *American Annals of the Deaf, 132,* 124.

Day, P. S., & Meadow-Orlans, K. P. (1985). Analysis. In D. S. Martin (Ed.), *Cognition, education, and deafness* (pp. 34–40). Washington, DC: Gallaudet College Press.

DeConde, C. (1984). Children with central auditory processing disorders. In R. H.

Hull & K. L. Dilka (Eds.), *The hearing impaired child in school* (pp. 141–162). New York: Grune & Stratton.

Diefendorf, A., & Arthur, D. (1987). Monitoring children's hearing aids: Re-examining the problem. *Volta Review, 89,* 17–26.

Doll, E. A. (1965). *Vineland Social Maturity Scale.* Circle Pines, MN: American Guidance Service.

Dubose, R. F., & Langley, M. B. (1977). *Developmental Activities Screening Inventory.* Hingham, MA: Teaching Resources.

Dunn, L. M., & Dunn, L. M. (1981). *Peabody Picture Vocabulary Test–Revised.* Circle Pines, MN: American Guidance Service.

Dunst, C. J. (1980). *A clinical and educational manual for use with the Uzgiris and Hunt Scales of Infant Psychological Development.* Austin, TX: PRO-ED.

Eagney, P. (1987). ASL? English? Which? Comparing comprehension. *American Annals of the Deaf, 132,* 272–275.

Effect of degree of hearing loss on understanding of language and speech. (1984). Unpublished manuscript, Department of Communication Disorders, Central Michigan University, Mt. Pleasant.

Engen, E., & Engen, T. (1983). *Rhode Island Test of Language Structure.* Austin, TX: PRO-ED.

Erber, N. P. (1981). Speech perception by hearing-impaired children. In F. H. Bess, B. A. Freeman, & J. S. Sinclair (Eds.), *Amplification in education* (pp. 69–88). Washington, DC: Alexander Graham Bell Assoc.

Evans, L. D. (1983). *A comparison of the effects of the supplemental and alternate instructions on the Adaptation of the WISC-R for the Deaf.* Unpublished master's thesis, Central Michigan University, Mt. Pleasant.

Ewoldt, C. (1982). Diagnostic approaches and procedures and the reading process. In R. E. Kretschmer, *Reading and the hearing-impaired individual* [Special issue]. *Volta Review, 84,* 83–94.

Federal Register. (1977, August 23). Part II, Education of Handicapped Children, Implementation of Part B of the Education of the Handicapped Act. Vol. 42, 42474–42518.

Fewell, R. R., & Langley, M. B. (1984). *Developmental Activities Screening Inventory–II.* Austin, TX: PRO-ED.

Flynn, J. R. (1984). The mean IQ of Americans: Massive gains 1932 to 1978. *Psychological Bulletin, 95,* 29–51.

Frankenburg, W. K., Dodds, J. B., Fandal, A. W., Kazuk, E., & Cohrs, M. (1975). *Denver Developmental Screening Test.* Denver, CO: University of Colorado Medical Center.

Freeman, R. D., Carbin, C. F., & Boese, R. J. (1981). *Can't your child hear? A guide for those who care about deaf children.* Austin, TX: PRO-ED.

Freeman, R. D., Malkin, S. F., & Hastings, J. O. (1975). Psychosocial problems of deaf children and their families: A comparative study. *American Annals of the Deaf, 120,* 391–405.

French, J. L. (1964). *Pictorial Test of Intelligence.* New York: Houghton Mifflin.

Furth, H. (1964). *Thinking without language.* New York: Free Press.

Furth, H. (1973). *Deafness and learning: A psychosocial approach.* Belmont, CA: Wadsworth.

Geers, A. E., & Lane, H. S. (1984). *CID Preschool Performance Scale.* St. Louis, MO: Central Institute for the Deaf.

Gelfand, D., & Hartman, D. P. (1984). *Child behavior analysis and therapy* (2nd ed.) New York: Pergamon Press.

Gentile, A., & McCarthy, B. (1973). *Additional handicapping conditions among hearing impaired students–United States: 1971–1972* (Office of Demographic Studies Publication Series D, No. 14). Washington, DC: Gallaudet College Press.

Giangreco, J. C. (1966). The Hiskey–Nebraska Test of Learning Aptitude (Revised) compared to several achievement tests. *American Annals of the Deaf, 8,* 566–577.

Gibbons, S., Ulissi, S. M., & Brice, P. (1984, April). *Use of the K-ABC with hearing-impaired children.* Paper presented at the meeting of the National Association of School Psychologists, Philadelphia, PA.

Gildston, P. (1973). The hearing-impaired child in the classroom. In N. H. Northcott (Ed.), *The hearing-impaired child in the regular classroom: Preschool, elementary, and secondary years.* Washington, DC: Alexander Graham Bell Assoc.

Gjerdingen, D. (1987). Language acquisition and reading scores. *Newsounds, 12,* 3.

Goldsmith, L., & Schloss, P. J. (1986). Diagnostic overshadowing among school psychologists working with hearing-impaired learners. *American Annals of the Deaf, 131,* 288–293.

Gormley, K., & Sarachan-Deily, A. B. (1987). Evaluating hearing-impaired students' writing: A practical approach. *Volta Review, 89,* 157–166.

Graham, E. E., & Shapiro, E. (1953). Use of the Performance Scale of the WISC and the deaf child. *Journal of Consulting Psychology, 17,* 396–398.

Griswold, E. L., & Commings, J. (1974). The expressive vocabulary of preschool deaf children. *American Annals of the Deaf, 119,* 16–28.

Grove, C., & Rodda, M. (1984). Receptive communication skills of hearing impaired students: A comparison of four methods of communication. *American Annals of the Deaf, 129,* 378–385.

Guilford, J. P. (1978). *Fundamental statistics in psychology and education.* New York: McGraw-Hill.

Guilford, J. P., & Hoepfner, R. (1971). *The analysis of intelligence.* New York: McGraw-Hill.

Guilfoyle, G. R., & Silverman, T. (1975). *Vocabulary norms for deaf children.* Washington, DC: The Alexander Graham Bell Assoc.

Hall, J. W., & Derlacki, E. L. (1986). Effect of conductive hearing loss and middle ear surgery on binaural hearing. *Annals of Otology, Rhinology, and Laryngology, 95,* 525–530.

Hall, V. (1983). *The measurement of behavior* (rev. ed.). Austin, TX: PRO-ED.

Hallahan, D. P., Keller, C. E., & Ball, D. W. (1986). A comparison of prevalence rate variability from state to state for each of the categories of special education. *Remedial and Special Education, 7,* 8–14.

Hammill, D. (1986). *Detroit Tests of Learning Aptitude-2.* Austin, TX: PRO-ED.

Hammill, D. D. (1987). *Assessing the abilities and instructional needs of students.* Austin, TX: PRO-ED.

Hammill, D. D., Brown, V. L., Larsen, S. C., & Wiederholt, J. L. (1987). *Test of Adolescent Language-2.* Austin, TX: PRO-ED.

Hammill, D. D., & Larsen, S. (1988). *Test of Written Language–2.* Austin, TX: PRO-ED.

Hamp, N. W. (1972). Reading attainment and some associated factors in deaf and partially hearing children. *The Teacher of the Deaf, 70,* 203–215.

Harkins, J. (1985, Winter). Hearing-impaired children and youth. A demographic and academic profile. *Newsletter, Gallaudet Research Institute,* pp. 1–4.

Harris, R. I. (1978). Impulse control in deaf children: Research and clinical issues. In L. S. Liben (Ed.), *Deaf children: Developmental perspectives* (pp. 137–156). New York: Academic Press.

Harrison, J. (1985). Hearing impairments. In G. Scholl (Ed.), *The school psychologist and the exceptional child* (pp. 179–202). Reston, VA: Council for Exceptional Children.

Heimgartner, N. L. (1982). *Behavioral traits of deaf children.* Springfield, IL: Thomas.

Hirshoren, A., Hurley, O. L., & Kavale, K. (1979). Psychometric characteristics of the WISC-R Performance Scale with deaf children. *Journal of Speech and Hearing Disorders, 101,* 73–79.

Hirsh-Pasek, K., & Treiman, R. (1982). Recoding in silent reading: Can the deaf child translate print into a more manageable form? In R. E. Kretschmer (Ed.), *Reading and the hearing-impaired individual* [Special issue]. *Volta Review, 84,* 71–82.

Hiskey, M. S. (1966). *Manual for the Hiskey–Nebraska Test of Learning Aptitude.* Lincoln, NE: Union College Press.

Hobbs, P. (1980). *Assessment workshop learning assessment.* Washington, DC: Gallaudet College Press.

Hyde, M. B., Power, D. J., & Elias, G. C. (1980). *The use of the verbal and non-verbal control techniques by mothers of hearing-impaired infants* (Research Rep. No. 5). Australia: Mt. Gravatt College of Advanced Education, Centre for Human Development Studies.

Jaffe, B. F. (1977). Medical evaluation and medical management of children with sensorineural hearing loss. In F. B. Bess (Ed.), *Childhood deafness: Causation, assessment and management* (pp. 197–210). New York: Grune & Stratton.

James, R. P. (1984). A correlational analysis between the Raven's Matrices and WISC-R Performance Scales. *Volta Review, 86,* 336–341.

Jensema, C. J., Karchmer, M. A., & Trybus, R. J. (1978). *The rated speech intelligibility of hearing impaired children: Basic relationships and a detailed analysis* (Office of Demographic Studies Publication Series R, No. 6). Washington, DC: Gallaudet College Press.

Jenesema, C. J., & Trybus, R. J. (1978). *Communication patterns and educational achievement of hearing impaired students* (Office of Demographic Studies Publication Series T, No. 2). Washington, DC: Gallaudet College Press.

Johnson, D. D., Caccamise, F., Rothblum, A. M., Hamilton, L. F., & Howard, M. (1981). Identification and follow-up of visual impairments in hearing-impaired populations. *American Annals of the Deaf, 126,* 321–352.

Johnson, G. R., & Boyd, H. F. (1981). *Nonverbal Test of Cognitive Skills.* Columbus, OH: Merrill.

Jordan, I. K., Gustason, G., & Rosen, R. (1976). Current communication trends in programs for the deaf. *American Annals of the Deaf, 121,* 527–532.

Jordan, I. K., Gustason, G., & Rosen, R. (1979). An update on communication trends at programs for the deaf. *American Annals of the Deaf, 124,* 350–357.

Jordan, I. K., & Karchmer, M. A. (1986). Patterns of sign use among hearing impaired students. In A. N. Schildroth & M. A. Karchmer (Eds.), *Deaf children in America* (pp. 125–138). San Diego, CA: College-Hill.

Kagan, J. (1965). Impulsive and reflective children: Significance of conceptual tempo. In J. D. Krumboltz (Ed.), *Learning and the educational process* (pp. 131–166). Chicago: Rand McNally.

Kahn, J. V. (1976). Utility of the Uzgiris and Hunt Scales of Sensorimotor Development with severely and profoundly retarded children. *American Journal of Mental Deficiency, 80,* 663–665.

Kamphe, C. M., & Turecheck, A. G. (1987). Reading achievement of prelingually deaf students and its relationship to parental method of communication: A review of the literature. *American Annals of the Deaf, 132,* 11–15.

Kaplan, H. E. (1974). The Arthur Adaptation of the Leiter International Performance Scale: Its suitability tested for use with preschool children in various countries. *Psychological Service Center Journal, 14,* 21–27.

Karchmer, M. A., & Belmont, J. M. (1976, November). *On assessing and improving deaf performance in the cognitive laboratory.* Paper presented at the meeting of the American Speech and Hearing Association, Houston, TX.

Karchmer, M. A., & Kirwin, L. (1977). *The use of hearing aids by hearing impaired students in the United States* (Office of Demographic Studies Publication Series S, No. 2). Washington, DC: Gallaudet College Press.

Karchmer, M. A., Milone, M. N., & Wolk, S. (1979). Educational significance of hearing loss at three levels of severity. *American Annals of the Deaf, 124,* 97–109.

Kaufman, A. S. (1975). Factor analysis of the WISC-R at 11 age levels between 6½ and 16½ years. *Journal of Consulting and Clinical Psychology, 43,* 135–147.

Kaufman, A. S., & Kaufman, N. L. (1983). *Kaufman Assessment Battery for Children: Interpretive manual.* Circle Pines, MN: American Guidance Service.

Kellogg, C. E., & Morton, N. W. (1978). *Revised Beta Examination* (2nd ed.). San Antonio, TX: Psychological Corp.

King, C. (1981). *An investigation of similarities and differences in the syntactic abilities of deaf and hearing children learning English as a first or second language.* Unpublished doctoral dissertation, University of Illinois at Urbana-Champaign.

King, C. M., & Quigley, S. P. (1985). *Reading and deafness.* Austin, TX: PRO-ED.

King, W. L., & Seegmiller, B. (1973). Performance of 14- to 22-month-old black, firstborn male infants on two tests of cognitive development: The Bayley Scales and the Infant Psychological Development Scale. *Developmental Psychology, 8,* 317–326.

Kraus, N., Ozdamar, O., Stein, L., & Reed, N. (1984). Absent auditory brain stem response: Peripheral hearing loss or brain stem dysfunction? *Laryngoscope, 94,* 400–406.

Kretschmer, R. E. (1982). Reading and the hearing-impaired individual: Summation and application. In R. E. Kretschmer, *Reading and the hearing-impaired individual* [Special issue]. *Volta Review, 84,* 107–122.

Kretschmer, R. E., & Kretschmer, L. W. (1978). *Language development and intervention with the hearing impaired.* Baltimore, MD: University Park Press.

Lake, D. (1980). Syntax and sequential memory in hearing impaired children. In H. Reynolds & C. Williams (Eds.), *Proceedings of the Gallaudet conference on reading in relation to deafness* (pp. 193–212). Washington, DC: Gallaudet College, Division of Research.

Lane, H., & Grosjean, F. (Eds.). (1980). *Recent perspectives on American Sign Language.* Hillsdale, NJ: Erlbaum.

Layton, T. L., & Holmes, D. W. (1985). *Carolina Picture Vocabulary Test.* Austin, TX: PRO-ED.

Lee, L. (1974). *Developmental sentence analysis.* Evanston, IL: Northwestern University Press.

Leiter, R. G. (1940). *The Leiter International Performance Scale* (Vol. 1). Santa Barbara, CA: Santa Barbara College Press.

Leiter, R. G. (1969). *The Leiter International Performance Scale.* Chicago: Stoelting.

Leshowitz, B. (1982). Development of an infrared hearing aid. *Medical Instrumentation, 16,* 15–16.

Lesiak, J., & Bradley-Johnson, S. (1983). *Reading assessment for placement and programming.* Springfield, IL: Thomas.

Levine, E. S. (1971). Mental assessment of the deaf child. *Volta Review, 73,* 80–105.

Levine, E. S. (1974). Psychological tests and practices with the deaf: A survey of the state of the art. *Volta Review, 76,* 298–319.

Levine, E. S. (1981). *The ecology of deafness: Guide to fashioning environments and psychological assessments.* New York: Columbia University.

Liben, L. S. (1978). The development of deaf children: An overview of issues. In L. S. Liben (Ed.), *Deaf children: Developmental perspectives* (pp. 3–20). New York: Academic Press.

Lichtenstein, E. (1984). Deaf working memory processes and English language skills. In D. Martin (Ed.), *International symposium on cognition, education, and deafness: Working papers* (pp. 331–360). Washington, DC: Gallaudet College Press.

Ling, D. (1976). *Speech and the hearing impaired child: Theory and practice.* Washington, DC: Alexander Graham Bell Assoc.

Ling, D. (1986). Devices and procedures for auditory learning. *Volta Review, 88,* 19–28.

Longhurst, T., & Grubb, J. (1974). A comparison of language samples in four situations. *Language, Speech and Hearing Services in the Schools, 5,* 71–78.

MacMillan, D. L., & Meyers, C. E. (1977). The non-discriminatory testing provisions of 94-142. In M. I. Semmel & J. L. Heinmiller (Eds.), *Viewpoints* (pp. 39–56). Bloomington, IN: School of Education, Indiana University.

Madison, J. P. (1985). Analysis. In D. S. Martin (Ed.), *Cognition education, and deafness* (pp. 128–131). Washington, DC: Gallaudet College Press.

Markwardt, F. C. (1989). *Peabody Individual Achievement Test–Revised.* Circle Pines, MN: American Guidance Service.

Marlowe, J. A. (1987). Early identification and the hearing impaired child's right to become. *American Annals of the Deaf, 132,* 337–339.

Marston, D. B. (1989). A curriculum-based measurement approach to assessing academic performance: What it is and why do it. In M. Shinn (Ed.), *Curriculum-based measurement* (pp. 18–78). New York: Guilford Press.

Matkin, N. D. (1981). Amplification for children: Current status and future priorities. In F. H. Bess, B. A. Freeman, & J. S. Sinclair (Eds.), *Amplification in education* (pp. 192–201). Washington, DC: Alexander Graham Bell Assoc.

Mavilya, M. (1982). Assessment, curriculum, and intervention strategies for hearing impaired mentally retarded children. In D. Tweedie & E. H. Shroyer (Eds.), *The multihandicapped hearing impaired: Identification and instruction* (pp. 113–123). Washington, DC: Gallaudet College.

McQuaid, M. F., & Alovisetti, M. (1981). School psychology services for hearing impaired children in the New York and New England Area. *American Annals of the Deaf, 126,* 37–42.

Meadow, K. P. (1978). The natural history of a research project: An illustration of methodological issues in research with deaf children. In L. S. Liben (Ed.), *Deaf children: Developmental perspectives* (pp. 21–40). New York: Academic Press.

Meadow, K. (1980). *Deafness and child development.* Berkeley: University of California Press.

Miller, M. S. (1985). Experimental use of signed presentation of the Verbal Scale of the WISC-R with profoundly deaf children: A preliminary report. In D. S. Martin (Ed.), *Cognition, education, and deafness: Directions for research and instruction* (pp. 134–136). Washington, DC: Gallaudet College.

Mira, M. P. (1962). The use of the Arthur Adaptation of the Leiter International Performance Scale and the Nebraska Test of Learning Aptitude with preschool deaf children. *American Annals of the Deaf, 107,* 224–228.

Monsen, R. B. (1978). Toward measuring how well hearing-impaired children speak. *Journal of Speech and Hearing Research, 21,* 197–219.

Monsen, R. B. (1981). A usable test for the speech intelligibility of deaf talkers. *American Annals of the Deaf, 126,* 845–852.

Monsen, R. B., Moog, J. S., & Geers, A. E. (1988). *Central Institute for the Deaf Picture SPINE.* St. Louis, MO: Central Institute for the Deaf.

Moog, J. S. (1988). *Central Institute for the Deaf Phonetic Inventory.* St. Louis, MO: Central Institute for the Deaf.

Moog, J. S., & Geers, A. E. (1975). *Scales of Early Communication Skills.* St. Louis, MO: Central Institute for the Deaf.

Moog, J. S., & Geers, A. E. (1980). *Grammatical Analysis of Elicited Language: Complex Sentence Level.* St. Louis, MO: Central Institute for the Deaf.

Moog, J. S., & Geers, A. E. (1985). *Grammatical Analysis of Elicited Language: Simple Sentence Level.* St. Louis, MO: Central Institute for the Deaf.

Moog, J. S. & Kozak, J. (1983). *Teacher Assessment of Grammatical Structures.* St. Louis, MO: Central Institute for the Deaf.

Moog, J. S., Kozak, V. J., & Geers, A. E. (1983). *Grammatical Analysis of Elicited Language: Pre-Sentence Level.* St. Louis, MO: Central Institute for the Deaf.

Murphy, K. P. (1957). Tests of ability and attainments. In A. W. G. Ewing (Ed.), *Educational guidance and the deaf child* (pp. 213–251). Manchester: Manchester University Press.

Musgrove, W. J., & Counts, L. (1975). Leiter and Raven performances and teacher rankings: A correlational study with deaf children. *Journal of the Rehabilitation of the Deaf, 8,* 19–22.

Musket, C. H. (1981). Maintenance of personal hearing aids. In M. Ross, R. J. Roeser, & M. Downs (Eds.), *Auditory disorders in school children* (pp. 229–248). New York: Thieme & Straton.

Myklebust, H. E. (1964). *The psychology of deafness: Sensory deprivation, learning, and adjustment* (2nd ed.). New York: Grune & Stratton.

Nance, W. E. (1976). Studies of hereditary deafness: Present, past, and future. In R. Frisina (Ed.), *A bicentennial monograph of hearing impairment: Trends in the USA* (pp. 6–11). Washington, DC: Alexander Graham Bell Assoc.

Neuhaus, M. (1967). Modifications in the administration of the WISC Performance subtests for children with profound hearing losses. *Exceptional Children, 33,* 573–574.

Newborg, J., Stock, J. R., Wnek, L., Guidubaldi, J., & Svinicki, J. (1984). *Battelle Developmental Inventory.* Allen, TX: DLM Teaching Resources.

Newcomer, P. L. (1990). *Diagnostic Achievement Battery–2.* Austin, TX: PRO-ED.

Newcomer, P. L., & Bryant, B. (1986). *Diagnostic Achievement Test for Adolescents.* Austin, TX: PRO-ED.

Newcomer, P. L., & Hammill, D. D. (1988). *Test of Language Development–2P.* Austin, TX: PRO-ED.

Northern, J. L., & Downs, M. P. (1978). *Hearing in children* (2nd ed.). Baltimore, MD: Williams and Wilkins.

O'Brien, D. H. (1987). Reflection–impulsivity in total communication and oral deaf and hearing children: A developmental study. *American Annals of the Deaf, 132,* 213–217.

Orlansky, M., & Bonvillian, J. (1984). The role of iconicity in early sign language acquisition. *Journal of Speech and Hearing Disorders, 49,* 287–292.

Paul, P. V. (1984). *The comprehension of multimeaning words from selected frequency levels by deaf and hearing subjects.* Unpublished doctoral dissertation, University of Illinois, Urbana-Champaign.

Paul, P. V. (1985). Reading and other language-variant populations. In C. M. King & S. P. Quigley (Eds.), *Reading and deafness* (pp. 251–289). Austin, TX: PRO-ED.

Phelps, L., & Ensor, A. (1986). Concurrent validity of the WISC-R using deaf norms and the Hiskey–Nebraska. *Psychology in the Schools, 23,* 138–141.

Pintner, R. (1918). The measurement of language ability and language progress of deaf children. *Volta Review, 20,* 755–764.

Porter, J., & Holzberg, B. C. (1979). From theory to practice: The changing role of the school psychologist within programs for exceptional children. *American Annals of the Deaf, 124,* 444–449.

Porter, L. J., & Kirby, E. A. (1986). Effects of two instructional sets on the validity of the *Kaufman Assessment Battery for Children–Nonverbal Scale* with a group of severely hearing impaired children. *Psychology in the Schools, 23,* 37–43.

Porteus, S. D. (1965). *The Porteus Maze Test* (rev.). New York: Psychological Corp.

Poull, L. E., Bristol, A. S., King, H. B., & Peatman, L. B. (1931). *Randall's Island Performance Series.* New York: Appleton.

Powers, A., Elliot, R., Jr., & Funderburg, R. (1987). Learning disabled hearing impaired students: Are they being identified? *Volta Review, 132,* 99–105.

Public Law 94-142. (1975). *Federal Register,* 22676-22692 (§121a.532).

Psychological Corporation. (1982). *Stanford Achievement Test.* San Antonio, TX: Author.

Psychological Corporation. (1989). *Stanford Achievement Test.* San Antonio, TX: Author.

Quigley, S. P., & Kretschmer, R. E. (1982). *The education of deaf children.* Austin, TX: PRO-ED.

Quigley, S. P., & Paul, P. V. (1984). *Language and deafness.* San Diego: College-Hill.

Quigley, S. P., & Paul, P. V. (1986). A perspective on academic achievement. In D. M. Luterman, *Deafness in perspective* (pp. 55–86). San Diego: College-Hill.

Quigley, S. P., & Paul, P. V. (1989). English language development. In M. C. Wang, M. C. Reynolds, & H. J. Walberg (Eds.), *Handbook of special education: Research and practice* (Vol. 3, pp. 3–21). New York: Pergamon Press.

Quigley, S. P., Steinkamp, M. W., Power, D. J., & Jones, B. W. (1978). *Test of Syntactic Abilities.* Austin, TX: PRO-ED.

Quigley, S. P., Wilbur, R. B., Power, D. J., Montanelli, D. S., & Steinkamp, M. W. (1976). *Syntactic structures in the language of deaf children.* Urbana, IL: Institute for Child Behavior and Development, University of Illinois.

Ratcliffe, K. J., & Ratcliffe, M. W. (1979). The Leiter Scales: A review of validity findings. *American Annals of the Deaf, 124,* 38–44.

Raven, J., & Summers, B. (1986). *Manual for Raven's Progressive Matrices and Vocabulary Scales.* San Antonio, TX: Psychological Corp.

Rawlings, B., & Jensema, C. (1977). *Two studies of the families of hearing-impaired children* (Office of Demographic Studies Publication Series R, No. 5). Washington DC: Gallaudet College Press.

Rawlings, B., & Ries, P. W. (1973). *Characteristics of hearing impaired children by hearing status, United States: 1970–71.* Washington, DC: Office of Demographic Studies, Gallaudet College.

Ray, S. (1979). *Manual for the Adaptation of the WISC-R for the Deaf.* Natchitoches, LA: Steven Ray Publishing.

Ray, S., & Ulissi, S. M. (1982). *An Adaptation of the Wechsler Preschool and Primary Scale of Intelligence for Deaf Children.* Natchitoches, LA: Steven Ray Publishing.

Reed, M. (1970). Deaf and partially hearing children. In P. Mittler (Ed.), *The psychological assessment of mental and physical handicaps* (pp. 403–441). London: Methuen.

Reid, K., Hresko, W. P., Hammill, D. D., & Wiltshire, S. (1991). *Test of Early Reading Ability–Deaf or Hard of Hearing.* Austin, TX: PRO-ED.

Ries, P., Bateman, D., & Schildroth, A. (1975). *Ethnic background in relation to other characteristics of hearing impaired students in the United States* (Office of Demographic Studies Publication Series D, No. 15). Washington, DC: Gallaudet College.

Riko, K., Hyde, M. L., & Alberti, P. W. (1985). Hearing loss in infancy: Incidence, detection and assessment. *Laryngoscope, 95,* 137–145.

Rittenhouse, R. K. (1987). The attitudes of teachers toward mainstreaming of hearing-impaired high schoolers. *Journal of the Rehabilitation of the Deaf, 20,* 11–14.

Ritter, D. R. (1976). Intellectual estimates of hearing impaired children: A comparison of three measures. *Psychology in the Schools, 13,* 397–399.

Robbins, N. L., & Hatcher, C. W. (1981). The effects of syntax on the reading comprehension of hearing-impaired children. *Volta Review, 83,* 105–115.

Rodda, M., & Grove, C. (1987). *Language, cognition and deafness*. Hillsdale, NJ: Erlbaum.

Rogers, S. J., & Soper, E. (1982). Assessment considerations with hearing-impaired preschoolers. In G. Ulrey & S. J. Rogers (Eds.), *Psychological assessment of handicapped infants and young children* (pp. 115–122). New York: Thieme-Stratton.

Ross, A. (1976). *Psychological aspects of learning disabilities and reading disorders*. New York: McGraw-Hill.

Ross, M. (1978). Classroom acoustics and speech intelligibility. In J. Katz (Ed.), *Handbook of clinical audiology* (2nd ed., pp. 469–478). Baltimore, MD: Williams & Wilkins.

Ross, M. (1981). An introduction. In M. Ross & L. W. Nober (Eds.), *Special education in transition: Educating hard-of-hearing children* (pp. 1–10). Reston, VA: Council for Exceptional Children.

Ross, M. (1986). A perspective on amplification: Then and now. In D. M. Luterman, *Deafness in perspective* (pp. 35–53). San Diego, CA: College-Hill.

Saigal, S., Lunyk, O., Larke, R. P., & Chernesky, M. A. (1982). The outcome in children with congenital cytomegalovirus infection: A longitudinal follow-up study. *American Journal of Diseases of Children, 136*, 896–901.

Salvia, J., & Ysseldyke, J. E. (1981). *Assessment in special and remedial education*. Boston: Houghton Mifflin.

Sarachan-Deily, A. B., & Love, R. J. (1974). Underlying grammatical rule structure in the deaf. *Journal of Speech and Hearing Research, 17*, 689–698.

Sattler, J. M. (1982). *Assessment of children's intelligence and special abilities* (2nd ed.). Boston: Allyn and Bacon.

Scherer, P. (1981). *Total Communication Receptive Vocabulary Test*. Northbrook, IL: Mental Health and Deafness Resources.

Scherer, P. (1983). Psycho-educational evaluation of hearing impaired preschool children. *American Annals of the Deaf, 128*, 118–124.

Schildroth, A. (1986). Hearing impaired children under age 6: 1977 & 1984. *American Annals of the Deaf, 131*, 85–90.

Schlesinger, H. (1986). Total communication in perspective. In D. Luterman, *Deafness in perspective* (pp. 87–116). San Diego: College-Hill.

Schlesinger, H. S., & Meadow, K. P. (1972). *Sound and sign: Childhood deafness and mental health*. Berkeley: University of California Press.

Schnittjer, C. J., & Hirshoren, A. (1981). The prevalence of behavior problems in deaf children. *Psychology in the Schools, 18*, 67–72.

Shah, C. P., Chandler, D., & Dale, R. (1978). Delay in referral of children with impaired hearing. *Volta Review, 80*, 206–215.

Sharp, H. C. (1958). A note on the reliability of the Leiter International Performance Scale, 1948 revision. *Journal of Consulting Psychology, 22*, 320.

Shepard, N. T., Davis, J. M., Gorga, M. P., & Stelmachowicz, P. G. (1981). Characteristics of hearing-impaired children in the public schools: Part 1—Demographic data. *Journal of Speech and Hearing Disorders, 46*, 123–128.

Shinn, M. (1989). *Curriculum-based measurement*. New York: Guilford Press.

Silverman, S. R., Lane, H. S., & Doehring, D. G. (1960). Deaf children. In H. Davis & S. R. Silverman (Eds.), *Hearing and deafness* (2nd ed., pp. 413–451). New York: Holt, Rinehart & Winston.

Sinclair, J. S., & Freeman, B. A. (1981). The status of classroom amplification in American education. In F. H. Bess, B. A. Freeman, & J. S. Sinclair (Eds.), *Amplification in education* (pp. 205–215). Washington, DC: Alexander Graham Bell Assoc.

Smith, A. J., & Johnson, R. E. (1977). *Manual for the Smith–Johnson Nonverbal Performance Scale.* Los Angeles: Western Psychological Services.

Spragins, A. (1979). Psychological assessment of the school-aged hearing impaired child. In R. K. Mulliken & M. Evans (Eds.), *Assessment of children with low-incidence handicaps.* Stratford, CT: NASP.

Stein, L. K., Palmer, P., & Weinberg, B. (1982). Characteristics of a young deaf-blind population. *American Annals of the Deaf, 127,* 828–837.

Stuckless, E. R., & Birch, J. W. (1966). The influence of early manual communication on the linguistic development of deaf children. *American Annals for the Deaf, 111,* 452–460, 499–504.

Stutsman, R. (1931). *Merrill–Palmer Scale of Mental Tests.* New York: Harcourt, Brace & World.

Sullivan, P. M. (1982). Administrative modifications of the WISC-R Performance Scale with different categories of deaf children. *American Annals of the Deaf, 127,* 780–788.

Sullivan, P. M. (1985). Review of Wechsler Intelligence Scale for Children–Revised: For the deaf. In J. V. Mitchell, Jr. (Ed.), *The ninth mental measurement yearbook* (pp. 1354–1355). Lincoln: University of Nebraska.

Sullivan, P. M., & Vernon, M. (1979). Psychological assessment of hearing impaired children. *School Psychology Digest, 8,* 271–289.

Taylor, L. (1969). *A language analysis of the writing of deaf children.* Unpublished doctoral dissertation, Florida State University, Tallahassee.

Terman, L. M., & Merrill, M. A. (1960). *Stanford–Binet Intelligence Scale, 3rd revision.* Boston: Houghton-Mifflin.

Terman, L. M., & Merrill, M. A. (1973). *Stanford–Binet Intelligence Scale, 1972 norms edition.* Boston: Houghton-Mifflin.

Thompson, M., Biro, P., Vethivelu, S., Pious, C., & Hatfield, N. (1987). *Language assessment of hearing-impaired school age children.* Seattle: University of Washington Press.

Thorndike, R. L., Hagen, E. P., & Sattler, J. M. (1986). *Stanford–Binet Intelligence Scale* (4th ed.). Chicago, IL: Riverside.

Trott, L. A. (1984). Providing school psychological services to hearing-impaired students in New Jersey. *American Annals of the Deaf, 129,* 319–323.

Trybus, R. J., & Karchmer, M. A. (1977). School achievement scores of hearing impaired children: National data on achievement status and growth patterns. *American Annals of the Deaf, Directory of Programs and Services, 122,* 62–69.

Trybus, R., Karchmer, M., Kerstette, P., & Hicks, W. (1980). The demographics of deafness resulting from maternal rubella. In E. R. Stuckless (Ed.), Deafness and rubella: Infants in the 60's, adults in the 80's [Special issue]. *American Annals of the Deaf, 125,* 977–984.

Tyack, D., & Gottsleben, R. (1974). *Language sampling, analysis and training.* Palo Alto, CA: Consulting Psychologists Press.

Uzgiris, I., & Hunt, J. M. (1975). *Assessment in Infancy: Ordinal Scales of Psychological Development.* Champaign: University of Illinois Press.

Vernon, M. (1972). Mind over mouth: A rationale for total communication. *Volta Review, 74*, 529–540.

Vernon, M. C. (1974). Deaf and hard-of-hearing. In M. V. Wisland (Ed.), *Psychoeducational diagnosis of exceptional children* (pp. 190–212). Springfield, IL: Thomas.

Vernon, M. C. (1982). Multihandicapped deaf children: Types and causes. In D. Tweedie & E. H. Shroyer (Eds.), *The multi-handicapped hearing impaired: Identification and instruction* (pp. 11–28). Washington, DC: Gallaudet College Press.

Vernon, M., & Alles, B. F. (1986). Psychoeducational assessment of deaf and hard-of-hearing children and adolescents. In P. J. Lazarus & S. S. Strichart (Eds.), *Psychoeducational evaluation of children and adolescents with low-incidence handicaps.* New York: Grune & Stratton.

Vernon, M., Bair, R., & Lotz, S. (1979). Psychological evaluation and testing of children who are deaf-blind. *School Psychology Digest, 8*, 291–295.

Vernon, M. C., & Brown, D. W. (1964). A guide to psychological tests and testing procedures in the evaluation of deaf and hard-of-hearing children. *Journal of Speech and Hearing Disorders, 29*, 414–423.

Vernon, M., Grieve, B., & Shaver, K. (1972). Handicapping conditions associated with the congenital rubella syndrome. In E. R. Stuckless (Ed.), Deafness and rubella: Infants in the 60's, adults in the 80's [Special issue]. *American Annals of the Deaf, 125*, 993–1001.

Vernon, M., & Koh, S. (1970). Early manual communication and deaf children's achievement. *American Annals of the Deaf, 115*, 527–536.

Wachs, T. D. (1970). Report on the utility of a Piaget-based infant scale with older retarded children. *Developmental Psychology, 2*, 449.

Wachs, T. D., & DeRemer, P. (1978). Adaptive behavior and Uzgiris–Hunt Scale performance of young developmentally disabled children. *American Journal of Mental Deficiency, 83*, 171–176.

Watson, B. U. (1983). Test–retest stability of the Hiskey–Nebraska Test of Learning Aptitude in a sample of hearing-impaired children and adolescents. *Journal of Speech and Hearing Disorders, 48*, 145–149.

Watson, B., Goldar, D., & Kroese, J. (1983, August). *The Hiskey–Nebraska Test of Learning Aptitude.* Paper presented at the annual meeting of the American Psychological Association. (ERIC Document Reproduction Service No. ED 236 173)

Watson, B., Goldar, D., Kroese, J., & Lotz, W. (1986). Nonverbal Intelligence and academic achievement in the hearing impaired. *Volta Review, 88*, 151–157.

Watson, B. U., Sullivan, P. M., Moeller, M. P., & Jensen, J. K. (1982). Nonverbal intelligence and English language ability in deaf children. *Journal of Speech and Hearing Disorders, 47*, 199–204.

Watson, B. U., Sullivan, P. M., Teare, J. F., & Thompson, R. W. (1984). Intellectual evaluation. In M. J. Osberger (Ed.), *Language and learning skills of hearing impaired students* (pp. 32–37). Washington, DC: American Speech & Language Monograph.

Wechsler, D. (1967). *Wechsler Preschool and Primary Scale of Intelligence.* San Antonio, TX: Psychological Corp.

Wechsler, D. (1974). *Wechsler Intelligence Scale for Children–Revised.* San Antonio, TX: Psychological Corp.

Wechsler, D. (1981). *Wechsler Adult Intelligence Scale–Revised.* San Antonio, TX: Psychological Corp.

Werner, E. E. (1965). Review of the Leiter International Performance Scale. In O. K. Buros (Ed.), *Sixth Mental Measurement Yearbook* (pp. 814–816). Highland Park, NJ: Gryphon Press.

White, O. R., Haring, N. G., Edgar, E. B., Affleck, J. Q., & Hayden, A. H. (1981). *Uniform Performance Assessment Scale.* San Antonio, TX: Psychological Corp.

Wilber, R. (1987). *American Sign Language: Linguistic and applied dimensions* (2nd ed.). Austin, TX: PRO-ED.

Wilson, K. (1979). *Inference and language processing in hearing and deaf children.* Unpublished doctoral dissertation, Boston University.

Wolff, A. B., & Harkins, J. E. (1986). Multihandicapped students. In A. N. Schildroth & M. A. Karchmer (Eds.), *Deaf children in America* (pp. 55–82). San Diego, CA: College-Hill.

Wood, D. J. (1984). Social and educational adjustment of deaf chidren in relation to mental retardation. In J. Dobbing, A. D. B. Carke, J. A. Corbett, J. Hogg, & R. O. Robinson (Eds.), *Scientific studies in mental retardation* (pp. 285–293). London: Royal Society of Medicine and MacMillan Press.

Wood, D., Wood, H., Griffiths, A., & Howarth, I. (1986). *Teaching and talking with deaf children.* New York: Wiley.

Worthington, D. W., Stelmachowicz, P., & Larson, L. (1986, March). Audiological evaluation. In M. J. Osberger (Ed.), *Language and learning skills of hearing-impaired students* (American Speech–Language–Hearing Association Monographs No. 23, pp. 12–20). Rockville, MD.

Yarnall, G. D. (1983). Comparison of operant and conventional audiometric procedures with multihandicapped (deaf-blind) children. *Volta Review, 85,* 69–82.

Zieziula, F. R. (1982). *Assessment of hearing-impaired people: A guide for selecting psychological, educational, and vocational tests.* Washington, DC: Gallaudet College Press.

Zimmerman, I. L., & Woo-Sam, J. (1972). Research with the Wechsler Intelligence Scale for Children. *Psychology in the Schools, 9,* 232–271.

Zwiebel, A., & Mertens, D. M. (1985a). A comparison of intellectual structure in deaf and hearing children. *American Annals of the Deaf, 130,* 27–31.

Zwiebel, A., & Mertens, D. M. (1985b). A factor analytic study of intellectual development in deaf and hearing children. In D. S. Martin (Ed.), *Cognition, education, and deafness: Directions for research and instruction* (pp. 151–152). Washington, DC: Gallaudet College Press.

Author Index

Subject Index

Academic achievement. *See* Assessment of achievement

Achievement. *See* Assessment of achievement

Acquired hearing loss, 29

Adaptation of the Wechsler Preschool and Primary Scale of Intelligence for Deaf Children, 51
  ages appropriate for, 83, 84, 129, 130, 155
  cognitive ability according to ages, 124, 125
  description of, 92–93
  reliability of, 93
  standardization of, 93
  strengths and limitations of, 94
  subtests of, 93
  technical adequacy of, 93–94
  use with hearing-impaired children, 94
  validity of, 94

Adaptation of the WISC-R for the Deaf, 45, 51, 53, 61, 63, 111
  ages appropriate for, 129, 130, 155
  description of, 131–132
  normative data for, 55
  reliability of, 132
  standardization of, 132
  strengths and limitations of, 132–133
  technical adequacy of, 132
  use with hearing-impaired students, 132
  validity of, 132

Adolescents. *See* Assessment of school-age children and adolescents

Air conduction, 35

Alpern-Boll Developmental Profile, 123

American Sign Language (ASL)
  as communication method, 40–42
  for communication of test instructions, 52, 54
  and *Kaufman Assessment Battery for Children*, 111
  and reading skills, 161, 207

Amplification aids, 40, 63–66, 71

Arithmetic and mathematics, 164, 178–179, 208, 209

Arthur Adaptation of the Leiter International Performance Scale
  ages appropriate for, 83, 84, 129, 130, 155, 156
  description of, 117–118
  description of items, 118
  measures of cognitive ability according to ages, 124, 125
  normative data for, 82
  reliability of, 118
  standardization of, 118
  strengths and limitations of, 119
  technical adequacy of, 118–119
  use of interpreters for, 69
  use with hearing-impaired children, 119
  validity of, 118–119

ASL. *See* American Sign Language (ASL)

Assessment. *See also* names of specific tests
  behavior of students during, 73
  checklist for considerations after assessment, 77
  checklist for considerations prior to assessment, 69–70
  checklist of considerations during assessment, 73, 74–75
  choice of WISC-R normative data, 63